INTRODUCTION

Welcome to the Haddonstone catalogue, containing the world's most comprehensive collection of fine ornamental and architectural cast stone.

Established in 1971, Haddonstone has expanded to become an international group with offices and manufacturing facilities in both the United Kingdom and the United States of America. Today, we continue to manufacture all UK orders in the UK, whilst 95% of all US orders are made by the company in the US.

If you are an existing client, Haddonstone trusts that you will find this catalogue continues to inspire. If this is your first introduction to the company, we hope that you will shortly be joining the many leading architects, landscape designers, contractors, specifiers, interior designers and private clients that we already serve.

This catalogue has been divided into colour-coded sections for ease of use. The new Specialist Services section highlights a selection of products and services outside the scope of the main catalogue.

CONTENTS

WHY HADDONSTONE?

Haddonstone is a unique form of cast limestone with a surface texture similar to Portland stone. The material matures and weathers like natural stone yet, piece for piece, normally costs significantly less than quarried stone.

The ability to mould the Haddonstone material into almost any shape ~ faithfully reproducing new designs or producing replicas that are virtually indistinguishable from an antique original ~ has won the company numerous contracts ranging from leading international hotels and retail developments to listed National Trust properties and prestige residential projects.

The material used in every design, from the smallest planter to the largest Corinthian column, exceeds the compressive cube strength requirements of the United Kingdom Cast Stone Association and complies with all relevant UK and European standards, whilst TecStone also meets the requirements of all US standards.

Each design is hand made by Haddonstone in the UK or USA using moulds created within the company's extensive mould shops and studios. Using these same facilities Haddonstone can even manufacture non-standard architectural stone pieces to practically any shape, size or colour.

As Haddonstone maintains original models and/or moulds for every single design in the standard collection, and utilises the very latest vapour curing technology, customers can be reassured that the high quality of each stone produced is incredibly consistent whilst retaining the individuality of a hand-made product. The company even offers a five year warranty on cast stone garden ornaments.

Haddonstone can also be an enjoyable investment. At a Sotheby's auction, four Haddonstone Plaited Baskets sold for more than twenty times their current retail value.

Haddonstone ~ one of the few things in life that can grow more beautiful and valuable with the passing of the years.

VISIT US

At East Haddon, in the rolling countryside of Northamptonshire in England, Haddonstone has beautiful show gardens and an interior showroom where visitors can see many of the designs illustrated in this catalogue in their proper settings, see opposite. The garden and showroom are open every week from Monday to Friday ~ public holidays and Christmas period excepted ~ between the hours of 9.00 am and 5.00 pm. The gardens are also open on occasional weekends as part of the National Garden Scheme (Yellow Book) to raise money for charity. Brown tourism signs guide visitors to the gardens from the A428.

Haddonstone pieces may also be viewed at stockists across the UK as well as the RHS gardens at Wisley and Harlow Carr. In addition, Haddonstone, TecLite, TecStone and Technistone designs can be seen at Pennine Stone Ltd, Askern Road, Carcroft, Doncaster DN6 8DE. Haddonstone's catalogue can be obtained from the Building Centre, Store Street, London WC1 or viewed online at:
www.haddonstone.com/view-catalogue

In the USA, Haddonstone offices have a permanent showroom display, whilst Haddonstone designs may also be viewed at stores and distributors across North America.

GARDEN & LANDSCAPE

Ever since English gardens began to be influenced by those of Italy, urns, fountains and statues have found an honourable, often the most honourable, place in their scheme. They contribute very much to the embellishment and magnificence of a garden, whether large or small, terraced or open-ground.

"Garden ornaments provide emphasis and accent in a garden, drawing the eye in a particular direction. Most ornaments, because they are solid and static objects such as urns, seats, columns or statues, provide a contrast with the living things around them."

David Hicks, 1929-1998

GARDEN & LANDSCAPE INSPIRATIONS

By studying the following pages, you will see how, with imagination and inspiration, architects and designers have used Haddonstone designs to great effect in a variety of gardens and landscapes.

Each project has been achieved by using either standard Haddonstone components or custom-made designs created by utilising the company's skilled craftsmen and extensive mould-making facilities.

Whether standard or custom-made, within reason, the only constraint is your imagination...

Colonnade at the Grade I listed Dyffryn Gardens near Cardiff.

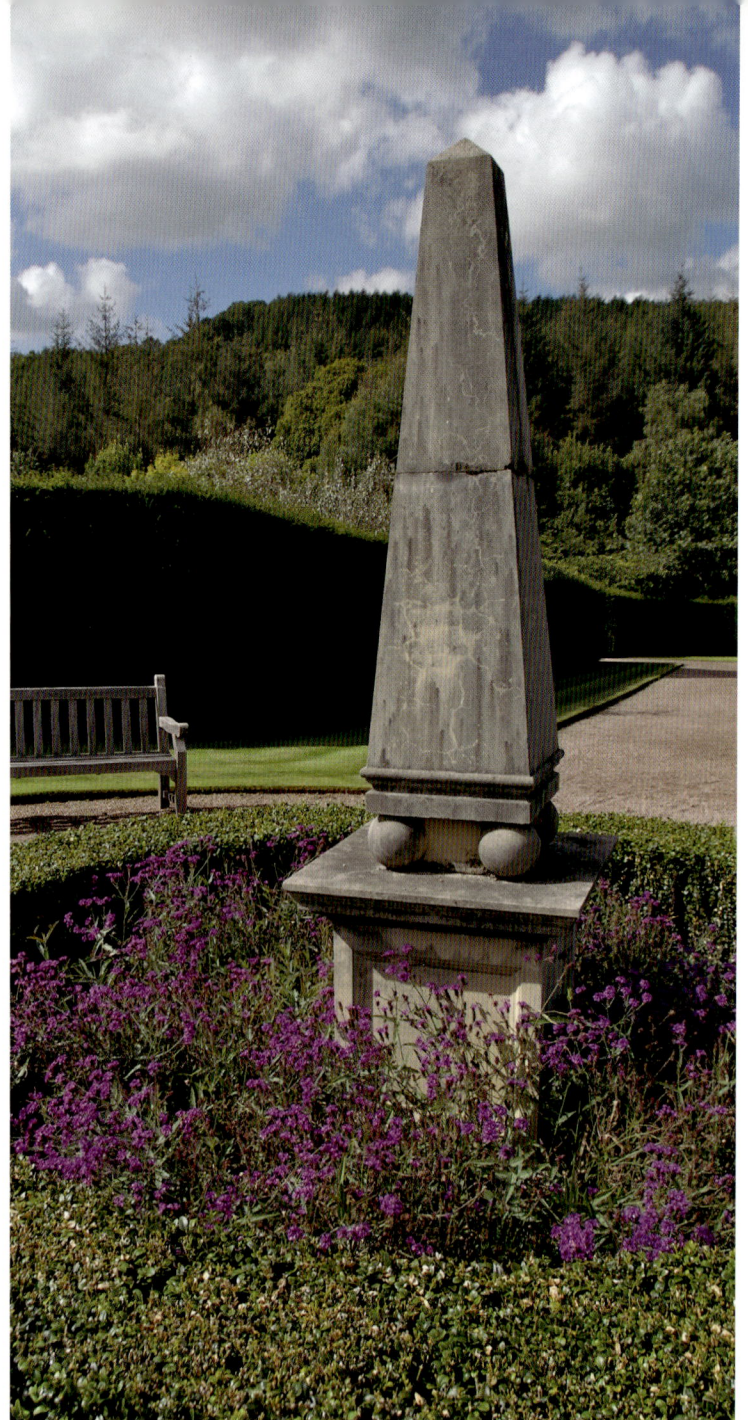

Haddonstone's obelisk is used to great effect at the RHS Gardens, Rosemoor.

Haddonstone has been used extensively at this major South Korean project.

Evocative urban garden incorporating Large Versailles Vases and Pedestals.

Design: Anthony Noel. Image: Andrew Lawson

Haddonstone balustrading can be used to enhance both residential and commercial projects.

The unique landscape at this private residence in Dorset incorporates both standard and custom-made designs including a special Triple Lotus Bowl Fountain and two Naiad statues, replicating the work of John Bacon RA by Croggon of Lambeth.

Haddonstone's Pavilion, Pergola and ornaments enhance the historic garden of an important Grade I listed property located in Surrey.

Standard architectural components including steps, risers and finials combine to create a unique garden feature at this magnificent home counties residence.

GARDEN & LANDSCAPE
INSPIRATIONS

A Haddonstone pergola provides an focal point at Roosevelt Park, Chicago.

Architects: Scholz Design. Photographer: Beth Singer Photographer Inc.

Roman Pool Surround and ornaments at a splendid residence in Pittsburgh.

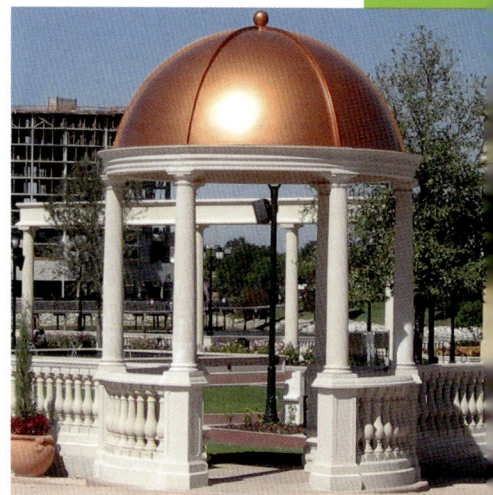

Temple and balustrading enhance Altamonte Springs, Florida.

Haddonstone landscape ornaments and architectural stonework combine with great effect at this Ohio residence.

Majestic balustrading at a prestigious Leicestershire hotel.

Client: Kilworth House Hotel

Intriguing shapes from custom copings at the University of Southampton.

These massive custom spheres were created for Northampton's Racecourse.

Massive M1 columns create a focal point at an entrance to Manchester's Trafford Centre.

Haddonstone landscape ornaments and architectural designs combine to create a magnificent entrance at the West Midlands Golf Club.

GARDEN & LANDSCAPE INSPIRATIONS

Haddonstone Pergola and ornaments at King James Quay, Old Portsmouth.

Special Copings are used to provide seating at the Eden Project in Cornwall.

Haddonstone obelisks at The National Exhibition Centre in Birmingham.

A beautiful Orangery constructed in Northern Scotland solely using Haddonstone standard architectural components and decorated with Margam Swagged Urns.

Clarence Urn
A215

This elegant urn, inspired by the designs of the Regency period, has been crafted by Haddonstone as a complementary piece to the Regency and Trafalgar Urns. The simple design has leaf moulding to the rim and gadrooning to the bowl. Identical in proportion to the Large Clarence Urn A214, see page 21.

Width at top: 540mm (21")
Width at base: 242mm (9½")
Height: 430mm (17")
Weight: 40kg (88 lb)

Recommended pedestals: B300, B310, B331, B400, B420, B440.

(Registered Design No. 2045998)

Croyland Vase
A245

A small campana-shaped vase featuring a stylised leaf design. This vase was replicated from an original in a private Northamptonshire garden.

Width at top: 470mm (18½")
Width at base: 240mm (9½")
Height: 500mm (19¹¹⁄₁₆")
Weight: 32kg (70 lb)

Recommended pedestals: B300, B310, B400, B420, B440.

(Registered Design No. 2082024)

Magnolia Vase
A490

A simple campana-shaped vase with a circular base incorporating acanthus-leaf moulding around the bowl. The original dates back to the XVII century in the style of Christopher Wren.

Width at top: 395mm (15½")
Diameter of base: 280mm (11")
Height: 510mm (20")
Weight: 35kg (77 lb)

Recommended pedestals: B300, B310, B400, B420, B440.

Vine Urn
A705

This charming small urn features vine decoration and gadrooning to the body and overlapping leaf decoration around the rim. Ideal for use in conjunction with Haddonstone balustrading.

Width at top: 343mm (13½")
Width at base: 197mm (7¾")
Height: 430mm (17")
Weight: 21kg (45 lb)

Recommended pedestals: B130, B300, B310, B330, B400, B420, B440, B480.

(Registered Design No. 2039119)

Lotus Vase
A470

An octagonal Regency-style vase with a beautiful lotus-leaf design carved on the vase and base. Replicated from an XIX century Blashfield original.

Width at top: 405mm (16")
Width at base: 320mm (12½")
Height: 495mm (19½")
Weight: 40kg (88 lb)

West Lodge Urn
HA780

Featuring gadrooning to the bowl, this elegant small urn was originally replicated for West Lodge Park Hotel in Hertfordshire.

Height: 527mm (20¾")
Width overall: 660mm (26")
Width at base: 273mm (10¾")
Weight: 74kg (163 lb)
Recommended pedestals: B300, B310, B400, B420, B440.

Regency Urn
A530
Regency Pedestal
B330

This popular urn is shown on a simple pedestal and can also enhance balustrading.

Width at urn top: 485mm (19")
Width at urn base: 220mm (8¾")
Pedestal base width: 280mm (11")
Height of urn: 380mm (15")
Height of pedestal: 430mm (17")
Weight of urn: 30kg (66 lb)
Weight of pedestal: 33kg (73 lb)

Alternative pedestals: B130, B300, B310, B400, B420, B440, B480.

Trafalgar Urn
A620

An urn of early XIX century design with egg and dart moulding around the rim and a fluted base. This urn can be used as a decorative ornament on balustrade piers.

Width at top: 585mm (23")
Width at base: 240mm (9½")
Height: 430mm (17")
Weight: 48kg (106 lb)

Recommended pedestals: B300, B310, B331, B400, B420, B440, B695.

Sheraton Vase
A610

Designed by Haddonstone, this charming vase features gadrooning and fluting to the bowl, enriched around the rim with rods and ribbons in the style of Sheraton. Ideal for interior planting in conservatories and garden rooms.

Height: 355mm (14")
Width overall: 395mm (15½")
Width at base: 230mm (9")
Weight: 32kg (70 lb)

Recommended pedestals: B300, B310, B331, B400, B420, B440, B480.

House of Dun Urn
A420

Commissioned by the National Trust for Scotland to replace the originals at the House of Dun as part of the major restoration programme. The Trust has since granted permission to include the urn in the Haddonstone Collection.

Width at top: 330mm (13")
Width at base: 195mm (7¾")
Height: 425mm (16¾")
Weight: 24kg (53 lb)

Recommended pedestals: B130, B300, B310, B330, B400, B420, B440, B480.

GARDEN & LANDSCAPE PLANTERS - TRADITIONAL

Gothic Urn and Base A370

A Regency-period octagonal urn with single quatrefoil panels mounted on a waisted square base. These impressive urns line the Rose Walk at Lambeth Palace. Gothic Vase (see below), Gothic Jardiniere (page 33) and Large Gothic Jardiniere (page 32) also available.

Width at top of urn: 620mm (24½")
Width at base of urn: 355mm (14")
Width of base: 485mm (19")
Height of urn: 585mm (23")
Height overall: 745mm (29¼")
Weight overall: 150kg (330 lb)

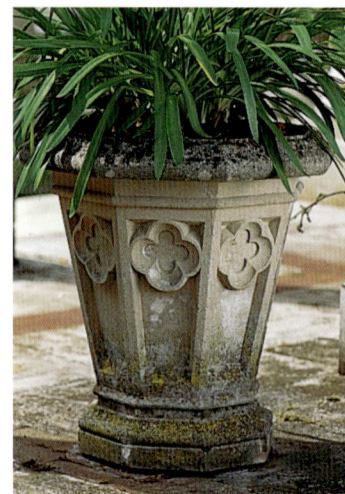

Florentine Urn
A290

Reproduced from an ornate early XIX century urn acquired from Florence, this design is swathed in a rich vine relief, with gadrooning around the base.

Width at top: 585mm (23")
Width at base: 335mm (13¼")
Height: 890mm (35")
Weight: 115kg (253 lb)

Recommended pedestals: B255, B265, B350, B370

Etruscan Vase
A280

The beautiful Etruscan Vase was commissioned by a private client and features a simple campana shape with gadrooning to the bowl and an egg and dart rim.

Width at top: 420mm (16½")
Width at base: 195mm (7½")
Height: 460mm (18")
Weight: 19kg (42 lb)

Recommended pedestals: B130, B300, B310, B330, B400, B420, B440, B480.

Versailles Vase
A690

A simple campana-shaped state vase with restrained gadrooning to the bowl. Identical in proportion to Large Versailles Vase A680, see page 22. This design was replicated from a Blashfield original.

Width at top: 535mm (21")
Width at base: 255mm (10")
Height: 685mm (27")
Weight: 50kg (110 lb)

Recommended pedestals: B255, B265, B300, B310, B331, B400, B420, B440, B695.

Gothic Vase
A380

Regency-style octagonal vase with single quatrefoil panels. Ideal for decorating a terrace. Gothic Urn and Base (see above), Gothic Jardiniere (page 33) and Large Gothic Jardiniere (page 32) also available.

Width at top: 565mm (22¼")
Width at base: 400mm (15¾")
Height: 590mm (23¼")
Weight: 70kg (154 lb)

Eastwell Urn
A260

A large, elegant tazza with elaborately interlaced ribbonwork decoration around the bowl. It can also be supplied in fountain form as a centrepiece (see C200 on page 84).

Width at top: 785mm (31")
Width at base: 350mm (13¾")
Height: 595mm (23½")
Weight: 89kg (195 lb)

Recommended pedestals: B255, B265, B350, B370

Shugborough Vase
A585

The Shugborough Vase is a replica of an original we were commissioned to replace at Shugborough Hall. The proportions of this vase allow its use as a decorative ornament to enhance Haddonstone balustrading.

Width at top: 320mm (12½")
Width overall: 420mm (16½")
Width at base: 215mm (8½")
Height: 430mm (17")
Weight: 40kg (88 lb)

Recommended pedestals: B300, B310, B330, B400, B420, B440, B480

Cliveden Vase
A220

The National Trust commissioned this replica to replace damaged vases at Cliveden, Buckinghamshire.

Width at top: 415mm (16¼")
Width overall: 520mm (20½")
Width at base: 285mm (11¼")
Height: 560mm (22")
Weight: 82kg (182 lb)

Recommended pedestals: B255, B265, B331

Large Acanthus Urn
Q997

Taken from a Doulton original of c1840, this elegant design features bold gadrooning and acanthus leaf decoration.

Width at top: 360mm (14¼")
Width overall: 595mm (23½")
Width at base: 380mm (15")
Height: 805mm (31¾")
Weight: 144kg (317 lb)

Recommended pedestals: B255, B265, B370

Warwick Castle Urn
A740

Haddonstone was commissioned by Warwick Castle to reproduce this urn as part of the castle's restoration project for the rose garden.

Width at top: 405mm (16")
Width overall: 560mm (22")
Width at base: 355mm (14")
Height: 510mm (20")
Weight: 78kg (173 lb)

Recommended pedestals: B255, B265, B370.

French Urn
A320

A facsimile of a Renaissance campana-shaped urn with medallion and intricate relief of vine leaves. The underside of the bowl and the neck are decorated with acanthus leaves.

Width at top: 660mm (26")
Width at base: 330mm (13")
Height: 650mm (25½")
Weight: 96kg (211 lb)

Recommended pedestals: B255, B265, B350, B370

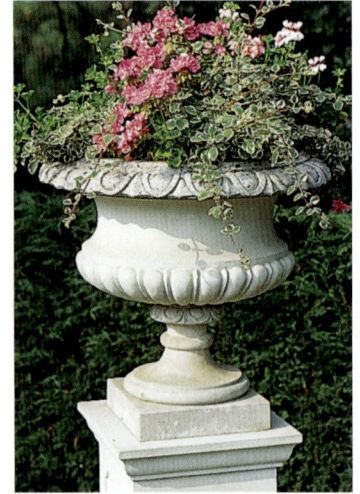

Small Haddo House Urn A395
Large Haddo House Urn A390

Haddonstone was commissioned by the National Trust for Scotland to replicate these urns. Haddo House is a splendid design by William Adam, built between 1732 and 1735 for William, 2nd Earl of Aberdeen. The campana-shaped urns that adorn the grounds are decorated with restrained gadrooning to the bowl incorporating scrolled handles.

Small Haddo House Urn:
Width at top: 570mm (22½")   Height: 755mm (29¾")
Width at base: 305mm (12")   Weight: 68kg (150 lb)
Recommended pedestals: B255, B265, B350

Large Haddo House Urn:
Width at top: 650mm (25½")   Height: 885mm (34¾")
Width at base: 330mm (13")   Weight: 95kg (209 lb)
Recommended pedestals: B255, B265, B350, B370

Zahra Vase
A790

The abstract pattern of this vase with stylised Ashoka buds, tendrils and leaf nodes results from a cultural blend of Islamic and Indian traditions.

Width at top: 580mm (22¾")
Width at base: 430mm (17")
Height: 660mm (26")
Weight: 120kg (264 lb)

Hadrian Vase
A404 (without handles)

The Hadrian Vase combines a half-gadrooned bowl with egg-and-dart rim, a circular socle and square base. The Hadrian Vase is also available with handles, see right.

Width at top: 760mm (30")
Width at base: 350mm (13¾")
Height: 685mm (27")
Weight: 158kg (348 lb)

Recommended pedestals: B255, B265, B350

Turn to Specialist Services - Archives for further ornament options

Hadrian Vase

A405 (with handles)

The Hadrian Vase combines a half-gadrooned bowl with egg-and-dart rim, two scroll and foliate carved handles, a circular socle and square base. The Hadrian Vase is also available without handles, see left.

Maximum width: 970mm (38")
Height: 840mm (33")
Width at base: 350mm (13¾")
Weight: 171kg (377 lb)

Recommended pedestals: B255, B265, B350

GARDEN & LANDSCAPE
PLANTERS - TRADITIONAL

Westonbirt Urn A755

Commissioned as a commemoration by the governors of Westonbirt School, Gloucestershire. The original was manufactured by Pulham from a design attributed to the architect Lewis Vulliamy who was active in the early XIX century. This scaled-down version is typical of his style, featuring spiralled gadrooning and egg-and-dart rim.

Width at top: 700mm (27¾") Height: 650mm (25½")
Width at base: 380mm (15¼") Weight: 129kg (285 lb)

Recommended pedestals: B255, B265, B370

Winslow Vase A770
Winslow Pedestal
B350

An unusual design with fluted decoration and leaf mouldings. Its elegant proportions make it ideal for entrances and walkways.

Width at vase top: 620mm (24½")
Width at vase base: 300mm (11¾")
Pedestal top width: 355mm (14")
Pedestal base width: 525mm (20¾")
Height of vase: 865mm (34")
Height of pedestal: 205mm (8")
Weight of vase: 84kg (186 lb)
Weight of pedestal: 57kg (125 lb)

Recommended pedestals: B255, B265, B350, B370

Swagged Adam
Vase A605

Adapted from Haddonstone's popular finial, see page 71, the Swagged Adam Vase is a stylish planter featuring drapery swags.

Width overall: 495mm (19½")
Width at base: 229mm (9")
Height: 530mm (20⅞")
Weight: 50kg (110 lb)

Recommended pedestals: B420, B440, B490, B495.

(Registered Design No. 2039118)

Ionian Vase
A425

This design in the Greek Revival style features a ribbed neck with a gadrooned bowl surmounted by a palmette band and an egg and dart rim design. Designed for use in conjunction with the Ionian Jardiniere (see page 28).

Width at top: 500mm (19¾")
Width at base: 270mm (10⅝")
Height: 845mm (33¼")
Weight: 104kg (229 lb)

Recommended pedestals: B255, B265, B331

(Registered Design No. 3010465)

Festooned Vase
A285

Designed for use in association with the Festooned Jardiniere (see page 28), this design by Haddonstone can be elevated on a variety of standard pedestals and plinths.

Width at top: 520mm (20½")
Width at base: 280mm (11")
Height: 850mm (33½")
Weight: 115kg (253 lb)

Recommended pedestals: B255, B265, B331

(Registered Design No. GB 3014439)

Fontainebleau Urn A300

This elegant urn is a replica of an XVIII century marble original. It is also available as a fountain centrepiece (see C230 on page 84).

Width at top: 915mm (36")
Width at base: 470mm (18½")

Height: 635mm (25")
Weight: 166kg (366 lb)

Recommended pedestals: B120, B360

Jubilee Urn A440

To commemorate the occasion of our Silver Jubilee in 1996, Haddonstone produced a Jubilee Urn inspired by James Blashfield's XIX century artificial stone tazza. A special limited edition of twenty-five was launched at the Chelsea Flower Show. A standard edition is now a part of the Haddonstone Collection.

Width at top: 810mm (32")
Width at base: 330mm (13")

Height: 775mm (29¾")
Weight: 145kg (319 lb)

Recommended pedestals: B120, B255, B265, B350

(Registered Design No. 2056413)

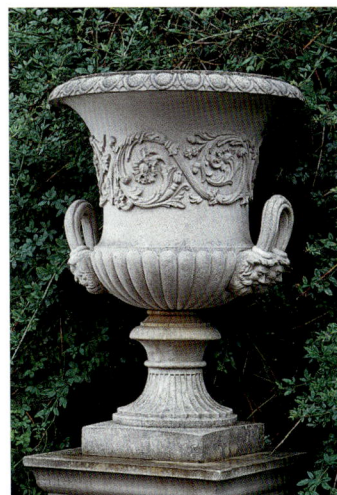

State Vase with handles A600
State Vase without handles A590
(not illustrated)

This imposing mid-Victorian design has been translated from a cast-iron original and is available with or without handles.

Width at top: 560mm (22")
Width at base: 300mm (11¾")
Height: 785mm (31")
Weight: 81kg (179 lb)

Recommended pedestals: B255, B265, B350, B370

Large Clarence Urn A214

An elegant Regency-style urn, identical in proportion to the Clarence Urn A215, see page 14.

Width at top: 780mm (30¾")
Width at base: 350mm (13¾")
Height: 605mm (23¾")
Weight: 104kg (229 lb)

Recommended pedestals: B255, B265

(Registered Design No. 2083499)

Large Versailles Vase A680

A handsome campana-shaped vase with gadrooning to the bowl. Identical in proportion to Versailles Vase A690, see page 16.

Width at top: 785mm (31")   Height: 1065mm (42")
Width at base: 380mm (15")   Weight: 179kg (395 lb)

Recommended pedestals: B120, B370

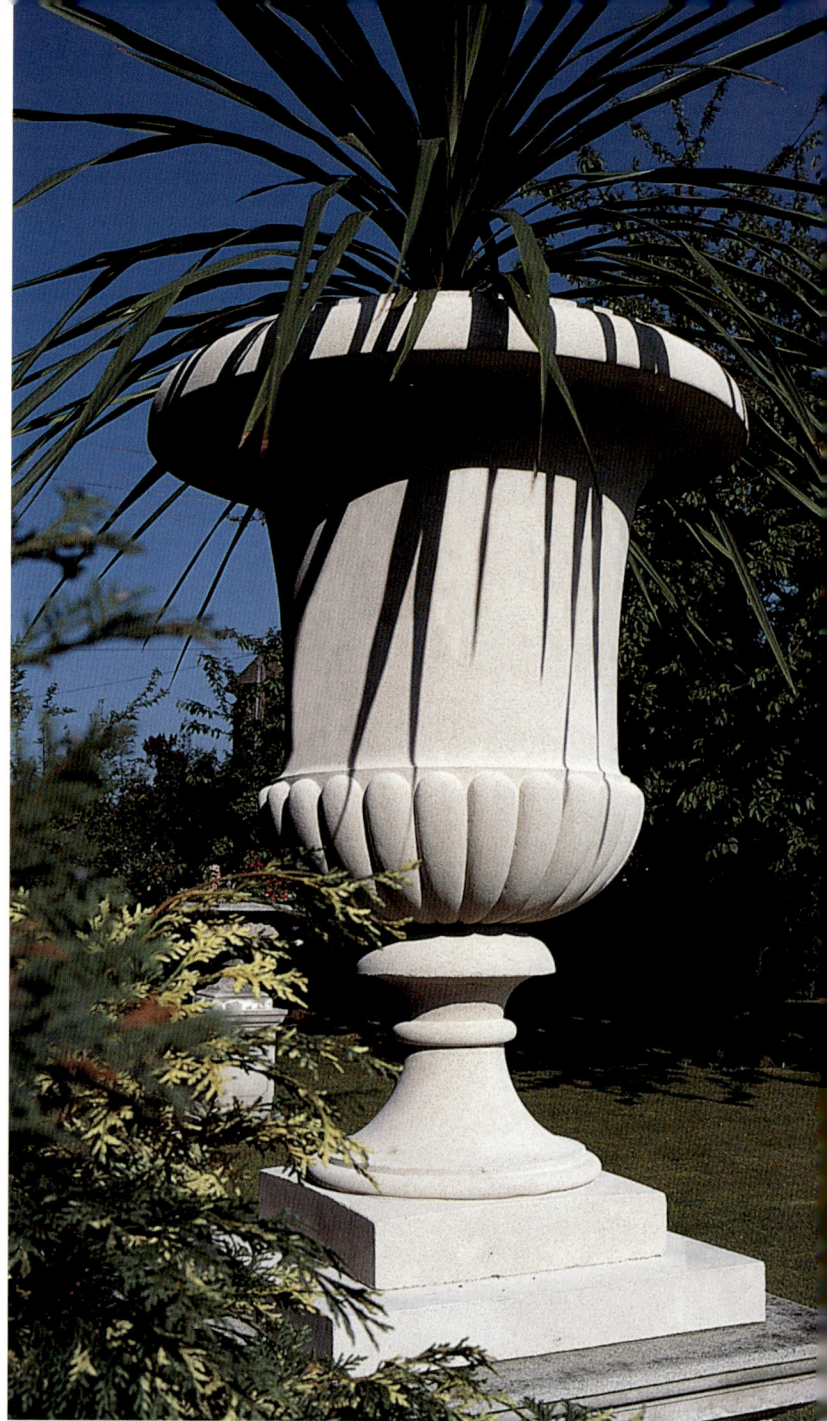

Campana Vase A212

The campana-shaped bowl features stylised acanthus leaf decoration.

Width at top: 755mm (29¾")   Height: 1035mm (40¾")
Width at base: 460mm (18⅛")   Weight: 187kg (412 lb)

Recommended pedestal: B120.

Tatham Tazza Q998

The Coade original for this fine design dates from c1812 and is known as the Tatham Tazza after Charles Heathcote Tatham (1772-1842), an architect of considerable repute who studied in Italy.

Width at top: 890mm (35")
Width at base: 460mm (18⅛")
Height: 660mm (26")
Weight: 127kg (280 lb)

Recommended pedestals: B120, B360

Gallé Vase A325

Replicated for the National Trust Ascott Estate, where the originals stand in the Venus Fountain Garden. The bowl of this striking vase has a wide rim and is decorated with a leaf design having strong art-nouveau influences.

Width at top: 850mm (33½")
Width at base: 420mm (16½")
Height: 985mm (38¾")
Weight: 213kg (470 lb)

Recommended pedestals: B120, B370

Waterloo Urn A750

A large, imposing urn in classical form with deep gadrooning. Stockport Borough Council commissioned Haddonstone to produce a series of Waterloo Urns to line the terraces at Lyme Hall, Cheshire.

Width at top: 785mm (31")
Width at base: 535mm (21")
Height: 760mm (30")
Weight: 205kg (452 lb)

Recommended pedestal: B120

Turn to Specialist Services - Archives for further ornament options

Plaited Jardiniere
A520

This is a replica of an exquisite Victorian jardiniere with a combination of basketwork design to the bowl and leaf moulding to the rim. Neat and compact, it is an immensely versatile piece.

Width at top: 790mm (31")
Width at base: 395mm (15½")
Height: 330mm (13")
Weight: 75kg (162 lb)

Tudor Jardiniere
A630

An interwoven strapwork design with rope decoration around the rim and foot. This jardiniere is designed for placing on walls and piers as well as at ground level.

Width at top: 535mm (21")
Width at base: 360mm (14¼")
Height: 380mm (15")
Weight: 38kg (84 lb)

Small Tudor Jardiniere
A625

In response to requests from our clients for a smaller jardiniere we introduced this piece to the range which complements the popular original Haddonstone design and is ideal for interior planting in conservatories and garden rooms.

Width at top: 395mm (15½")
Width at base: 245mm (9¾")
Height: 290mm (11½")
Weight: 26kg (57 lb)

Elizabethan Jardiniere
A270

A versatile container which complements a traditional or contemporary setting.

Width at top: 660mm (26")
Width at base: 430mm (17")
Height: 470mm (18½")
Weight: 79kg (175 lb)

Small Elizabethan Jardiniere
A275

The attractive strapwork decoration on this design complements the popular Elizabethan Jardiniere. Also, the Elizabethan Box (see page 30).

Width at top: 470mm (18½")
Width at base: 300mm (11¾")
Height: 345mm (13⅝")
Weight: 41kg (90 lb)

(Registered Design No. 2074670)

Large Elizabethan Jardiniere
A272

Created following numerous requests from clients, this version of the popular Elizabethan Jardiniere design provides an excellent planting capacity.

Width at top: 825mm (32½")
Width at base: 510mm (20")
Height: 610mm (24")
Weight: 112kg (247 lb)

GARDEN & LANDSCAPE PLANTERS - TRADITIONAL

Herculean Bowl HA385

The Herculean Bowl - an impressively large jardiniere which will make an impact in any setting. The design features festoons of fruit including pears, plums and grapes, bound together with ribbons and swags.

Height: 1000mm (39⅜")
Width overall: 1200mm (47¼")
Width at base: 600mm (23⅝")
Weight: 340kg (749 lb)

Please note: will require mechanical lifting on site in all instances.

Small Scrolled Jardiniere A575

Haddonstone introduced this jardiniere as a complementary design to the popular Haddonstone Scrolled Jardiniere. Illustrated in our terracotta colour.

Height: 360mm (14¼")
Width overall: 440mm (17¼")
Width at base: 203mm (8")
Weight: 46kg (101 lb)

(Registered Design No. 2054077)

Scrolled Jardiniere A580

Taken from a design by Mary Watts (1849-1938) for the Compton Potters' Arts Guild, this simple and attractive jardiniere was previously attributed to Gertrude Jekyll – a great admirer of Mary Watts and her contribution to the Arts and Crafts movement. Shown here in our terracotta colour.

Width at top: 535mm (21")
Width overall: 595mm (23½")
Width at base: 280mm (11")
Height: 485mm (19")
Weight: 95kg (209 lb)

Small Roman Jardiniere A534

Simple lines and good proportions are the features of this Haddonstone design, which is ideal for topiary box or bay.

Height: 380mm (15")
Width overall: 430mm (17")
Width at base: 203mm (8")
Weight: 55kg (121 lb)

Roman Jardiniere A535

Identical in proportion to the Small Roman Jardiniere. Suitable for either traditional or contemporary gardens and landscapes.

Height: 515mm (20¼")
Width overall: 565mm (22¼")
Width at base: 280mm (11")
Weight: 109kg (240 lb)

Spartan Bowl HA615

Adapted from the Herculean Bowl, this massive planter features elegant lines and bold mouldings.

Height: 1000mm (39⅜")
Width overall: 1200mm (47¼")
Width at base: 600mm (23⅝")
Weight: 340kg (749 lb)

Please note: will require mechanical lifting on site in all instances.

Roman Vase
TLHA540

This Italian vase with simple circular mouldings is suitable for large and small plantings. Illustrated in our terracotta colour.

Width at top: 610mm (24")
Width at base: 265mm (10½")
Height: 485mm (19")
Weight: 38kg (84 lb)

Large Roman Vase
TLHA545

Complementing the standard Roman Vase is this taller example, which also features simple circular mouldings. Illustrated in our terracotta colour.

Width at top: 790mm (31")
Width at base: 390mm (15½")
Height: 815mm (32")
Weight: 110kg (242 lb)

Compton Bowl
A225

Suitable for either traditional or contemporary gardens, this simple and attractive bowl is adapted from the Poppy Bowl, based upon a design by Mary Watts (1849-1938) for the Compton Potters' Arts Guild.

Width at top: 710mm (28")
Width at base: 320mm (12½")
Height: 535mm (21")
Weight: 94kg (207 lb)

(Registered Design No. 2072887)

Poppy Bowl
A525

Based upon a design by Mary Watts (1849-1938) for the Compton Potters' Arts Guild, this versatile bowl is ideal for terraces and patios. This design reflects the style of the Arts and Crafts movement.

Width at top: 710mm (28")
Width at base: 320mm (12½")
Height: 535mm (21")
Weight: 100kg (220 lb)

(Registered Design No.2072886)

GARDEN & LANDSCAPE PLANTERS - TRADITIONAL

Large Gothic Basket
A335

The new Large Gothic Basket design is a taller version of Haddonstone's popular Gothic Basket. First created as a bespoke design for a private client, this planter is ideal for enhancing terraces, patios and garden rooms.

Height: 647mm (25½")
Width at top: (762mm (30")
Width at base: 450mm (17¾")
Weight: 145kg (319 lb)

Ionian Smokers' Stand HA424S

An elegant design adapted from the Ionian Jardiniere (see right) for use by hotels, restaurants and retail premises. Features a removable stainless steel sleeve for cleaning. Suitable for both interiors and exteriors.

Width of top: 500mm (19¾")
Height: 510mm (20⅛")
Weight:106kg (233 lb)

(Registered Design No. 3010464)

Ionian Jardiniere
A424

This design has been created by Haddonstone in the Greek Revival style. The jardiniere features a palmette around a cylindrical form and has been designed for use in conjunction with the Ionian Vase (see page 20).

Width at top: 500mm (19¾")
Height: 510mm (20⅛")
Weight: 93kg (205 lb)

(Registered Design No. 3010464)

Festooned Jardiniere
A284

A bold design created by Haddonstone featuring festoons of fruit bound together with ribbons in the classical style. Designed for use in conjunction with the Festooned Vase (see page 20).

Width at top: 520mm (20½")
Width at base: 400mm (15¾")
Height: 565mm (22¼")
Weight: 84kg (185 lb)

(Registered Design No. GB 3014438)

Gothic Basket
A330

A neo-Gothic-style basket with interlaced strapwork and acanthus-leaf moulding around the base. The rim is decorated with leaf and ribbon moulding.

Width at top: 622mm (24½")
Width at base: 387mm (15¼")
Height: 413mm (16¼")
Weight: 56kg (123 lb)

(Registered Design No. 1059496)

Kensington Bowl
A450

This large and versatile twelve-sided planter features an entwined hop design around the bowl.

Width: 735mm (29")
Height: 405mm (16")

Diameter at base: 455mm (18")
Weight: 102kg (226 lb)

Marlborough Bowl
A495

In the style of a Greek kylix, this elegant bowl is a Haddonstone design featuring a square base with gadrooning to the bowl.

Height: 365mm (14⅜")
Width overall: 600mm (23⅝")
Width at base: 330mm (13")
Weight: 72kg (159 lb)

Recommended pedestals: B255, B265, B350.

Byzantine Bowl
A210

Replicated from a Verona marble bowl of Byzantine design. Within foliate borders, it is decorated with four oval panels featuring stylised mythological creatures. These panels are divided by ornate strapwork.

Width: 530mm (21")
Height: 440mm (17½")
Diameter at base: 280 mm (11")
Weight: 78kg (172 lb)

Romanesque Bowl
TLHA550

An extremely useful bowl featuring Romanesque coin-moulding motifs in a band around the rim. It is also available as a freestanding fountain (see page 92, TLHC521).

Diameter: 815mm (32")
Width at base: 435mm (17⅛")
Height: 330mm (13")
Weight: 62kg (137 lb)

Plaited Basket
A510

A delightful oval basket with plaited rim. See also, the Plaited Trough A515, page 36.

Length: 510mm (20")
Width: 395mm (15½")
Height: 215mm (8½")
Weight: 17kg (37 lb)

Haddonstone Box
A400

A design composed of bouquets of flowers with ribbon and knot detail.

Width: 420mm (16½")
Height: 420mm (16½")
Weight: 71kg (156 lb)

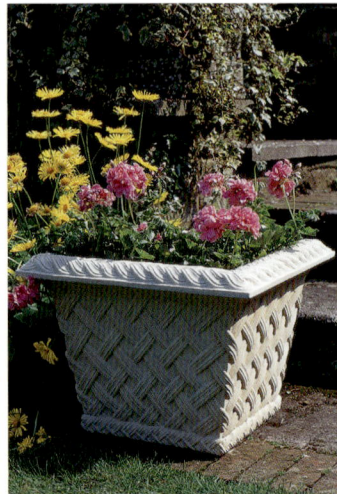

Belton Box
A195

A small planting box in Victorian style having a basketwork design of rod and ribbon to all sides. Ideal as a planter for wall tops, steps, or either side of an entrance doorway. The design complements that of our Belton Troughs (see page 36).

Width at top: 330mm (13")
Width at base: 165mm (6½")
Height: 260mm (10¼")
Weight: 18kg (40 lb)

Elizabethan Box
A265

An alternative shape designed to complement our Small Elizabethan Jardiniere (see page 24) with the attractive strapwork decoration that has become so popular.

Width at top: 470mm (18½")
Width at base: 300mm (11¾")
Height: 345mm (13⅝")
Weight: 49kg (108 lb)

Maidford Bowl
A480

This versatile design by Haddonstone, in the style of James Gibbs, has a fluted bowl with stylised leaf moulding to the rim and base. Named after the Manorial Lordship of Maidford Halse in Northamptonshire.

Width overall: 600mm (23⅝")
Height: 280mm (11")
Width at base: 343mm (13½")
Weight: 46kg (101 lb)

Turn to Specialist Services - Archives for further ornament options

Large Italian Jardiniere HA435

This large jardiniere complements the popular existing Italian Jardiniere designs.

Width at top: 1015mm (40")
Width at base: 790mm (31⅛")
Height: 760mm (30")
Weight: 400kg (881 lb)

(Registered Design No. 2061157)

Please note: will require mechanical lifting on site in all instances.

Italian Jardiniere
A430

A versatile jardiniere with reticulated rose and rod decoration with rope moulding around the rim and foot.

Width at top: 630mm (24¾")
Width at base: 495mm (19½")
Height: 405mm (16")
Weight: 73kg (161 lb)

Italian Quadrant Planter (1 section)
A431

The Italian Quadrant Planter provides a solution to the problem of how to ornament a difficult corner. Decorated on one side, yet plain on the other two faces, the planter can be: positioned in a corner; two can be placed side by side to create a wall trough; three can wrap round a corner; whilst four can create a compartmentalised planter ideal for containing invasive plants or herbs.

Italian Quadrant Planter (2 section)
A432

Italian Quadrant Planter (3 section)
A433

Italian Quadrant Planter (4 section) A434

Top radius: 500mm (19¾")
Base radius: 415mm (16⅜")
Height: 515mm (20¼")
Weight (per section): 73kg (161 lb)

Andalos Jardiniere A150

An Arabesque design. The twelve-sided bowl displays an hexagonal decoration, whilst the hexagonal base features a twelve-sided decoration. Also available is the freestanding Andalos Fountain C100, see page 94.

Width at rim: 725mm (28½")
Width at base: 560mm (22")
Height: 770mm (30¼")
Weight: 171kg (377 lb)

Corredo Jardiniere A230
Corredo Jardiniere Plinth A240

The original of this imposing Italian planter bearing two armorial devices was probably a dowry gift in the XVI century. A plinth is available.

Jardiniere width: 860mm (33⅞")
Jardiniere base: 450mm (17¾")
Jardiniere height: 635mm (25")
Plinth width: 660mm (26")
Plinth height: 172mm (6¾")

Jardiniere weight: 153kg (337 lb)
Plinth weight: 77kg (170 lb)

Large Gothic Jardiniere HA345
Large Gothic Upper Base HA355 (in 8 sections)

This imposing jardiniere and base has been created to meet clients' requests for a larger version of the popular Gothic Jardiniere. The octagonal design incorporates double-quatrefoil panels on each face. The Upper Base fits around the Jardiniere, making the overall height of the ensemble 1190mm (46⅞").

Overall width of jardiniere: 1252mm (49¼")
Overall width of jardiniere base: 966mm (38")
Height of jardiniere: 1190mm (46⅞")
Weight of jardiniere: 1336kg (2943 lb)
Overall width of base: 1998mm (78⁹⁄₁₆")
Height of base: 160mm (6¼")
Weight of base: 302kg (664 lb)

Please note: will require mechanical lifting on site in all instances.

Gothic Jardiniere
A340

Upper Base A350
Lower Base A360

A Regency Gothic octagonal jardiniere with double-quatrefoil panels. It has alternate acanthus and rose relief bosses. Shown on an Upper Base in four sections. For Lower Base in eight sections see diagram. It is also available as a freestanding fountain (see page 94, C251).

It is essential that your Gothic Jardiniere and bases are sited on a firm and level area. An 8 to 1 sand/cement bedding mortar should be used to ensure that the weight of the Jardiniere and bases is spread evenly, avoiding any pivoting or twisting strain. We cannot accept responsibility for cracking or breakage if this instruction is ignored.

Weight of jardiniere:
   224kg (494 lb)
Weight of Upper Base:
   128kg (282 lb)
Weight of Lower Base:
   342kg (754 lb)

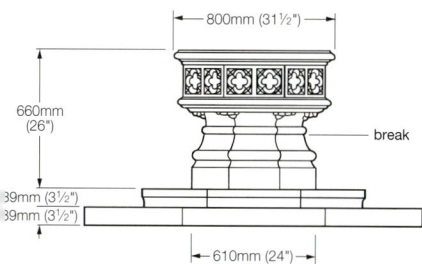

800mm (31½")
660mm (26")
39mm (3½")
39mm (3½")
break
610mm (24")

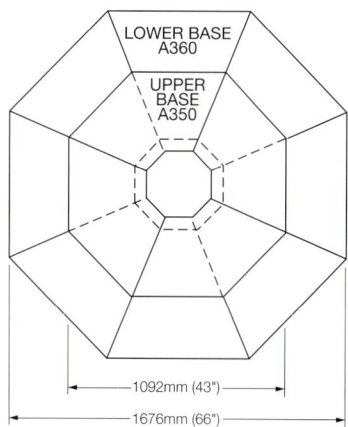

LOWER BASE A360
UPPER BASE A350
1092mm (43")
1676mm (66")

Victorian Jardiniere
A710
Upper Plinth A720
Lower Plinth A730

inspired by an Austin & Seeley design, this imposing ensemble is an elegant example of the XIX century naturalist style of ornament. The surprising combination of basketwork and dragon's feet is characteristic of this style. These jardinieres are used by the Royal Horticultural Society at Wisley. See diagrams below for dimensions.

Jardiniere weight: 205kg (452 lb)
A720 plinth weight: 86kg (190 lb)
A730 plinth weight: 118kg (260 lb)
Ensemble weight: 409kg (902 lb)

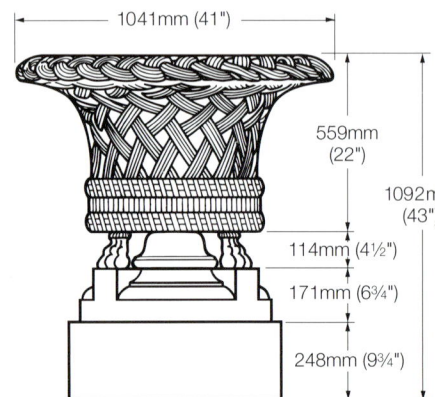

1041mm (41")
559mm (22")
1092m (43")
114mm (4½")
171mm (6¾")
248mm (9¾")

Victorian Jardiniere A710
with A720 and A730 Plinths.

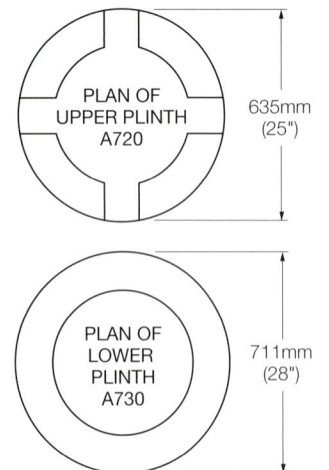

PLAN OF UPPER PLINTH A720
635mm (25")

PLAN OF LOWER PLINTH A730
711mm (28")

It is essential that the Victorian Jardiniere and plinths are sited on a firm and level area. An 8-1 sand/cement bedding mortar should be used to ensure that the weight of the jardiniere and bases is spread evenly, avoiding any pivoting or twisting strain. We cannot accept responsibility for cracking or breakage if this instruction is ignored.

Well Head C600

This highly decorative well head takes the form of a Corinthian capital.
Shown with Overthrow WA900 by Haddoncraft Forge.

Width at top: 1000mm (39¼")
Width at base: 850mm (33½")
Height: 900mm (35½")
Weight: 352kg (776 lb)

Victorian Jardiniere A710
Upper Plinth A720
Lower Plinth A730

Victorian Trough and Support
A735

The design of this charming rectangular trough, taken from a Vicenza stone original, is embellished with festoons of ribbon-tied roses and acanthus leaves, with gadrooning to the rim.

Length: 650mm (25¾")   Height: 395mm (15¾")
Width: 370mm (14½")   Weight: 73kg (160 lb)

Belton Wall Trough
A200

A simple Victorian basketwork design with rod and ribbon detailing and a plain back. Can be used as a window box. The design complements the Belton Box, see page 30.

Length: 865mm (34")
Width: 305mm (12")
Height: 260mm (10¼")
Weight: 50kg (110 lb)

Belton Trough A190

A variation of the Belton Wall Trough with rod and ribbon detailing to all sides. The design complements the Belton Box, see page 30.

Length: 865mm (34")
Width: 380mm (15")
Height: 260mm (10¼")
Weight: 55kg (121 lb)

Plaited Trough
A515

Complementing the Plaited Basket A510 (see page 30), this basketweave design is ideal for low walls and terraces.

Length: 770mm (30¼")   Height: 215mm (8½")
Width: 395mm (15½")   Weight: 32kg (70 lb)

(Registered Design No.2074669)

Venetian Trough A650
Fluted Supports A670

Reproduced from an original XV century Venetian design, this trough looks attractive when elevated on supports and placed against a wall.

Length: 1170mm (46")
Width: 385mm (15⅛")
Height of trough only: 400mm (15¾")

Height of supports: 395mm (15½")
Weight of trough: 153kg (337 lb)
Weight of each support: 35kg (77 lb)

Adam Trough A110
Adam Supports A120

This Adam-style trough, adorned with festoons and medallions, is ideal for decorating terraces or porches. For Adam Box, see below.

Length: 1220mm (48")
Width: 345mm (13½")
Height of trough only: 355mm (14")

Height of supports: 140mm (5½')
Weight of trough: 176kg (388 lb)
Weight of each support: 11kg (25 lb)

Adam Box
A100

An Adam-style container decorated with festoons and medallions, ideal for use on walls or terraces. For Adam Trough, see above.

Length: 610mm (24")
Width: 305mm (12")
Height: 380mm (15")
Weight: 55kg (121 lb)

Arabesque Trough A160
Arabesque Supports A170

Arabesque-style trough featuring an interlaced flower and leaf pattern set in banded panels. Can be raised on supports if desired.

Length: 1015mm (40")
Width: 345mm (13½")
Height of trough only: 355mm (14")
Height of supports: 127mm (5")
Weight of trough: 112kg (247 lb)
Weight of each support: 10kg (22 lb)

GARDEN & LANDSCAPE PLANTERS - TRADITIONAL

Roman Trough
A555

This stylish trough with a strigillated design has been created by Haddonstone for use in both traditional and contemporary schemes.

Length: 1100mm (43⅝")
Width: 400mm (15¼")
Height: 380mm (15")
Weight: 156kg (344 lb)

(Registered Design No. 2056402)

Small Alpine Trough
A140 (not illustrated)

This rustic trough is an ideal container for a miniature alpine garden.

Length: 850mm (33½")
Width: 560mm (22")
Height: 255mm (10")
Weight: 102kg (224 lb)

Large Alpine Trough
A130

The Large Alpine Trough is much sought after by alpine specialists.

Length: 1090mm (43")
Width: 660mm (26")
Height: 280mm (11")
Weight: 156kg (344 lb)

Promenade Trough
HA527 (USA only)

The Promenade Trough is available exclusively to clients of Haddonstone (USA) Ltd. Featuring an impressive planting area, this rectangular trough is ideal for large landscape schemes. It is possible to cast lettering or dates into this trough during production. Please ask for details.

Length: 62½"   Height: 23⅜"
Width: 28¼"   Weight: 1400 lb

Please note: will require mechanical lifting on site in all instances.

GARDEN & LANDSCAPE PLANTERS - CONTEMPORARY

Haddonstone, long associated with classical and traditional design, is now also renowed for contemporary style. The Art Deco and Cubist inspired planters on the following pages first brought Haddonstone's Modernist designs to the fore. Most feature geometric patterns and all are suitable for either residential or commercial projects.

Large Key HA955

Width: 500mm (19¾")
Height: 510mm (20¼")
Weight: 156kg (344 lb)

Key TLHA950

Width: 305mm (12")
Height: 305mm (12")
Weight: 20kg (44lb)

Block TLHA915

Width: 305mm (12")
Height: 305mm (12")
Weight: 20kg (44 lb)

Puzzle TLHA965

Width: 305mm (12")
Height: 305mm (12")
Weight: 20kg (44 lb)

Rib TLHA970

Width: 305mm (12")
Height: 305mm (12")
Weight: 20kg (44 lb)

Strap TLHA975

Width: 305mm (12")
Height: 305mm (12")
Weight: 20kg (44 lb)

Small Puzzle TLHA966
Small Key TLHA951
Small Rib TLHA971

Width: 100mm (4")
Height: 112mm (4½")
Weight (each): 1kg (2lb 3oz)

GARDEN & LANDSCAPE
PLANTERS - CONTEMPORARY

Classic
TLHA930

Width at top: 650mm (25⅝")
Width at base: 355mm (14")
Height: 545mm (21½")
Weight: 55kg (121 lb)

Cube
TLHA935

Width: 420mm (16½")
Height: 420mm (16½")
Weight: 46kg (101 lb)

Meander
TLHA960

Width: 420mm (16½")
Height: 420mm (16½")
Weight: 51kg (112 lb)

Arc
TLHA900

Width: 420mm (16½")
Height: 430mm (16¹⁵⁄₁₆")
Weight: 54kg (119 lb)

Crucible
HA910

Crucible Fountain also available, see page 95.

Width: 500mm (19¾")
Height: 620mm (24⅜")
Weight: 102kg (225 lb)

Turn to Specialist Services - Archives for further ornament options

Sunburst
HA980

Width: 450mm (17¾")
Height: 545mm (21½")
Weight: 140kg (308 lb)

Flute
HA940

Width at top: 600mm (23¾")
Width at base: 340mm (13⅜")
Height: 660mm (26")
Weight: 141kg (311 lb)

Chalice
HA920

Width: 420mm (16½")
Height: 840mm (33¹⁄₁₆")
Weight: 158kg (348 lb)

Large Highland Park Fire Pit HA413 (USA only)

The Large Highland Fire Pit is an innovation from Haddonstone (USA) Ltd. Ideal for yards and terraces, the Fire Pit provides a unique focal point – and warmth as the sun goes down! Available in both manual and automatic versions. Black firecrystals not supplied.

Width at top: 40"
Width at base: 32"
Height: 17"
Weight: 432 lb

Design: Mark Salzman

Large Highland Park Planter
A414

Width at top: 1016mm (40")
Width at base: 812mm (32")
Height: 430mm (17")
Weight: 182kg (400 lb)

Small Highland Park Planter
A415

Width at top: 762mm (30")
Width at base: 635mm (25")
Height: 355mm (14")
Weight: 86kg (190 lb)

Small Octagonal Jardiniere HA503
Medium Octagonal Jardiniere HA504

Featuring bold ogee mouldings, these jardinieres complement the Large Octagonal Jardiniere, see right.

Small Octagonal Jardiniere
Maximum width face to face: 615mm (24 1/4")
Height: 390mm (15 3/8")
Weight: 140kg (308 lb)

Medium Octagonal Jardiniere
Maximum width face to face: 1010mm (39 3/4")
Height: 635mm (25")
Weight: 450kg (991 lb)
Please note: will require mechanical lifting on site in all instances.

Bay Planter
HA185

The stylish Bay Planter is a new addition to the Haddonstone Collection. Also available as a self-circulating fountain, see page 94.

Height: 400mm (15³/₄")
Width at top: 1850mm (72⁷/₈")
Weight: 690kg (1520 lb)

Small Lagoon Planter HA460 (not illustrated)
Lagoon Planter HA463
Large Lagoon Planter HA465 (not illustrated)

These designs also available as self-circulating fountains, see page 92.

	HA460	HA463	HA465
Height:	600mm (23⁵/₈")	600mm (23⁵/₈")	600mm (23⁵/₈")
Top width:	1220mm (48")	1570mm (61³/₄")	1775mm (69⁷/₈")
Weight:	535kg (1178 lb)	857kg (1888 lb)	1092kg (2405 lb)

Large Octagonal Jardiniere HA505

Featuring bold ogee mouldings, this octagonal jardiniere allows shrub roots to reach the underlying soil, as the design is produced without a base.

Max width face to face: 1230mm (48¹/₂")
Height: 770mm (30¹/₄")
Weight: 800kg (1762 lb)

Please note: all planters on this page will require mechanical lifting on site in all instances.

43

The Robert A.M. Stern Collection

Robert A.M. Stern is the founding partner of the architectural firm that bears his name. The firm has an international reputation as a leading design practice with wide experience in residential, commercial, office, hospitality, healthcare and institutional work. Attention to detail and a commitment to design quality has resulted in the creation of the Robert A.M. Stern Collection comprising a wide range of interior and exterior products. Each partner company has been identified as a market-leader with a reputation for outstanding design, superb performance and unparalleled customer service. Haddonstone is proud to have been selected on this basis. The first planter and pedestal designs from the resultant collection are shown on these pages.

Olympian Vase
A911

Maximum width: 413mm (16¼")
Width at base: 300mm (11¹³/₁₆")
Height: 914mm (36")
Weight: 110kg (242 lb)

Small Olympian Bowl
A915 Excludes B332 Pedestal

Maximum width: 630mm (24¹³/₁₆")
Width at base: 292mm (11½")
Height: 324mm (12¾")
Weight: 60kg (131 lb)
Recommended Stern pedestals: B940, B950.

Small Olympian Urn
A913 Excludes B332 Pedestal

Maximum width: 505mm (19⅞")
Width at base: 286mm (11¼")
Height: 526mm (20¾")
Weight: 60kg (131 lb)
Recommended Stern pedestals: B940, B950.

Olympian Urn
A912

Maximum width: 760mm (29¹⁵/₁₆")
Width at base: 410mm (16⅛")
Height: 784mm (30⅞")
Weight: 198kg (435 lb)
Recommended Stern pedestal: B930.

Olympian Bowl
A914

Maximum width: 945mm (37¼")
Width at base: 420mm (16½")
Height: 480mm (18⅞")
Weight: 152kg (335 lb)
Recommended Stern pedestal: B930.

Athenian Urn

A923 Excludes B332 Pedestal

Width at top: 760mm (29 15/16")
Width at base: 308mm (12 1/8")
Height: 622mm (24 1/2")
Weight: 87kg (192 lb)

Recommended Stern pedestal: B920.

Small Athenian Bowl

A926 Excludes B332 Pedestal

Width at top: 750mm (29 1/2")
Width at base: 230mm (9 1/16")
Height: 340mm (13 3/8")
Weight: 43kg (95 lb)

Recommended Stern pedestal: B900.

Small Athenian Vase

A922 Excludes B332 Pedestal

Width at top: 420mm (16 1/2")
Width at base: 190mm (7 1/2")
Height: 527mm (20 3/4")
Weight: 28kg (62 lb)

Recommended Stern pedestal: B900.

Athenian Vase

A921

Width at top: 625mm (24 5/8")
Width at base: 308mm (12 1/8")
Height: 790mm (31 1/8")
Weight: 96kg (211 lb)

Recommended Stern pedestal: B920.

Athenian Bowl

A925

Width at top: 866mm (34 1/8")
Width at base: 308mm (12 1/8")
Height: 418mm (16 1/2")
Weight: 62kg (135 lb)

Recommended Stern pedestal: B920.

Small Athenian Urn

A924

Width at top: 568mm (22 3/8")
Width at base: 230mm (9 1/16")
Height: 467mm (18 3/8")
Weight: 43kg (95 lb)

Recommended Stern pedestal: B910.

Athenian Vase

A927

Incorporating scrolled foot

Width at top: 625mm (24 5/8")
Width at base: 396mm (15 9/16")
Height: 764mm (30 1/8")
Weight: 96kg (211 lb)

GARDEN & LANDSCAPE PEDESTALS AND PLINTHS

IMPORTANT PEDESTAL SITING It is essential that your Haddonstone pedestal is sited on a firm and level area to suit site conditions and loadings. An 8 to 1 sand/cement bedding mortar should be used to ensure that the weight of the pedestal and urn is spread evenly across the base of the pedestal, avoiding any pivoting or twisting strain. We cannot accept responsibility for cracking or breakage if this instruction is ignored. Technical Sheets available for all Athenian and Olympian pedestals.

48" Olympian Pedestal B950
Shown with
Small Olympian Bowl A915

Width at top: 330mm (13")
Width at base: 508mm (20")
Height: 1219mm (48")
Weight: 113kg (249 lb)

40" Olympian Pedestal B940
Shown with
Small Olympian Urn A913

Width at top: 356mm (14")
Width at base: 508mm (20")
Height: 1016mm (40")
Weight: 120kg (264 lb)

32" Athenian Pedestal B920
Shown with
Athenian Bowl A925

Width at top: 356mm (14")
Width at base: 611mm (24")
Height: 815mm (32⅛")
Weight: 140kg (308 lb)

32" Olympian Pedestal B930
Shown with
Olympian Bowl A914

Width at top: 507mm (20")
Width at base: 610mm (24")
Height: 813mm (32")
Weight: 163kg (359 lb)

38" Slender Athenian Pedestal B900
Shown with
Small Athenian Vase A922

Width at top: 216mm (8½")
Width at base: 409mm (16⅛")
Height: 968mm (38⅛")
Weight: 83kg (183 lb)

38" Athenian Pedestal B910
Shown with
Small Athenian Urn A924

Width at top: 275mm (10⅞")
Width at base: 520mm (20½")
Height: 968mm (38⅛")
Weight: 114kg (251 lb)

42" Athenian Classic Pedestal
B901
Shown with
Caesar Augustus HE815

Width at top: 255mm (10")
Width at base: 409mm (16⅛")
Overall Height: 1066mm (42")
Weight: 93kg (205 lb)

36" Athenian Classic Pedestal
B921
Shown with
Ionian Vase A425

Width at top: 395mm (15½")
Width at base: 611mm (24")
Overall Height: 920mm (36¼")
Weight: 168kg (370 lb)

43" Athenian Classic Pedestal
B911
Shown with
Versailles Vase A690

Width at top: 324mm (12¾")
Width at base: 520mm (20½")
Overall Height: 1085mm (42¾")
Weight: 133kg (293 lb)

B370 Pedestal
(Shown with
Eastwell Urn)

B360 Pedestal
(Shown with
Fontainebleau Urn)

B350 Pedestal
(Shown with
Florentine Urn)

B120 Pedestal
(Shown with
Large Versailles Vase)

B265 Pedestal
(Shown with
State Vase)

B255 Pedestal
(Shown with
Westonbirt Urn)

Dado Pedestal
B370

Classical column pedestal
design with deep recessed
compound moulding.

Width at base: 457mm (18")
Height: 279mm (11")
Weight: 61kg (134 lb)

IMPORTANT
PEDESTAL SITING

It is essential that your Haddonstone
pedestal is sited on a firm and level
area to suit site conditions and
loadings. An 8 to 1 sand/cement
bedding mortar should be used
to ensure that the weight of the
pedestal and urn is spread evenly
across the base of the pedestal,
avoiding any pivoting or twisting
strain. We cannot accept
responsibility for cracking or
breakage if this instruction is ignored.

Large Winslow
Pedestal B360

Large pedestal, identical in
proportion to the Winslow
Pedestal B350, below. For use
with larger urns and vases.

Width at base: 750mm (29½")
Width at top: 508mm (20")
Height: 293mm (11½")
Weight: 212kg (467 lb)

Winslow Pedestal
B350

Robustly moulded pedestal,
ideal for raising urns and vases
slightly above ground level.

Width at base: 525mm (20¾")
Width at top: 355mm (14")
Height: 205mm (8")
Weight: 57kg (125 lb)

Georgian Pedestal
B120

Imposing pedestal with deep
recessed compound mouldings.

Width at base: 700mm (27½")
Width at cap: 735mm (29")
Width of block: 546mm (21½")
Height (inc. block): 908mm (35¾")
Weight: 389kg (857 lb)

36"Queen Anne
Pedestal B265

Pedestal featuring a deeply
fielded panel to the pedestal shaft.

Cap and base width: 485mm (19")
Height: 915mm (36")
Weight: 170kg (375 lb)

27"Queen Anne
Pedestal B255

Pedestal featuring a deeply
fielded panel to the pedestal shaft.

Cap and base width: 485mm (19")
Height: 685mm (27")
Weight: 153kg (337 lb)

30"Queen Anne Plinth B310

Queen Anne-period fielded plinth with plain mouldings around cap and base.

Width at cap: 329mm (12$\frac{15}{16}$")
Width at base: 337mm (13$\frac{1}{4}$")
Height: 775mm (30$\frac{1}{2}$")
Weight: 87kg (192 lb)

27"Queen Anne Plinth B300

Queen Anne-period fielded plinth with plain mouldings around cap and base.

Width at cap: 329mm (12$\frac{15}{16}$")
Width at base: 337mm (13$\frac{1}{4}$")
Height: 695mm (27$\frac{1}{2}$")
Weight: 77kg (170 lb)

20" Elizabethan Plinth B400

Featuring a moulded cap.

Width at cap: 377mm (14$\frac{7}{8}$")
Width at base: 337mm (13$\frac{1}{4}$")
Height: 499mm (20")
Weight: 73kg (161 lb)

28" Elizabethan Plinth B420

Featuring a moulded cap.

Width at cap: 377mm (14$\frac{7}{8}$")
Width at base: 337mm (13$\frac{1}{4}$")
Height: 721mm (28")
Weight: 90kg (198 lb)

31" Elizabethan Plinth B440

Featuring a moulded cap.

Width at cap: 377mm (14$\frac{7}{8}$")
Width at base: 337mm (13$\frac{1}{4}$")
Height: 798mm (31")
Weight: 91kg (201 lb)

Raphael Pedestal B480

Small pedestal in high Renaissance style has richly decorated panels on each of four faces. The cap and base have bead and reel ornamentation.

Width at base: 265mm (10$\frac{1}{2}$")
Cap top width: 235mm (9$\frac{1}{4}$")
Overall height: 670mm (26$\frac{1}{2}$")
Weight: 74kg (163 lb)

(Registered Design No.2038958)

Regency Pedestal B330

Width at top: 220mm (8$\frac{3}{4}$")
Width at base: 280mm (11")
Height: 430mm (17")
Weight: 33kg (73 lb)

Large Regency Pedestal B331

Width at top: 305mm (12")
Width at base: 355mm (14")
Height: 455mm (18")
Weight: 80kg (176 lb)

Gothic Pedestal B130

Cap top width: 200mm (7$\frac{7}{8}$")
Width at base: 292mm (11$\frac{1}{2}$")
Height: 774mm (30$\frac{1}{2}$")
Weight: 76kg (167 lb)

GARDEN & LANDSCAPE PEDESTALS AND PLINTHS

IMPORTANT PEDESTAL SITING

It is essential that your Haddonstone pedestal is sited on a firm and level area to suit site conditions and loadings. An 8 to 1 sand/cement bedding mortar should be used to ensure that the weight of the pedestal and urn is spread evenly across the base of the pedestal, avoiding any pivoting or twisting strain. We cannot accept responsibility for cracking or breakage if this instruction is ignored.

Tuscan Pedestal B170
(Shown with Apollo)

B490 Pedestal
(Shown with Helena)

B495 Pedestal
(Shown with Bust of Pan)

B100 Pedestal
(Shown with Bacchante)

B150 Pedestal
(Shown with antique lead figure)

B140 Pedestal
(Shown with Brutus)

B340 Pedestal
(Shown with Andromeda)

B335 Pedestal
(Shown with Venus)

Tuscan Pedestal
B170

Width at top: 350mm (13¾")
Width at foot: 406mm (16")
Height: 1054mm (41½")
Weight: 145kg (319 lb)

Adam Pedestal
B490

Width at base: 358mm (14")
Width at top: 345mm (13⁹⁄₁₆")
Height: 887mm (35")
Weight: 103kg (227 lb)

(Registered Design No. 2038747)

Adam Pedestal
B495

Width at base: 358mm (14")
Width at top: 345mm (13⁹⁄₁₆")
Height: 1087mm (42¾")
Weight: 123kg (271 lb)

(Registered Design No. 2038747)

Doric Pedestal
B100

Width at top: 350mm (13¾")
Width at foot: 445mm (17½")
Height: 1190mm (46¾")
Weight: 137kg (302 lb)

Jacobean Pedestal
B150

Width at base: 385mm (15¼")
Width at top: 360mm (14³⁄₁₆")
Height: 620mm (24½")
Weight: 121kg (267 lb)

Ionic Pedestal
B140

Width at top: 345mm (13⁹⁄₁₆")
Width at foot: 400mm (15¾")
Height: 1140mm (45")
Weight: 136kg (300 lb)

Octagonal Pedestal
B340

Width at top: 425mm (16¾")
Height: 380mm (15")
Width overall: 485mm (19")
Face to face: 450mm (17¾")
Weight: 108kg (238 lb)

Small Octagonal Pedestal B335

Width at top: 375mm (14¾")
Height: 310mm (12¼")
Width overall: 435mm (17")
Face to face: 400mm (15¾")
Weight: 81kg (179 lb)

TS Tech Sheet No. M65   TS Tech Sheet No. GAR4 Security Fixings

Crescent Sundial X712

The Crescent holds the gnomon, which casts a shadow onto the hour band. Engraved along the hour band is the Latin inscription "HORA QUASI UMBRA" which translates as "time is but a shadow". Manufactured in high specification mirror polished stainless steel, the sundial is ideal for Haddonstone's Baluster Sundial Plinth D145 (not included - see below), or Georgian Sundial Plinth D265 (not included - see right).

Width at base: 215mm (8 1/2")
Height: 280mm (11")
Weight 3.2kg (7 lb)

Arcadian Wall Sundial GD360

Includes gnomon. Designed for south facing walls, this decorative ornament gives an insight into the workings of a wall sundial.

Height: 450mm (17 3/4")
Depth: 30mm (1 3/8")
Width: 340mm (13 3/8")
Weight: 9kg (20 lb)

Georgian Sundial Plinth D265
(Shown above with Crescent Sundial X712)

A beautiful baluster sundial, after James Gibbs.
For Bird Bath, see page 56.

Table Diameter: 335mm (13 1/4")
Width of base: 335mm (13 1/4")
Height: 845mm (33 1/4")
Weight: 73kg (161 lb)
(Registered Design No 2030286)

Baluster Sundial Plinth D145

See left. For dimensions, see Baluster Sundial D140 on page 52.
(Registered Design No. 2030823)

Note: Plinths and dials are priced separately – see price list.

GARDEN & LANDSCAPE SUNDIALS

Baluster Sundial Plinth D140

This simple baluster sundial design features cyma reversa moulding to both the square base and table. In each corner the table top has been decorated with vermiculated rustication (see below for details of X700 Brass Dial).

Width at top: 320mm (12½")
Width of base: 320mm (12½")

Height: 875mm (34½")
Weight: 51kg (112 lb)

(Registered Design No. 2030823)

Baluster Sundial Plinth D145 (Illustrated on page 51)

As Baluster Sundial D140 (see above) but without recess in the top, thereby allowing customers to use their own sundial plate or Crescent Sundial, see page 51.

(Registered Design No. 2030823)

Adam Sundial Plinth D135
(for Dial and Gnomon X710)

This octagonal sundial plinth is similar to the Adam Sundial Plinth D130 (see page 54); however, it features a larger table for use with the large sundial plate and gnomon X710.

D135 table width: 520mm (20½")
Plinth base width: 430mm (17")
Height of plinth: 1070mm (42")
D135 plinth weight: 164kg (362 lb)

Georgian Sundial Plinth D260

A beautiful baluster sundial, after James Gibbs. See right for X700 Brass Dial. For Bird Bath, see page 56.

Table Diameter: 335mm (13¼")
Width of base: 335mm (13¼")
Height: 845mm (33¼")
Weight: 73kg (161 lb)

Georgian Sundial Plinth D265
(Illustrated on page 51)

As D260 but without recess on the top. Ideal for customer's own sundial or the Crescent Sundial, see page 51.

(Registered Design No. 2030286)

Brass Dials and Gnomons

Designed exclusively for use with the Haddonstone collection of sundials, both of these beautiful solid-brass dials and gnomons feature the Haddonstone sundial verse:

"Make time, save time while time lasts.
All time is no time when time is past."

Note: Plinths and dials are priced separately – see price list.

Brass Dial and Gnomon X700
(for D140, D150, D250 & D260 Plinths)

Diameter of dial: 290mm (11½")
Height of gnomon: 125mm (5")
Weight: 1.1kg (2½ lb)

Brass Dial and Gnomon X710
(for D280 & D135 Plinths)

Diameter of dial: 405mm (16")
Height of gnomon: 185mm (7¼")
Weight: 2.7kg (6 lb)

Arcadian Sundial
GD350

A baluster-style sundial featuring a sun motif at the centre of the dial, surrounded by clouds, moon and stars. Includes gnomon.

Height: 575mm (22⅝")
Max width: 375mm (14¾")
Total weight: 49kg (108 lb)
Heaviest component: 35kg (77 lb)

Doric Sundial Plinth
D150

This classical design with fluted shaft and moulded capital and base looks ideal on terraces or raised platforms (see left for details of X700 Brass Dial).

Diameter of table: 355mm (14")
Width at base: 445mm (17½")
Height: 1080mm (42½")
Weight: 137kg (302 lb)

XVIII Century Sundial Plinth D250

A well-proportioned baluster sundial with artificial leaf design around the bowl and table (see left for details of X700 Brass Dial).

Diameter of table: 335mm (13¼")
Width at base: 455mm (18")
Height: 990mm (39")
Weight: 112kg (248 lb)

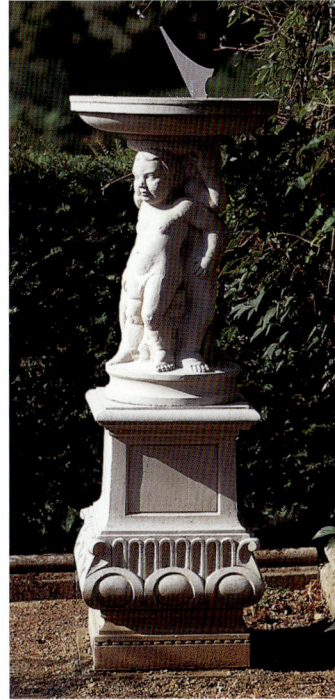

Jacobean Sundial & Pedestal D280/B150

A circular sundial table supported by three putti and mounted on a pedestal enriched with fluting and ovolo ornament (see left for details of X710 Brass Dial). See also Figured Bird Bath (page 56) and Figured Fountain (page 84).

Diameter at top: 520mm (20½")
Width of base: 385mm (15¼")
Height overall: 1340mm (52¾")
Weight overall: 195kg (429 lb)

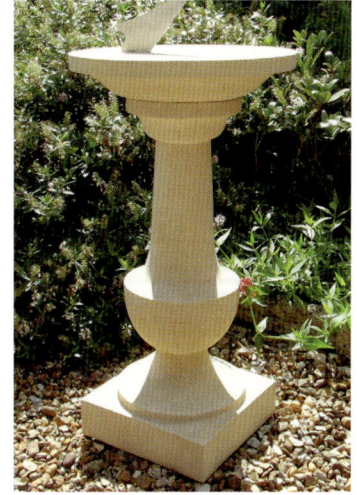

Roman Sundial
HD285

Featuring a stainless steel gnomon to project a shadow across the Roman numerals cast into the sundial top. See also Baluster Bird Bath (page 55) and Baluster Bird Table (page 55).

Diameter at top: 375mm (14¾")
Width of base: 260mm (10¼")
Height: 670mm (26⅜")
Weight: 43kg (95 lb)

Note: Plinths and dials are priced separately – see price list.

Armillary Sphere X714 (for B495 Pedestal/D130 Plinth)

Designed exclusively for Haddonstone, the Armillary Sphere is calibrated to tell solar time and features the Haddonstone sundial verse. Made from solid brass throughout, the Armillary Sphere has three rings depicting the equator, the meridian and a colure. The gnomon, casts a shadow onto the equator band which is engraved with Roman numerals. The sphere is supported by a cruxiform stand on a circular base for securing to the plinth. Fixing screws are supplied. The Sphere can be calibrated for any country in the world.

Designed exclusively for Haddonstone, the Armillary Sphere features the Haddonstone sundial verse:

"Make time, save time while time lasts.
All time is no time when time is past."

Diameter: 530mm (20⅞")
Height: 660mm (26")
Width of base: 190mm (7½")
Weight: 7kg (15½ lb)

Recommended pedestals: B495, D130

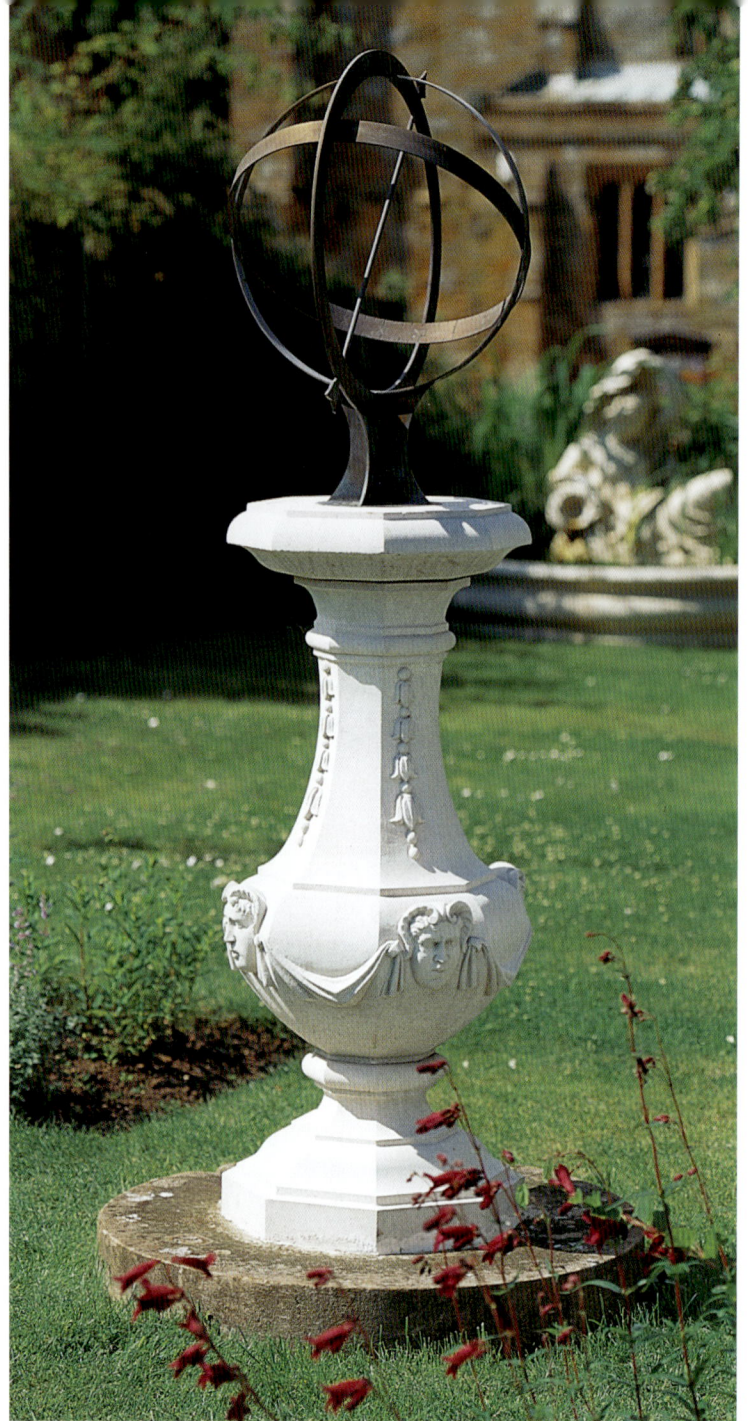

Adam Sundial Plinth D130 (for Armillary Sphere X714)

An octagonal sundial plinth, in the style of Robert Adam, decorated with masks and margents of husks. An elegant support for the Armillary Sphere sundial. See also, Adam Sundial Plinth page 52.

Width of table: 430mm (17") Height of plinth: 1070mm (42")
Width of plinth base: 430mm (17") Weight of plinth: 152kg (335 lb)

(Registered Design No. 2013394)

Adam Pedestal B495 (for Armillary Sphere X714)

This stylish design - featuring a fluted shaft with palmette decoration to the base and capital - provides an alternative pedestal for the exclusive Armillary Sphere Sundial, see left.

Width at base: 358mm (14") Height: 1087mm (42¾")
Width at top: 345mm (13⁹⁄₁₆") Weight: 123kg (271 lb)

(Registered Design No 2038747)

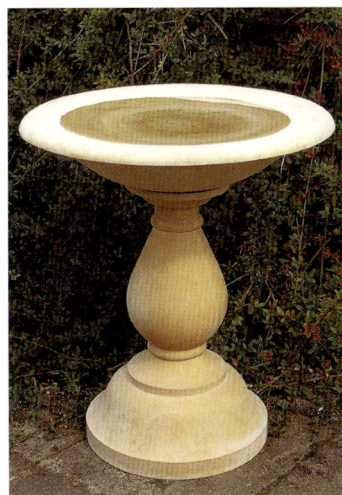

Arcadian Bird Table
GC353

A recent addition to the range.

Height: 580mm (22⁷/₈")
Maximum width: 420mm (16½")
Weight: 50kg (110 lb)

Arcadian Bird Bath
GC350

A stylish baluster bird bath.

Height: 610mm (24")
Max width: 560mm (22")
Total weight: 58kg (128lb)
Heaviest component: 35kg (77 lb)

Baluster Bird Table
HC334

A new Haddonstone design.

Height: 710mm (28")
Maximum width: 560mm (22")
Weight: 68kg (150 lb)

Baluster Bird Bath
HC335

A simple baluster bird bath.

Width at rim: 560mm (22")
Width at base: 260mm (10¼")
Height: 710mm (28")
Weight: 58kg (128 lb)

Regency Bird Bath HC500
Regency Pedestal HB330

A very popular small bird bath in the Regency style. See also
Regency Fountain, page 84.

Width at top of bird bath: 510mm (20")
Width at base of bird bath: 220mm (8¾")
Width at pedestal foot: 280mm (11")
Height (without pedestal): 340mm (13½")
Height of pedestal: 430mm (17")
Weight of bird bath: 36kg (79 lb)
Weight of pedestal: 42kg (93 lb)

Figured Bird Bath
C330

The pedestal for this charming bird bath is formed by three entwined putti who support the circular bird bath bowl with plain moulding and a fluted design to the rim. See also Jacobean Sundial (page 53) and Figured Fountain (page 84).

Width at top: 520mm (20½")
Width at base: 340mm (13½")
Height: 725mm (28½")
Weight: 75kg (165 lb)

Design: Mark Saltzman

Georgian Bird Bath
HC340

This is a beautiful baluster-style bird bath, after James Gibbs. The strigillated baluster shaft is decorated with artificial leaf mouldings at the base. For Georgian Sundial, see pages 51-52.

Width at rim: 685mm (27")
Width at base: 335mm (13¼")
Height: 915mm (36")
Weight: 91kg (200 lb)

(Registered Design No.2013393)

Highland Park Bird Bath HC345

A stylish design to suit both contemporary and traditional gardens.

Width at top: 768mm (30¼")
Width at base: 368mm (14½")
Height: 870mm (34¼")
Weight: 85kg (187 lb)

Hazelwood Bird Bath
HC280

An attractive Victorian design with shell decoration on the pedestal.

Width at rim: 585mm (23")
Width at base: 380mm (15")
Height: 850mm (34")
Weight: 76kg (167 lb)

GARDEN & LANDSCAPE STATUARY

"There is nothing adds so much to the Beauty and Grandeur of Gardens, as fine Statues"

Batty Langley, 1728

Isis HE810

Acquired by Charles Townley, the famous collector, during his second Grand Tour of Italy (1771-74). Townley himself believed the bust represented Isis, considered by the ancients as the ideal mother and wife as well as patron of nature and magic.

Width of bust: 450mm (17³/₄")
Width of socle: 240mm (9¹/₂")
Height: 690mm (27¹/₄")
Weight: 65kg (143 lb)
Recommended pedestals: B170, B490, B495, B901

Apollo E700

Apollo was a great and powerful deity, one of the leading figures in all of mythology. Young and handsome, he became best known for his oracles and for his interest in music. A twin of Diana, or Artemis, Apollo is represented here in the classical style of Phidias, the 5th century BC Greek sculptor.

Height: 515mm (20¹/₄")
Max. base width: 235mm (9¹/₄")
Weight: 52kg (115 lb)
Recommended pedestals: B170, B490, B495

Diana E705

Diana, or Artemis, is the virgin huntress of classical mythology, sacred to all things natural and wild, protector of women in labour and newborn children. She was a proud and beautiful goddess and a formidable warrior. She assisted in the birth of Apollo, her twin brother, and the bond between them was very strong. Created here in the style of Phidias, the 5th century BC Greek sculptor.

Height: 530mm (20⁷/₈")
Max. base width: 295mm (11⁵/₈")
Weight: 48kg (106 lb)
Recom. pedestals: B170, B490, B495

Aurora HE800

Aurora, goddess of Dawn, after Michelangelo. The original forms an integral part of the Michelangelo's famous Tomb of Lorenzo di Piero de' Medici (1492-1519) in the Church of San Lorenzo, Florence. Machiavelli's 'The Prince' is dedicated to Lorenzo.

Width of bust: 285mm (11¹/₄")
Width of socle: 200mm (7⁷/₈")
Height: 550mm (21³/₄")
Weight: 24kg (53 lb)
Recommended pedestals: B130, B480, B490, B495

Aristotle HE805

One of the most important founding figures in Western philosophy, Aristotle (384-322 BC) was a student of Plato and teacher of Alexander the Great.

Width of bust: 350mm (13³/₄")
Width of socle: 175mm (6⁷/₈")
Height 567mm (22³/₈")
Weight: 29kg (64 lb)
Recommended pedestals: B130, B480, B490, B495

Antinous HE840

Antinous (111-130 AD) was an important member of Emperor Hadrian's entourage. Deified by Hadrian after his death, Antinous came to be considered the personification of youthful beauty.

Width of bust: 550mm (21⅝")   Height: 790mm (31⅛")
Width of socle: 250mm (9⅞")   Weight: 84kg (185 lb)
Recommended pedestals: B170, B490, B495, B901

Eros HE845

This fine torso is a Roman copy of a Greek bronze original attributed to the sculptor Praxiteles. In Greek mythology Eros was the primordial god of sexual love and beauty. Inscribed "1378 TORSE ANTIQVE D'AMOVR. L'AMOVR GREC MUSE VATIC". The original marble is in the Vatican Museum.

Width: 440mm (17⁵⁄₁₆")
Height: 970mm (38¼")
Weight: 103kg (227 lb)
Recommended pedestals: B255, B265

Apollo Belvedere
HE830

From the full size Roman marble copy, after the ancient Greek statue by Leochares embodying masculine beauty in all its plentitude, it is one of the most celebrated sculptures from classical antiquity. The original is in the Vatican Museum. Often paired with Diana Chasseresse.

Width of bust: 565mm (22¼")
Width of socle: 250mm (9⅞")
Height: 790mm (31⅛")
Weight: 83kgs (183 lb)
Recommended pedestals: B170, B490, B495, B901

Diane Chasseresse
HE835

From the full size Roman marble copy, after the ancient Greek statue depicting Diana the Huntress by Leochares. Prominently displayed at Fontainebleau in the sixteenth century, the original marble is now in the Louvre, Paris. Often paired with Apollo Belvedere.

Width of bust: 420mm (16½")
Width of socle: 220mm (8⅝")
Height 740mm (29½")
Weight: 50kg (110 lb)
Recommended pedestals: B170, B490, B495, B901

Caesar Augustus HE815

Caesar Augustus (63BC – 14AD), was the first Emperor of the Roman Empire, ruling alone from 31 BC. This bust is replicated from a marble statue excavated in 1863 at Prima Porta near Rome and now displayed at the Vatican Museum. Caesar Augustus, whose great uncle was Julius Caesar, is depicted in armour as commander-in-chief of the Roman army.

Width of bust: 500mm (19³/₄")
Width of socle: 230mm (9¹/₈")
Height: 740mm (29¹/₂")
Weight: 67kg (148 lb)

Recommended pedestals: B170, B490, B495, B901

Antoninus Pius HE820

Antoninus Pius, Roman Emperor from 138-161 AD, was the adoptive son and successor to Hadrian. He instigated the construction of the Antonine Wall between the Firths of Clyde and Forth.

Width of bust: 640mm (25¼")   Height: 860mm (33⁷/₈")
Width of socle: 220mm (8⁵/₈")   Weight: 92kg (203 lb)

Recommended pedestals: B170, B490, B495, B901

Septimus Severus HE825

Septimius Severus (145-211 AD) was Roman Emperor from 193 AD. Severus was considered a strong, able ruler who sought glory through military exploits.

Width of bust: 520mm (20¹/₂")   Height: 840mm (33¹/₈")
Width of socle: 230mm (9¹/₄")   Weight: 80kg (176 lb)

Recommended pedestals: B170, B490, B495, B901

Brutus E195

Taken from an original carved by Michelangelo, which now stands in the Bargello Museum, Florence, this bust conveys the power of Brutus to an extraordinary degree of grandeur.

Width of bust overall: 750mm (29½")
Width of socle: 320mm (12½")
Height: 970mm (38¼")
Weight: 142kg (313 lb)

Recommended pedestals: B140, B265

Bacchus
E190

A bust of the god of wine wearing an animal skin and cloak, usually mounted on our Doric Pedestal (see page 50).

Width of bust: 690mm (27")
Width of socle: 290mm (11½")
Height of bust: 965mm (38")
Weight: 96kg (211 lb)

Recommended pedestals: B100, B170, B265

Bacchante
E180

Originating in Italy, circa 1870, this bust depicts a Bacchante, a reveller in the court of Bacchus, god of wine. Featuring vine-entwined hair and a loosely draped robe, she is designed for display on our Doric Pedestal (see page 50).

Width of bust: 560mm (22")
Width of socle: 290mm (11½")
Height: 880mm (34⅝")
Weight: 100kg (220 lb)

Recommended pedestals: B100, B170, B265

Pan Term
E690

This magnificent term depicts Pan, the Arcadian god of hills and woods, who is the protecting deity of flocks and herdsmen. He is portrayed as having the body of a man, but with the beard and horns of a goat, playing his syrinx. A beautiful lion's skin, complete with mask, robes his body and drapes the term pedestal shaft. Traditionally used for terminating a path or hedge, or alternatively is ideal for positioning in a temple or grotto or as a focal point in a garden scheme.

Height: 2020mm (79½")
Width at base: 700mm (27½")
Weight: 426kg (939 lb)

Bust of Pan
E695

This bust is taken from our Pan Term E690.

Height: 770mm (30¼")
Width overall: 540mm (21¼")
Width at base: 250mm (9⅞")
Weight: 85kg (187 lb)

Recommended pedestal: B310, B440, B490, B495.

Byron
E175

Lord Byron was famously described as being "mad, bad and dangerous to know" by Lady Caroline Lamb. Byron (1788-1824) was an icon of his age and the subject of a major exhibition at the National Portrait Gallery in London during 2003.

Haddonstone's Byron is taken from a fine marble original carved by Edward Hodges Baily RA in c1826. During his lifetime, Byron was much admired for his extraordinary beauty of appearance as well as his poetic genius. Haddonstone's replica captures the very essence of Byron.

Width of bust: 520mm (20½")
Width of socle: 214mm (8½")
Height: 790mm (31")
Weight: 71kg (156 lb)

Recommended pedestals: B490, B495

Helena E170

This beautiful bust, from an original by the renowned XIX century sculptor Charles Francis Fuller, depicts a young Roman maiden whom we have called Helena. Shown here on an Adam Pedestal (see page 50).

Height: 695mm (27⅜")
Width overall: 457mm (18")
Width of base: 250mm (9⅞")
Weight: 55kg (121 lb)

Recommended pedestals: B310, B440, B490, B495.

63

GARDEN & LANDSCAPE STATUARY

THE FOUR ELEMENTS

HADDONSTONE WAS COMMISSIONED BY STOCKPORT BOROUGH COUNCIL TO REPRODUCE THIS CHARMING GROUP OF ELEMENTS FOR THE DUTCH GARDEN AT LYME HALL, CHESHIRE. THE ORIGINALS WERE CARVED IN THE EARLY 1800S FOR ELVEDEN HALL, NORFOLK.

Earth HE600

Height: 1010mm (39¾")
Max. base width: 455mm (18")
Weight: 113kg (249 lb)

Fire HE610

Height: 1010mm (39¾")
Max. base width: 405mm (16")
Weight: 121kg (266 lb)

Air HE620

Height: 980mm (38½")
Max. base width: 395mm (15½")
Weight: 102kg (225 lb)

Water HE630

Height: 995mm (39¼")
Max. base width: 410mm (16¼")
Weight: 119kg (262 lb)

Recommended pedestals: B255, B265, B370

THE FOUR SEASONS

THIS SERIES OF STATUES DEPICTING THE SEASONS WAS SPECIALLY COMMISSIONED BY HADDONSTONE.

Spring stands demurely holding a sprig of pussy willow in her right hand, Summer stands gracefully holding a sheaf of corn in her hand, Autumn is depicted holding freshly harvested grapes within her skirts, whilst Winter stands with oak entwined hair and her left arm warmly wrapped with drapery. See also Water Nymph page 79.

Height: 1430mm (56¼")
Max. base width: 360mm (14¼")
Weight: 140kg (308 lb)

Recommended pedestals: B255, B265, B370

Spring HE750

(Registered Design No 2086381)

Autumn HE760

(Registered Design No 2092420)

Winter HE765

(Registered Design No 2092835)

Summer HE755

(Registered Design No 2091580)

Piper HE660

This charming figure of a young boy playing a pipe has been modelled by Haddonstone from an antique copy of the original that stood in the Villa Borghese until purchased by Napoleon Bonaparte and subsequently displayed in the Louvre. Shown on Dado Pedestal (see page 48).

Height: 1380mm (54¼")
Max. base width: 355mm (14")
Weight: 140kg (308 lb)

Recommended pedestals: B255, B265, B370

(Registered Design No. 2065719)

Shepherdess HE655

The Shepherdess statue has been created to provide the Gardener design with a partner. She is depicted in the style of a rustic, in period dress with bonnet, laced bodice, flowing skirt and buckle shoes. In her right hand she holds a wrought iron crook and under her left arm she gently cradles a small lamb.

Height: 1380mm (54¼")
Max base width: 350mm (13¾")
Weight: 132kg (291 lb)

Recommended pedestals: B255, B265, B370

Andromeda E640

Taken from a XIX century Italian original, Andromeda stands, scantily clad, clutching a robe to her right breast whilst manacled to a rocky outcrop. In classical mythology Andromeda was chained to a rock before being found by the hero Perseus who released her, slew a monster and obtained her as his wife.

Height: 1030mm (40¾")
Max. base width: 345mm (13½")
Weight: 80kg (176 lb)

Recommended pedestals: B255, B340, B350

(Registered Design No. 2022882)

Venus E680

Venus, the goddess of love and fertility, is replicated from a late XIX century Italian white-marble sculpture. She is depicted with flowing locks, resting against a rocky promontory, a robe loosely draped around her body.

Height: 840mm (33")
Max. base width: 280mm (11")
Weight: 57kg (126 lb)

Recommended pedestals: B335, B400

(Registered Design No. 2024380)

The Gardener HE650

Inspired by the engaging lead figure that once stood at Burton Agnes in Yorkshire, Haddonstone created this statue of an XVIII century gardener, in period dress, resting on his spade.

Height: 1380mm (54¼")
Max. base width: 355mm (14")
Weight: 140kg (308 lb)

Recommended pedestals: B255, B265, B370

(Registered Design No. 2083190)

Music
HE670

Music holds a classical lyre in her left hand, an instrument attributed to the Greek God Hermes. Originally created for the restoration of Leazes Park in Newcastle, this design is identical in proportion to Poetry.

Height: 1800mm (71")
Width at base: 650mm (25⅝")
Weight: 465kg (1024 lb)

Please note: will require mechanical lifting on site in all instances.

Poetry
HE671

This elegant statue, representing Poetry, stands clutching a bound volume of verse. Originally created for the restoration of Leazes Park in Newcastle, this design is identical in proportion to Music.

Height: 1800mm (71")
Width at base: 650mm (25⅝")
Weight: 395kg (870 lb)

Please note: will require mechanical lifting on site in all instances.

Turn to Specialist Services - Archives for further ornament options

GARDEN & LANDSCAPE STATUARY

Equine Head E570

The original of this impressive Equine Head was excavated at Civitavecchia near Rome and acquired by the Medici family who sent it to Florence in 1585. It was later adapted to serve as a fountain spout in the courtyard of the Medici Palace.

Depth of bust: 890mm (35")
Width of bust base: 340mm (13½")
Width of socle: 380mm (15")
Height: 1010mm (39¾")
Weight: 183kg (403 lb)

Recommended pedestals: B120, B265

Large Lion Finial HE461

This massive lion was originally created for a project in Qatar. Identical in proportion to the Lion Finial E460.

Base width: 780mm (30¾")
Height: 2040mm (80⅜")
Weight: 2000kg (4405 lb)

Please note: will require mechanical lifting on site in all instances.

Lion Finial E460
Lion Base A370B

This lion sejant may also be used as a fountain (see page 79). Shown mounted on a waisted octagonal base.

Width at lion base: 280mm (11")
Width of base: 355mm (14")
Height of lion: 610mm (24")
Height of base: 280mm (11")
Weight of lion: 35kg (77 lb)
Weight of base: 35kg (77 lb)

XVIII Century Lion E450
XVIII Century Lion Pedestal B200

Well-proportioned lion couchant, which can be mounted on the B200 pedestal. Suitable for terraces or tops of steps. See Specialist Services - Archives for Large XVIII Century Lion.

Length of lion: 610mm (24")
Width of lion: 280mm (11")
Height of lion: 405mm (16")
Weight of lion: 56kg (125 lb)
Length of pedestal at foot: 645mm (25½")
Width of pedestal at foot: 330mm (13")
Height of pedestal: 240mm (9½")
Weight of pedestal: 57kg (126 lb)

Aquila (left hand) HE357
Aquila (right hand) HE358

Aquila was the immortal eagle of Zeus, king of the gods. Since ancient times, the eagle has been considered a symbol of power and victory. This pair of eagles was originally created as part of the restoration of Leazes Park in Newcastle.

Height overall: 825mm (32½")
Width overall: 750mm (29½")
Diameter of base: 410mm (16⅛")
Weight (each): 130kg (286 lb)

Eagle Owl E565

Eagle Owls are among the largest and most magnificent of the owls - noted for their large size, conspicuous ear tufts, eagle-like bills and enormously powerful talons. This Haddonstone design captures the power of this bird of prey.

Height: 720mm (28⅜")
Width at base: 317mm (12½")
Weight: 56kg (123 lb)

Recommended pedestals: B150, B331, B400, B420, B440, B695

(Registered Design No. 2084729)

Eagle (left hand) HE350 Eagle (right hand) HE355

These powerful representations of the noble eagle are ideal for positioning on a gateway, at the entrance to a garden walk, or to frame a landscape vista. Adapted from original designs by Doulton of Lambeth.

Height overall: 930mm (36⅝")
Width overall: 800mm (31½")
Width at base: 370mm (14½")
(Registered Design No. 2065693)

Depth overall: 580mm (22¾")
Depth at base: 370mm (14½")
Weight (each): 174kg (383 lb)
(Registered Design No. 2065694)

Recommended pedestal: B120

GARDEN & LANDSCAPE
GARDEN PET MEMORIALS

Haddonstone has introduced a unique range of Garden Pet Memorials. Exceptionally crafted, yet unobtrusive, these provide both a beautiful ornament and a discreet receptacle for a cherished pet's remains.

Each design (not the Memorial Block, Memorial Marker or Memorial Stone) incorporates a pedestal which can accommodate one or two Poly-Urns for your pet's ashes (one supplied with memorial). To personalize these memorials an inscription panel is recess fixed into the pedestal. Garden Pet Memorials are designed to be used as a garden ornament and may be placed in a pet's favourite area of the garden. Memorials can easily be relocated at a future time if required.

In addition to Garden Pet Memorials, Haddonstone engraves some standard ornaments, see page 184. Garden Cremation Memorials also available, see page 182.

Memorial Stone
MEM850

(Shown with standard engraved inscription with optional enamel lettering infill)

Height: 450mm (17¾")
Height above ground: approx 305mm (12")
Width: 210mm (8¼")
Weight: 7kg (15 lb)

Memorial Vase & Pedestal MEM300

(Standard engraved inscription shown)

Width at top: 510mm (20")
Pedestal base width: 338mm (13¼")
Height: 980mm (38⅝")
Weight: 88kg (194 lb)

Small Bird (optional) MEM800

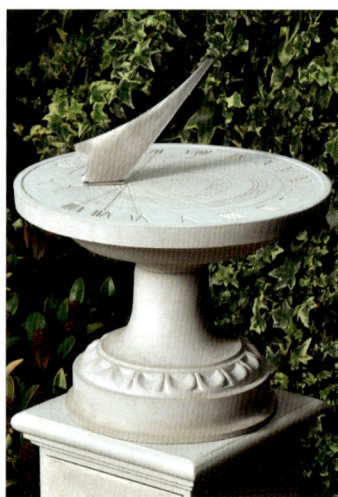

Memorial Celestial Sundial & Pedestal
MEM200 (detail below left)
Memorial Classical Sundial & Pedestal
MEM100 (detail below right)

Sundial diameter: 375mm (14¾")
Pedestal base width: 338mm (13¼")
Stone height: 880mm (34⅝")
Weight: 81kg (178 lb)

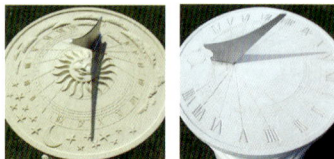

Celestial (detail)   Classical (detail)

Memorial Fountain & Pedestal MEM500

Fountain diameter: 305mm (12")
Pedestal base width: 338mm (13¼")
Height: 890mm (35")
Weight: 88kg (194 lb)

Memorial Marker
MEM840 (right)

(Shown with standard engraved inscription with optional enamel lettering infill)

Dimensions: 300 x 300 x 38mm
 (11¹³⁄₁₆ x 11¹³⁄₁₆ x 1½")
Weight: 7kg (15 lb)
Other sizes available on request.

Memorial Bird Bath & Pedestal MEM400

Width at top: 485mm (19")
Pedestal base width: 338mm (13¼")
Height: 927mm (36½")
Weight: 96kg (211 lb)

GARDEN & LANDSCAPE FINIALS

Finials are normally used to adorn gate piers, entrances or balustrading. They provide a decorative alternative to the geometric Ball & Base designs (see page 74). Many of Haddonstone's finials have been replicated from notable country houses including National Trust properties. Alongside these standard designs, Haddonstone is also able to create custom designs to meet individual requirements or to replicate an existing design as part of a restoration project.

Ven Finial
E715

Replicated as part of the restoration of the William-and-Mary-style country house of Ven in Dorset, this exquisite finial is now included in the Haddonstone Collection.

Height: 826mm (32½")
Width overall: 390mm (15¼")
Width at base: 245mm (9¾")
Weight: 43kg (95 lb)

Vine House Finial
E730

Sir Christopher Wren has been authoritatively associated with the original finial from which this Haddonstone design has been developed.

Height: 790mm (31")
Width overall: 410mm (16")
Width at base: 230mm (9")
Weight: 45kg (100 lb)

Swagged Adam Finial
E740

An Adam-style finial with a scalloped lid surmounted by a naturalistic bud. The main decoration to the finial comprises drapery swags terminated with disc moulding and lion masks over a fluted body. The lid may be removed, allowing this finial to be planted during the spring and summer months. See also Swagged Adam Vase, page 20.

Height: 762mm (30")
Width overall: 495mm (19½")
Width at base: 229mm (9")
Weight: 64kg (141 lb)

(Registered Design No. 2039118)

GARDEN & LANDSCAPE FINIALS

Margam Swagged Urn E510

A very elegant Georgian urn with formal floral and lion-head decoration. Haddonstone was commissioned to restore the original urns at Margam Orangery, South Wales, as part of the British project for the 1975 European Architectural Heritage Year. Originally manufactured by the illustrious Coade company.

Width overall: 585mm (23")
Width at base: 255mm (10")
Height: 660mm (26")
Weight: 75kg (165 lb)

Ham House Pineapple E380

The National Trust granted the right for Haddonstone to include in its Collection a perfect replica of the beautiful Coade Stone pineapples adorning the perimeter pedestals at Ham House, Richmond.

Height: 820mm (32¼")
Width overall: 455mm (18")
Width at base: 300mm (11¾")
Weight: 95kg (209 lb)

Pineapple and Base E590

An early XVIII century pineapple design.

Height: 585mm (23")
Width overall: 345mm (13½")
Width at base: 280mm (11")
Weight: 43kg (95 lb)

Margam Masked Urn E500

A Georgian-style urn adorned in high relief with naturalistic vines and satyr heads. This piece was also restored for Margam Orangery, South Wales.

Width overall: 560mm (22")
Width at base: 255mm (10")
Height: 915mm (36")
Weight: 78kg (172 lb)

Rugby Finial E595

Replicated from an original design on behalf of Rugby Borough Council, this finial features strong gadrooning to the body with moulded top surmounted by a flame.

Height: 1300mm (51¼")
Width overall: 450mm (17¾")
Width at base: 290mm (11½")
Weight: 107kg (236 lb)

Large Basket of Fruit
E220

This neo-Gothic-style basket with interlaced strapwork overflows with ripe fruits in a naturalistic style.

Height: 455mm (18")
Width overall: 470mm (18½")
Width at base: 230mm (9")
Weight: 45kg (98 lb)

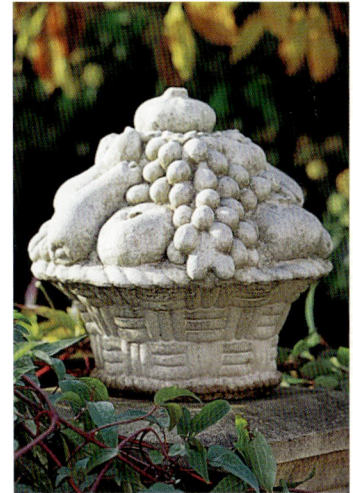

Lyme Hall Urn
E480

This splendid ram's-head finial was originally commissioned for Lyme Hall by Stockport Borough Council. It can be mounted on a pedestal at low level or at parapet level to dramatic effect.

Width overall: 660mm (26")
Width at base: 290mm (11½")
Height: 1145mm (45")
Weight: 115kg (254 lb)

Dogmersfield Finial
E280

A replica of a finial designed for Dogmersfield Park, Hampshire, in 1742.

Height: 1500mm (59")
Width overall: 650mm (25½")
Width at base: 385mm (15")
Weight: 158kg (348 lb)

Festoon of Fruit
E230

The Festoon of Fruit comprises a fluted vase, gadrooned stem and waved top line with a beautifully detailled cornucopia of fruit

Height: 600mm (23½")
Width overall: 390mm (15½")
Width at base: 230mm (9")
Weight: 48kg (106 lb)

Basket of Fruit
E200

This small basket with relief basketweave pattern contains ornate and rotund fruits, and is ideal as a table centrepiece.

Height: 310mm (12¼")
Width overall: 310mm (12¼")
Width at base: 190mm (7½")
Weight: 21kg (46 lb)

Turn to Specialist Services - Archives for further ornament options

GARDEN & LANDSCAPE BALLS AND BASES

6¾" Ball E100A & Base E100B

Height: 265mm (10½")
Diameter of ball: 170mm (6¾")
Width at base: 230mm (9")
Weight: 10kg (22 lb)

8" Ball E105A & Base E100B

Height: 295mm (11¾")
Diameter of ball: 200mm (8")
Width at base: 230mm (9")
Weight: 12kg (27 lb)

9" Ball E110A & Collared Base E110C

Height: 455mm (18")
Diameter of ball: 230mm (9")
Width at base: 230mm (9")
Weight: 23kg (51 lb)

Acanthus-Leaf Ball E080A & Collared Base E120C

Height: 620mm (24½")
Max diameter: 400mm (15¾")
Width at base: 330mm (13")
Weight: 63kg (139 lb)

14" Ball E130A & Base E120B

Height: 595mm (23½")
Diameter of ball: 355mm (14")
Width at base: 330mm (13")
Weight: 64kg (141 lb)

Vanbrugh Ball E710A & Base E120B

Height: 560mm (22")
Width: 370mm (14½")
Width at base: 330mm (13")
Weight: 59kg (130 lb)

13" Ball E120A & Collared Base E120C on Pier Cap S940C

Acanthus-leaf Ball E080A & Collared Base E120C on Pier Block S140B and Pier Cap S940C

Vanbrugh Ball E710A & Base E120B on Pier Cap S940C

11" Ball E115A & Base E120B

Height: 520mm (20½")
Diameter of ball: 280mm (11")
Width at base: 330mm (13")
Weight: 42kg (93 lb)

13" Ball E120A & Collared Base E120C

Height: 620mm (24½")
Diameter of ball: 330mm (13")
Width at base: 330mm (13")
Weight: 58kg (128 lb)

17" Ball E140A & Collared Base E140C

This ball and base is of similar design to the E120 13" Ball and Collared Base. Ball supplied with lifting socket.

Height: 775mm (30½")
Diameter of ball: 430mm (17")
Width at base: 430mm (17")
Weight: 119kg (262 lb)

21" Ball E150A & Collared Base E150C

Ball supplied with lifting socket.

Height: 945mm (37¼")
Diameter of ball: 535mm (21")
Width at base: 560mm (22")
Weight of ball: 143kg (315 lb)
Weight of base: 82kg (181 lb)

TS Tech Sheet No. M59   For Pier Caps, see pages 136-137

24" Ball E160A also available (USA only)

Circular Table

This table features a circular top with a simple decorated centre panel and moulded edging. This can be mounted on four D460 Lion Supports.

Circular Table Top D450
Diameter: 1370mm (54")
Thickness: 80mm (3⅛")
Weight: 186kg (410 lb)

Lion Support D460
Width at base: 290mm (11½")
Height: 710mm (28")
Weight: 45kg (99 lb) each

Scrolled Bench Seats

Bench seats with vine and scrollwork supports, available in straight and curved form. The standard curved and straight sections can be arranged in various combinations to suit individual requirements; the standard combinations are shown in the Seat Data table below.

Width of seat top: 405mm (15¹⁵⁄₁₆")
Overall height of seat: 457mm (18")
Lengths and weights: (see table)

TS Tech Sheet No. M75 & M76

IMPORTANT
INSTALLATION DETAILS
It is essential that your Haddonstone seat or table is sited on a firm and level area. Although the top is reinforced, it may crack if subjected to a pivoting or twisting strain. An 8 to 1 sand/cement bedding mortar must be used to ensure that each support bears an equal weight. The properties of this mixture give a secure hold that can be broken without difficulty if the seat has to be re-sited. We cannot accept responsibility for breakage if this instruction is ignored.

HD311 Straight 51" Bench Seat including 2 Scrolled Seat Supports

HD332 Double Curved 54" Bench Seat including 5 Scrolled Seat Supports

HD321 Curved 52" Bench Seat including 3 Scrolled Seat Supports

SCROLLED BENCH SEAT DATA							
TYPE	CODE	SUPPORTS REQUIRED (D400A)	LENGTH/ OUTER GIRTH (excluding joints)	OUTER CHORD	RADIUS		OVERALL WEIGHT (Supports 25kg each)
					INNER	OUTER	
Single 51 Straight	HD311	2	1295mm (51")	N/A	N/A	N/A	135kg (297 lb)
Single 52 Curved	HD321	3	1380mm (54¼")	1320mm (52")	920mm (36¼")	1325mm (52¼")	156kg (344 lb)
Single 54 Curved	HD331	3	1400mm (55")	1365mm (54")	1385mm (54½")	1790mm (70½")	160kg (352 lb)
Double 54 Curved	HD332	5	2800mm (110¼")	N/A	1385mm (54½")	1790mm (70½")	295kg (650 lb)
Single 60 Curved	HD341	3	1540mm (60½")	1525mm (60")	3100mm (122")	3505mm (138")	171kg (377 lb)

Note ⌐_ Type number on curved seats indicates approx. outer chord length in inches

HD431 Curved 47" Egg and Dart Bench Seat including 3 Chimera Seat Supports

HD421 Straight 51" Egg and Dart Bench Seat including 2 Chimera Seat Supports

Egg and Dart Seat Tops

A range of ornate bench seat tops decorated with an egg and dart design with a leaf motif to each corner. Designed specifically for use with the D405 Chimera Seat Support, they may also be used with the D400 Support.

(Registered Design No. 2042756)

TS Tech Sheet No. M77

Chimera Seat Support D405

Exquisite design in the form of a Chimera, a mythological beast popular in the XVIII century. May be used with standard seat tops.

Length (base): 383mm (15")
Width (base): 135mm (5¼")
Height: 393mm (15½")
Weight: 25kg (55 lb)

(Registered Design No. 2042755)

Hadrian Seat HD520

Responding to requests from numerous clients, Haddonstone has created an elegant bench seat of modest proportions incorporating a panelled back, scrolled arm rests, chimera supports and an egg and dart seat top. Rebates are provided for fixings (not supplied), required if used in a public area only. Engraving possible, see page 184. HD525 version also available, featuring scrolled support based on D400A design, see page 76.

Length: 1335mm (52½")   Depth: 495mm (19½")

(Registered Design No. 3003646)

					RADIUS		
TYPE	CODE	SUPPORTS (D405A)	LENGTH/OUTER GIRTH	OUTER CHORD	INNER	OUTER	OVERALL WEIGHT (Support 25kg ea.)
Straight 51	HD421	2	1295mm (51")	N/A	N/A	N/A	140kg (308 lb)
Curved 47	HD431	3	1240mm (48⅞")	1190mm (46⅞")	845mm (33⅜")	1250mm (49¼")	163kg (359 lb)

EGG AND DART SEAT DATA

Raphael Seat D510

Designed for a livery company in the City of London. Using four rams couchant, this is an interesting variation on the original Raphael Seat. For dimensions see Raphael Seat D500 below.

(Registered Design No.2006991)

TS Tech Sheet No. M70 & M71

Raphael Seat D500

The imposing Raphael Seat incorporates decorative panels thought to be inspired by Raphael's grotesque decorations in the Vatican with both Etruscan and early English Renaissance influences.

Length: 2217mm (87 ½")
Depth: 609mm (24")
Height: 1194mm (47")
Weight: 875kg (1930 lb)

(Registered Design No. 2006991)

TS Tech Sheet No. M70 & M71

Original concept for Ram Supports: Lingard + Styles, landscape architects

GARDEN & LANDSCAPE FOUNTAINS - CENTREPIECE

General Note: Simple precautions should be taken to avoid frost damage to fountains. Water should be drained off before winter every year and not replaced until spring when any risk of hard frost has passed.

Single Dolphin Fountain HC171

Height: 740mm (29⅛")
Weight: 25kg (55 lb)

Recommended Pump: X210

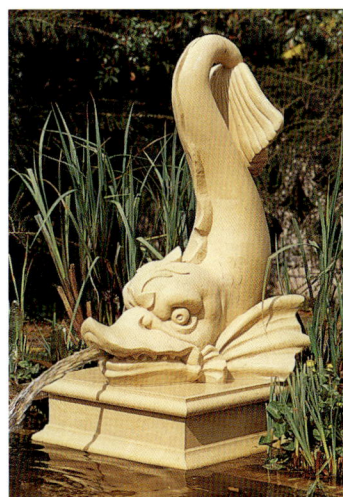

Water Nymph HC390

This charming design features a water nymph in a classical pose. The fountain can be positioned either adjacent to a pool or used as a centrepiece. Can be supported on an A240 Plinth, see page 32. A complementary design to Haddonstone's Seasons statues (see page 65).

Height: 1005mm (39½")
Base diameter: 435mm (17⅛")
Weight: 135kg (297 lb)

(Registered Design No. 3003645)

Recommended Pump: X210

Large Dolphin Fountain C172

The dolphin is considered the king of the fish. In classical ornament the dolphin often appears as an attribute of Neptune, the Roman god of the sea. This piece was inspired by early XVI century Italianate designs. For pedestal see S310S string on page 136.

Height: 905mm (35½")
Length overall: 700mm (27½")
Width overall: 670mm (26½")
Weight: 94kg (207 lb)

Recommended pump: X220

Lion Fountain C300 Fountain Base C305

The lion sejant shown as a fountain with water spouting from its mouth. It is mounted on a waisted octagonal base. Also available as a finial, see page 68.

Width at lion base: 280mm (11")
Width at base: 355mm (14")
Height of lion: 610mm (24")
Height of base: 280mm (11")
Weight of lion: 36kg (79 lb)
Weight of base: 31kg (68 lb)

Recommended pump: X210

West Lodge Fountain HC780

Replicated for the West Lodge Park Hotel in Hertfordshire, this elegant fountain is ideal for use as a centrepiece in a small pool. One of the latest additions to the Haddonstone Collection. Shown with S160S.

Height: 527mm (20¾")
Width overall: 660mm (26")
Width at base: 273mm (10¾")
Weight: 74kg (163 lb)

Recommended pump: X210

GARDEN & LANDSCAPE FOUNTAINS - CENTREPIECE

Neapolitan Fountain
C3700

A centrepiece fountain featuring a Boy-holding-dolphin centrepiece, the dolphin's mouth being the fountain head. Supported by an ornate base, the fountain bowl is the shape of a round shell.

Width of shell: 955mm (37")
Height of shell: 255mm (10")
Width of base: 495mm (19½")
Overall height: 1395mm (55")
Weight: 210kg (463 lb)

Recommended pump: X220

TS Tech Sheet No. F30

Boy-holding-dolphin Centrepiece
C370A

Height: 510mm (20")
Width at base: 180mm (7")
Weight: 15kg (33 lb)

Recommended pump: X201

General Note: Simple precautions should be taken to avoid frost damage to fountains. Water should be drained off before winter every year and not replaced until spring when any risk of hard frost has passed.

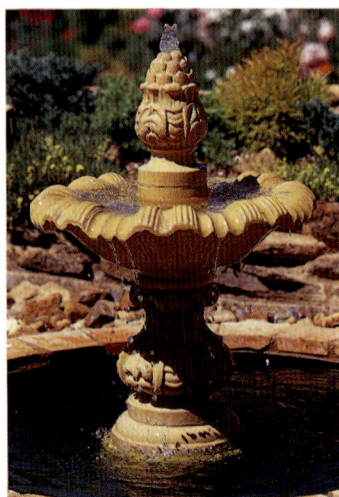

Small Neapolitan Fountain
C3750

This charming small fountain features an ornate shell bowl with a naturalistic bud fountain head. Ideal for use as a centrepiece in a small pool.

Width of shell: 460mm (18")
Width of base: 250mm (9⅞")
Overall height: 655mm (25¾")
Weight: 36kg (79 lb)

Recommended pump: X201
Optional Pump Housing: HC3601

TS Tech Sheet No. F53

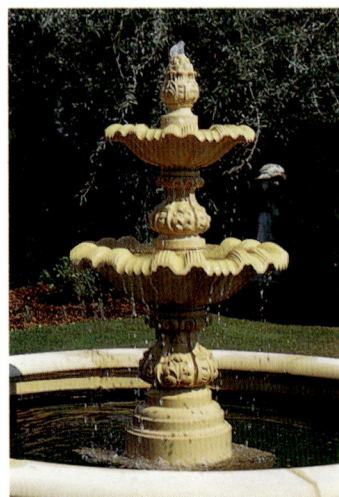

Neapolitan Small Double Fountain
C3650

Formed by two ornate shell bowls and pedestals with a naturalistic bud fountain head, this fountain is ideal as a centrepiece for the Small Pool.

Upper shell width: 460mm (18")
Lower shell width: 680mm (26¾")
Width of base: 325mm (12¾")
Overall height: 1175mm (46¼")
Weight: 99kg (218 lb)

(Registered Design No.2030925)

Recommended pump: X210
Optional Pump Housing: HC360H

TS Tech Sheet No. F52

Neapolitan Large Double Fountain
C3550

A large double fountain with ornate shell bowls and pedestals supporting an entwined triple-dolphin centrepiece. Suitable for a Medium Pool.

Upper shell width: 680mm (26¾")
Lower shell width: 955mm (37")
Base width: 495mm (19½")
Overall height: 1705mm (67⅛")
Weight: 262kg (578 lb)

(Registered Design No. 2030926)

Recommended pump: X230

TS Tech Sheet No. F51

Eton College Fountain C3600

The original for this exquisite triple fountain stood in the Cloister Court of Eton College, Windsor. The badly eroded original has now been replaced by a Haddonstone replica to restore this feature to its former glory.

The fountain comprises ornate pedestals supporting three decorative shell bowls surmounted by a naturalistic bud.

Upper shell width: 460mm (18")
Middle shell width: 680mm (26¾")
Lower shell width: 955mm (37")
Base width: 495mm (19½")
Overall height: 1860mm (73¼")
Weight: 269kg (593 lb)

Recommended pump: X230

TS Tech Sheet No. F50

Triple Lotus Bowl Fountain HC3500

Launched at the 1997 Chelsea Flower Show, each bowl of this powerful triple-tiered fountain is supported by fluted pedestals featuring stylised Ionic capitals with the top bowl surmounted by a naturalistic bud. This original design by Haddonstone is based around the standard Lotus Bowl. Ideal for use as a centrepiece to Haddonstone's L, XL and XXL pool surrounds, see page 87.

Upper bowl diameter: 800mm (31½")   Width of base: 500mm (19¾")
Middle bowl diameter: 1200mm (47¼") Overall Height: 2777mm (109⅜")
Lower bowl diameter: 1830mm (72")   Weight: 1300kg (2863 lb)

(Registered Design No. 2059936)   Recommended pump: X240

Please note: Lower bowl will require mechanical lifting on site in all instances.

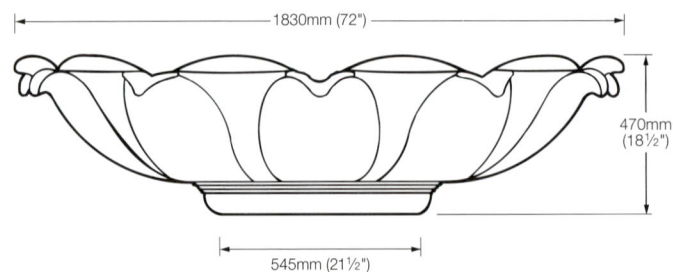

TS Tech Sheet No. F70 & F71

Lotus Bowl HC350 on Pedestal HD2900 or HD2901

The Lotus Bowl makes a spectacular fountain. It may be combined with three dolphins as its centrepiece and mounted on a Doric pedestal (HD2900 or HD2901). (For Triple Dolphin Fountain C1700 and Pedestal C180, see page 84.)

HC350 Weight: 690kg (1520 lb)
HD2900 Height: 1084mm (42¾")
HD2900 Weight: 181kg (399 lb)
HD2901 Height: 1190mm (46⅞")
HD2901 Weight: 194kg (427 lb)

TS Tech Sheet No. F20 & F21

Please note: will require mechanical lifting on site in all instances.

1830mm (72")
470mm (18½")
545mm (21½")

Double Lotus Fountain HC3510

Incorporating the top tiers of the Triple Lotus Fountain, this design was launched at the 1998 Chelsea Flower Show.

Diameter of upper bowl: 800mm (31½")
Diameter of lower bowl: 1200mm (47¼")
Width of base: 334mm (13³⁄₁₆")
Overall height: 1692mm (66⅝")
Weight: 367kg (808 lb)

(Registered Design No. 2076600)

Recommended pump: X230

TS Tech Sheet No. F72

Quadruple Lotus Bowl Fountain HC358

This imposing four-tiered fountain is supported by fluted pedestals featuring stylised Ionic capitals to the three upper bowls with the top bowl surmounted by a naturalistic bud. This original design by Haddonstone is based around the standard Triple Lotus Fountain. Shown in XXL Pool Surround. Bottom shell supplied in three segments.

Upper shell diameter: 800mm (31½")
Second shell diameter: 1200mm (47¼")
Third shell diameter: 1830mm (72")
Bottom shell diameter: 3660mm (144")
Width of base: 850mm (33½")
Overall height: 4470mm (176")
Weight: 6588kg (14511 lb)

Pump to be supplied by others. Please note: will require mechanical lifting in all instances.

GARDEN & LANDSCAPE FOUNTAINS - CENTREPIECE

Fontainebleau Fountain
C230

For details see Fontainebleau Urn A300 on page 21. Shown on a B360 Large Winslow Pedestal, see page 48. An inverted S310S string may also be used - see page 136.

Recommended pump: X220

TS Tech Sheet No. F40

General Note: Simple precautions should be taken to avoid frost damage to fountains. Water should be drained off before winter every year and not replaced until spring when any risk of hard frost has passed.

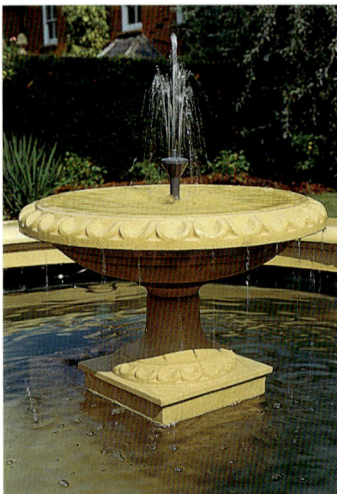

Regency Fountain
HC510

Also, Regency Bird Bath, page 55.

Width at rim: 510mm (20")
Width at base: 220mm (8¾")
Height: 340mm (13½")
Weight: 36kg (79 lb)

Recommended pump: X210

Regency Pedestal
HB330 (Illustrated on page 55)

Width at top: 220mm (8¾")
Width at base: 280mm (11")
Height: 430mm (17")
Weight: 42kg (93 lb)

Eastwell Fountain
C200

See also, the Eastwell Urn A260 on page 17. For pedestal see Winslow Pedestal B350 on page 48.

Width at top: 785mm (31")
Width at base: 350mm (13¾")
Height: 595mm (23½")
Weight: 89kg (195 lb)

Recommended pump: X210

Figured Fountain
C220

Shown raised on an optional Jacobean Pedestal B150 (see page 50) to create a stunning centrepiece fountain. See also Jacobean Sundial (page 53) and Figured Bird Bath (page 56).

Bowl diameter: 520mm (20½")
Height: 710mm (28")
Weight: 73kg (161 lb)
Recommended pump: X220

Triple Dolphin Fountain C1700
Pedestal C180

Three dolphins set on a pedestal as a fountain centrepiece. See also, Lotus Bowl page 82.

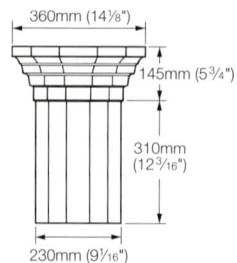

360mm (14⅛")
145mm (5¾")
310mm (12³⁄₁₆")
230mm (9¹⁄₁₆")

Pedestal C180

Dolphin height: 510mm (20")
Dolphin weight: 15kg (33 lb)
Pedestal weight: 35kg (77 lb)

Recommended pump: X220

TS Tech Sheet No. F22

GARDEN & LANDSCAPE FOUNTAINS - POOL SURROUNDS

Haddonstone pool surrounds are available in numerous combinations of kerb, vase and plinth sections to suit individual requirements. There are six standard sizes: HALF SMALL, SMALL, MEDIUM, LARGE, EXTRA LARGE and EXTRA EXTRA LARGE.

Straight pool components, including corners, are also available:

TS Tech Sheet No. P60 & P50

The vase section, which is in the shape of a conch shell, flanked by two dolphins, is supported by a base decorated with palmettes and scrolls. It can be used as a fountain, a planter, or both.

The kerb section has a continuous moulding enriched with ovolo and palmette designs.

The plinth lends appeal to the overall appearance of the pool, raising it from ground level.

Tech Sheets for pool assembly and recommended plumbing layout drawings are available on request. Plumbing Tech Sheets are:

TS Tech Sheet No. P42 for Half Small Pool

TS Tech Sheet No. P12 & P41 for Small Pool

TS Tech Sheet No. P11 & P12 for M, L, XL & XXL

For details of centrepiece fountains, see pages 79-84.

Glass fibre pool liners are available for the Half Small and Small pools only. Larger pools should be lined with a water-proofed render. Both are shown as typical sections, see page 86. Alternatively butyl liners may be used.

Please note that the use of a shallow liner in a Small or Half Small pool precludes the plumbing of vases. A plinth course is required to allow the use of a shallow liner.

Typical average weights:
Kerb sections: 31kg (68 lb)
Vase sections: 40kg (88 lb)
Kerb plinth: 31kg (68 lb)
Vase plinth: 50kg (110 lb)

Simple precautions should be taken to avoid frost damage to fountains. Water should be drained off before winter every year and not replaced until spring when any risk of hard frost has passed.

Half-Small Pool Surround C4HSKV illustrated without plinths (internal diameter 1780mm, 70") showing Lion Wall Fountain

TS Tech Sheet No. P40

For details of centrepiece fountains, see pages 79-84.

Turn to Specialist Services - Archives for further ornament options

PUMPS AND PLUMBING

Pool surrounds
Pumps and plumbing extra
– see price list.

Centrepiece and wall fountains, excluding Haddonstone Wall Fountain
Plumbing included. Pumps extra
– see price list.

Self-circulating fountains, including Haddonstone Wall Fountain
Pumps and plumbing included.

Please note:
Haddonstone's plumbing kits do not necessarily produce the effects shown in the catalogue. Details of standard and special effect fountain jets are available on request.

Small Pool Surround C4SKVP (internal diameter 1780mm, 70") showing Regency Fountain and Pedestal. For standard fountain jet, see page 89.

TS Tech Sheet No. P40

Medium Pool Surround C4MKVP (internal diameter 2705mm, 106½") showing Neapolitan Fountain

TS   Tech Sheet No. P30 & P50

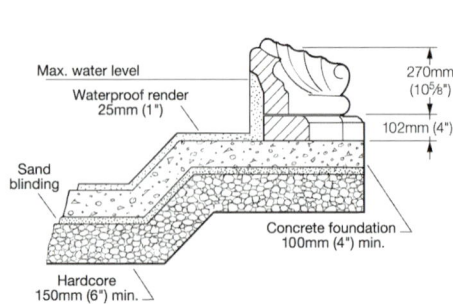

Max. water level
Waterproof render 25mm (1")
270mm (10⅝")
102mm (4")
Sand blinding
Concrete foundation 100mm (4") min.
Hardcore 150mm (6") min.

TYPICAL SECTION THROUGH C4M, C4L, C4XL & C4XXL POOLS

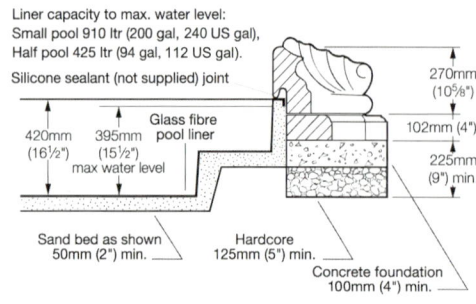

Liner capacity to max. water level:
Small pool 910 ltr (200 gal, 240 US gal).
Half pool 425 ltr (94 gal, 112 US gal).
Silicone sealant (not supplied) joint
Glass fibre pool liner
420mm (16½")
395mm (15½") max water level
270mm (10⅝")
102mm (4")
225mm (9") min.
Sand bed as shown 50mm (2") min.
Hardcore 125mm (5") min.
Concrete foundation 100mm (4") min.

TYPICAL SECTION THROUGH C4S & C4HS SMALL POOLS

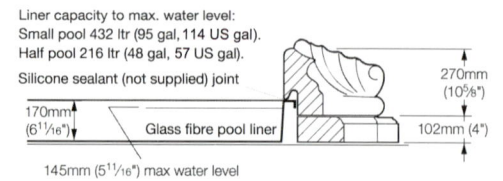

Liner capacity to max. water level:
Small pool 432 ltr (95 gal, 114 US gal).
Half pool 216 ltr (48 gal, 57 US gal).
Silicone sealant (not supplied) joint
170mm (6¹¹/₁₆")
Glass fibre pool liner
270mm (10⅝")
102mm (4")
145mm (5¹¹/₁₆") max water level

TYPICAL SECTION THROUGH SHALLOW POOL LINER FOR C4S & C4HS SMALL POOLS

GARDEN & LANDSCAPE
FOUNTAINS - POOL SURROUNDS

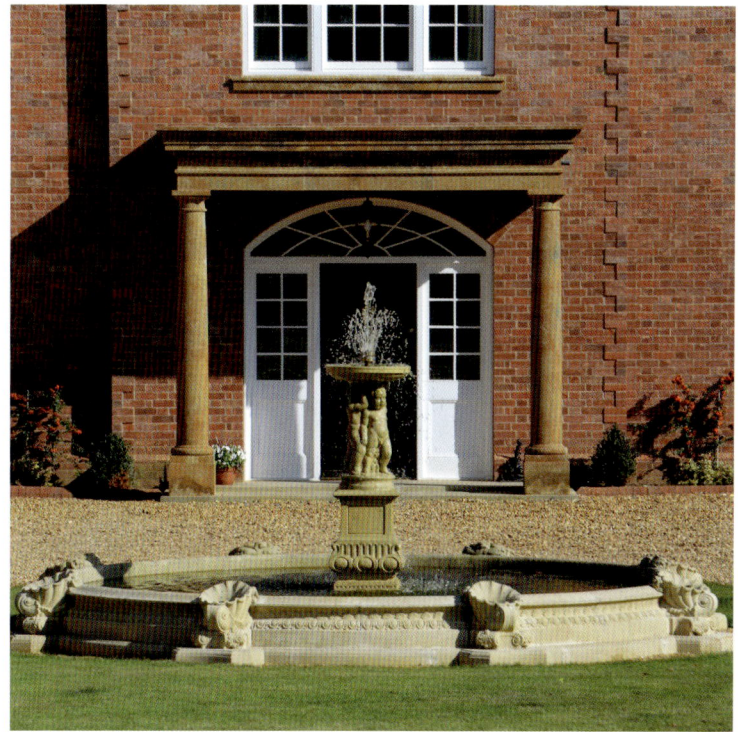

Large Pool Surround C4LKVP
(internal diameter 3660mm, 144")
showing Figured Fountain and
Jacobean Pedestal with special
effect fountain jet

TS Tech Sheet No. P20 & P50

Barton Grange Garden Centre, Lancashire

Extra Large Pool Surround C4XLKP illustrated without vases
(internal diameter 5450mm, 214½") showing Triple Lotus Bowl Fountain

TS Tech Sheet No. P10 & P50

Contractor: The Company of Landscapers

Extra Extra Large Pool Surround C4XXLKP illustrated without vases
(internal diameter 7500mm, 295") showing Triple Dolphin Fountain and
Pedestal in Lotus Bowl with special effect fountain jet

TS Tech Sheet No. P80 & P50

POOL TYPE	INSIDE DIAMETER	OUTSIDE DIAMETER KERB *	OUTSIDE DIAMETER KERB PLINTH **	WITH VASE SECTIONS						WITHOUT VASE SECTIONS			POOL LINER AVAILABLE
				C400 KERB	C420 VASE	C440 KERB PLINTH	C441 HALF PLINTH	C460 VASE PLINTH	WEIGHT	C400 KERB	C440 KERB PLINTH	WEIGHT	
C4HS HALF SMALL POOL	1780mm (70")	2100mm (82¾")	2306mm (90¾")	4	2	1	2	2	408kg (900 lb)	5	4	310kg (684 lb)	YES
C4S SMALL POOL	1780mm (70")	2100mm (82¾")	2306mm (90¾")	8	4	4	-	4	817kg (1800 lb)	10	8	620kg (1367 lb)	YES
C4M MEDIUM POOL	2705mm (106½")	3025mm (119¼")	3235mm (127½")	12	6	6	-	6	1078kg (2376 lb)	15	12	809kg (1784 lb)	NO
C4L LARGE POOL	3660mm (144")	3980mm (156¾")	4190mm (165")	16	8	8	-	8	1303kg (2872 lb)	20	16	958kg (2112 lb)	NO
C4XL EXTRA LARGE POOL	5450mm (214½")	5770mm (227¼")	5980mm (235½")	24	12	12	-	12	1968kg (4338 lb)	30	24	1506kg (3320 lb)	NO
C4XXL EXTRA EXTRA LARGE POOL	7500mm (295")	7820mm (308")	8030mm (316")	28	14	14	-	14	2587kg (5703 lb)	35	28	1974kg (4352 lb)	NO

* EXCLUDES VASES ** EXCLUDES VASES AND PLINTHS. REFER TO TECHNICAL SHEETS FOR DETAILS.

For details of centrepiece fountains, see pages 79-84.   Turn to Specialist Services - Archives for further ornament options

GARDEN & LANDSCAPE
FOUNTAINS - POOL SURROUNDS

Detail of a pool showing Haddonstone straight and outside corner pool sections featuring non-standard dolphin fountains. Straight kerb and plinth sections are supplied in 660mm (26") lengths. Inside and outside corners, vases and plinths are also available.

TS Tech Sheet No. P60

Pool and planting display using standard small and large Haddonstone pool surrounds.

Client: London Borough of Kensington and Chelsea

Torus Pool Surround showing West Lodge Fountain.

Torus Pool Surround HC485

A simple bull-nosed pool surround which can be used in conjunction with a Haddonstone standard Pool Liner and paving or flooring. Ideal for contemporary garden designs.

Internal diameter: 1720mm (67¾")
External diameter: 2320mm (91⅜")
Thickness: 50mm (2")
Weight (per slab): 25kg (55 lb)
Total weight: 200kg (440 lb)

Roman Pool Surround (Small) C470S showing Eastwell Fountain

TS   Tech Sheet No. P100, P105 & P110

Roman Pool Surround

This design extends the range of Haddonstone's pool surrounds. The design features a bold roll moulding and the flat coping forms a low sitting place. Also available are straight and corner stones allowing pools of differing shapes to be made. Glass fibre pool liners are available for the Half Small and Small pools only.

Height: 380mm (15")
Internal radius: 900mm (35½")
Ext. radius (base): 1080mm (42½")
C470S weight: 788kg (1738 lb)
C470HS weight: 394kg (869 lb)

ROMAN POOL TYPE	INSIDE DIAMETER (BASE)	OUTSIDE DIAMETER (BASE)	C470 KERB SECTIONS	WEIGHT	POOL LINER AVAILABLE
C470HS HALF SMALL POOL	1800mm (70⅞")	2160mm (85")	5	394kg (869 lb)	YES
C470S SMALL POOL	1800mm (70⅞")	2160mm (85")	10	788kg (1738 lb)	YES
C470M MEDIUM POOL	2770mm (109¹⁄₁₆")	3100mm (122")	15	1095kg (2412 lb)	NO
C470L LARGE POOL	3470mm (136¹¹⁄₁₆')	3800mm (149⅝")	18	1350kg (2974 lb)	NO

Roman Pool Straight Stone
C4706

Height: 380mm (15")
Length: 500mm (19¾")
Weight: 64kg (141 lb)

Roman Pool Outside Corner Stone C4707

Height: 380mm (15")
Length: 250mm (9¾")
Weight: 45kg (99 lb)

Roman Pool Inside Corner Stone
C4708

Height: 380mm (15")
Outside base length: 415mm (16¼")
Weight: 90kg (198 lb)

For details of centrepiece fountains, see pages 79-84.

Turn to Specialist Services - Archives for further ornament options

GARDEN & LANDSCAPE
FOUNTAINS - POOL SURROUNDS

Pebble Pool X435 (Shown with Neapolitan Small Double Fountain)

In response to numerous requests from clients, Haddonstone has introduced this sturdy pebble pool for digging into the ground, which can be used in conjunction with the following fountains:

C172   Large Dolphin Fountain on S310S Support, see page 79
C300   Lion Fountain on C305 Base, see page 79
HC390   Water Nymph on A240 Plinth, see page 79
C200   Eastwell Fountain on B350 Pedestal, see page 84
HC510   Regency Fountain on HB330 Pedestal, see page 84
C3650   Neapolitan Small Double Fountain (shown), see page 80
C3700   Neapolitan Fountain, see page 80

This robust pebble pool is manufactured from 100% recycled plastic and can be used without formal raised pool surrounds.

For dimensions, please refer to the diagram. Pebbles not supplied.

Pool Coping T770

As well as straight stones, inside and outside and 135° corner stones are available:

Weight: 63kg (139 lb) per 914mm (36")
Length: 914mm (36")

Inside and Outside Corner coping:
Size: 650mm x 650mm
(25½" x 25½") overall

TS Tech Sheet No. P70

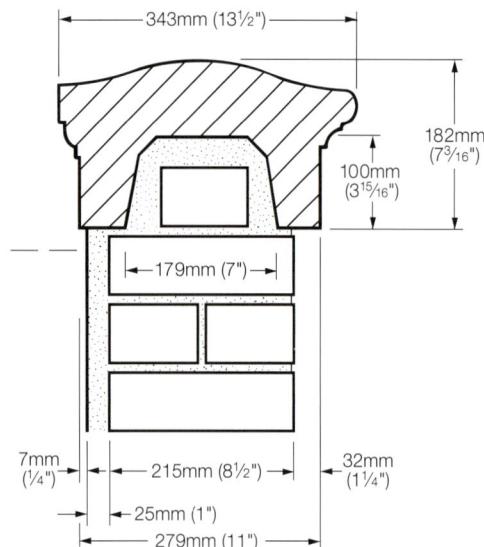

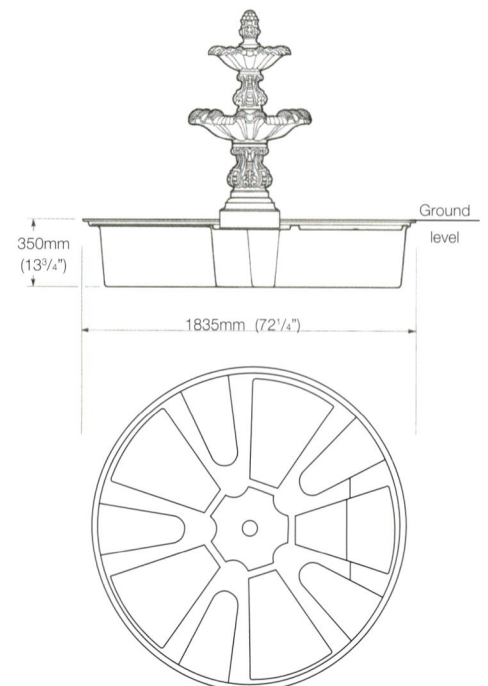

Please refer to our price list for details of fountains, pumps and plumbing.

For details of centrepiece fountains, see pages 79-84.

Jubilee Pool Surround C4801

Inspired by a pool surround in Haddonstone's Jubilee Show Garden in Northamptonshire, this design is intended to provide a simple surround for smaller water features.

This design can sit on an existing terrace or patio as it requires no additional excavation. Illustrated with the C3750 Small Neapolitan Fountain centrepiece (see page 80).

Outside base diameter: 1470mm (57⅞")
Height: 215mm (8½")
Weight: 212kg (467 lb)

TS Tech Sheet No. P95

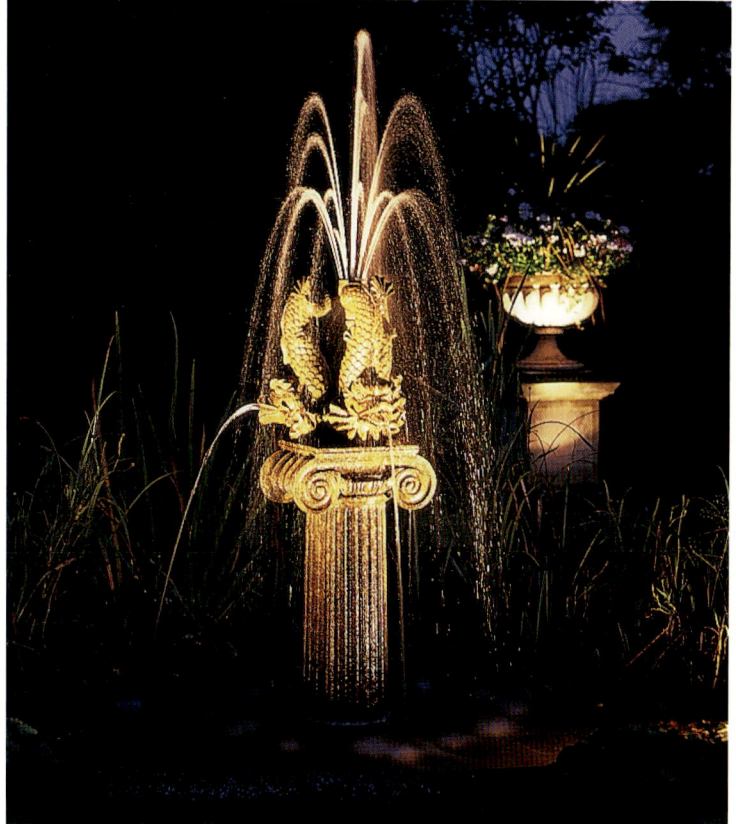

Arcadian Half Pool Surround GC405

Includes pool liner and cable gland. (Surround supplied in 4 sections). For Green Man Wall Fountain GC500A, see page 102.

Width: 1470mm (58") Projection: 735mm (29") Weight: 118kg (259 lb)

GARDEN & LANDSCAPE LIGHTING (UK only)

Haddonstone Ltd is able to offer lighting suitable for pool surrounds, fountains and gardens. The 12-volt system uses a transformer which can be submerged. As the transformer can be operated underwater, this enables long distances between the mains socket and the transformer to be bridged with conventional cables. Units can be connected to each transformer up to a maximum of 150 watts. A variety of other lighting effects and control systems are available. Please ask for details.

Lunaqua 10 (UK only)

A very versatile lighting system, which can be used either underwater or in a normal garden setting. The 50 watt spotlights are connected to the transformer via special plug-in connectors.

The spotlight is made of shockproof plastic with an integral swivel bracket allowing it to be turned through 180°, the angle of beam being 24°.

GARDEN & LANDSCAPE FOUNTAINS - SELF CIRCULATING

Small Lagoon Fountain HC380 (not illustrated)
Lagoon Fountain HC383
Large Lagoon Fountain HC385 (not illustrated)

New to the Haddonstone Collection, these impressive self-circulating fountains would add style to either a private garden or a commercial project. These designs are also available as planters, see page 43.

	HC380	HC383	HC385
Height:	600mm (23⅝")	600mm (23⅝")	600mm (23⅝")
Top width:	1220mm (48")	1570mm (61¾")	1775mm (69⅞")
Weight:	535kg (1178 lb)	857kg (1888 lb)	1092kg (2405 lb)

Please note: HC385 will require mechanical lifting on site in all instances.

Romanesque Fountain
TLHC521

Adapted from the Romanesque Bowl (see page 29), this low-level fountain bowl can provide an attractive self-circulating water feature to decorate any small interior or exterior setting. Includes pump. Shown with optional Brass Rose Jet X270.

Diameter: 815mm (32")
Height: 348mm (13¹¹⁄₁₆")
Weight: 67kg (148 lb)

Versailles Fountain
HC800

The design for this self-circulating fountain was inspired by the fountains within the renowned Bosquet de la Colonnade at Versailles. Ideally suited for interior and exterior settings ranging from terraces and kitchen gardens to conservatories and hotel foyers. Includes pump. Optional Brass Rose Jet X270 available.

Width of bowl: 913mm (36")
Overall width of base: 675mm (26½")
Height: 390mm (15⅜")
Weight: 210kg (463 lb)

(Registered Design No. 2077407)

General Note: Simple precautions should be taken to avoid frost damage to fountains. Water should be drained off before winter every year and not replaced until spring when any risk of hard frost has passed.

Bayeux Fountain
HC130

Inspired by Romanesque architecture, this robust self-circulating fountain features stylish leaf moulding around the fountain bowls. This design was created by Haddonstone to act as a focal point in a sheltered garden or conservatory. See page 99 for Bayeux Wall Fountain.

Includes pump.

Diameter of main bowl: 950mm (37 3/8")
Diameter of base: 572mm (22 1/2")
Overall height: 1525mm (60")
Weight: 222kg (489 lb)
Heaviest component: 147kg (323 lb)

Please note: will require mechanical lifting on site in all instances

93

Andalos Fountain
C100

The twelve-sided bowl displays an hexagonal Arabesque decoration, whilst the hexagonal base has a twelve-sided decoration. Rhythmical repetition of horseshoe arches suggests the fountain could have originated in a mosque complex. Includes pump. Jardiniere available, see page 32.

Width at rim: 725mm (28½")
Width at base: 560mm (22")
Height: 770mm (30¼")
Weight: 171kg (377 lb)

Bay Fountain HC185

The Bay Fountain is a new addition to the Haddonstone Collection. This stylish self-circulating fountain is ideal for enhancing a contemporary garden or landscape. Includes pump. Also available as a planter, see page 43.

Height: 400mm (15¾")
Width at top: 1850mm (72⅞")
Weight: 690kg (1520 lb)

Gothic Fountain
C251
Upper Base A350
Lower Base A360

Illustrated as a freestanding fountain with optional Gothic Upper Base. It can also be supplied with an optional Lower Base. For diagram see Gothic Jardiniere on page 33. Supplied with offset cable hole unless specified. Includes pump.

Fountain width: 800mm (31½")
Fountain height: 660mm (26")
Fountain weight: 224kg (494 lb)

TS Tech Sheet No. F75

GARDEN & LANDSCAPE
FOUNTAINS - SELF CIRCULATING

Eclipse Fountain
GC230

Table-top fountain.
Includes pump.

Height: 285mm (11¼")
Diameter: 305mm (12")
Weight: 26kg (57 lb)

Crucible Fountain
GC200

Includes pump.

Crucible planter also available, see page 40.

Height: 620mm (24⅜")
Width: 500mm (19¾")
Weight: 105kg (231 lb)

Original design concept: Alfresco Garden Furnishings

Lotus Bud Fountain GC320 Includes pump.

Will need topping up regularly - not suitable for continuous unattended running. Large bowl requires mechanical lifting on site in all instances.

Height: 1600mm (63")   Total weight: 582kg (1280 lb)
Max diameter: 1125mm (44¼")   Heaviest component: 267kg (587 lb)

Arcadian Double Fountain GC300 Includes pump.

Will need topping up regularly - not suitable for continuous unattended running.

Height: 1155mm (45½")   Total weight: 170kg (374 lb)
Max width: 845mm (33¼")   Heaviest component: 73kg (161 lb)

Turn to Specialist Services - Archives for further ornament options

GARDEN & LANDSCAPE FOUNTAINS - SELF CIRCULATING

X460 PLAN

Inspection cover

820mm (32¼")

1010mm (39¾")

Haddonstone launched the Pebble Bowl concept to enable fountains to be positioned in places where excavation is not possible, or desirable - making Pebble Bowls ideal for patios or garden rooms.

Each Pebble Bowl is also available with an optional GC710C Pebble Bowl Support to raise the fountain off the ground, see below left.

Each fountain centrepiece is also available with a robust Pebble Pool, which requires excavation, as follows:
X465 Pebble Pool [650mm (25½") diameter, 305mm (12") depth] or
X460/X461 Pebble Pool [ovoid 1010 x 820mm (39¾" x 32¼"), 410mm (16") depth]. See diagrams right, Ammonite Fountain GC101 shown.

The appropriate Pebble Pool is identified alongside each product description where relevant.

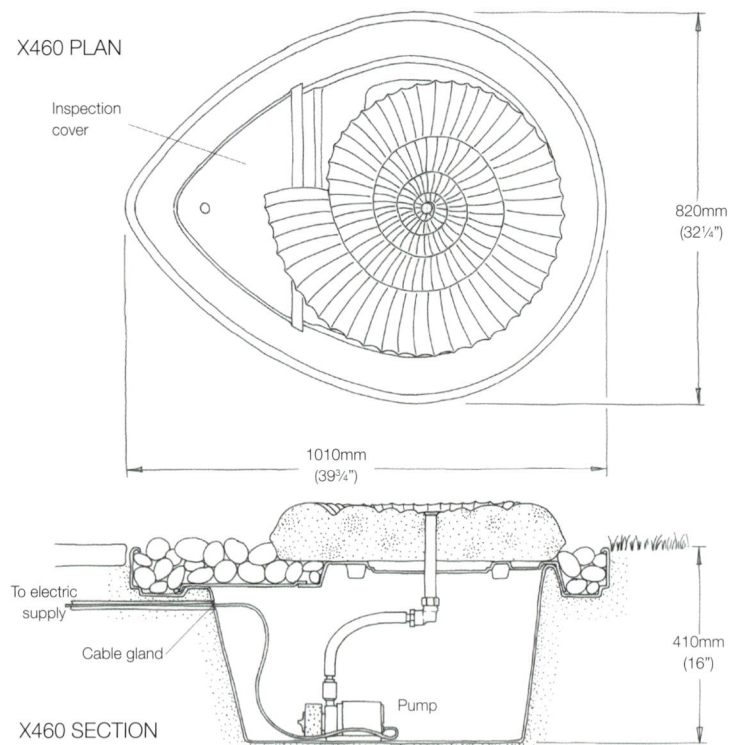

To electric supply

Cable gland

Pump

410mm (16")

X460 SECTION

Pebble Bowl Support GC710C

Shown with Lotus Flower Pebble Bowl Fountain, see page 97, (not included). Optional for all Arcadian Pebble Bowl Fountains.

Height: 210mm (8¼")
Overall diameter: 420mm (16½")
Weight: 39kg (86 lb)

AquaStack Fountain GC191 (with 7 sections)

Includes pump and X465 Pebble Pool. Pebbles not supplied.

Height of stone: 380mm (15")
Length of each section: 315mm (12⅜")
Total weight: 27kg (59 lb)

General Note: The innovative AquaStack system enables customers to build their own fountains by choosing the number of GC190A sections required - each being fitted over a central copper pipe at the preferred angle. GC190A height: 40mm (1⁹/₁₆")

AquaStack Pebble Bowl Fountain GC194 (with 12 sections)

Includes pump. For optional Pebble Bowl Support, see GC710C left.

Overall height: 650mm (25⅝")
Bowl width: 720mm (28½")

Total weight: 84kg (185 lb)
Heaviest component: 42kg (93 lb)

Ammonite Fountain GC101

Includes pump and X460 Pebble Pool. Pebbles not supplied.
Not available as a Pebble Bowl Fountain.

Height of stone: 120mm (4³⁄₄")
Width of stone: 625mm (24¹⁄₂")
Weight of stone: 53kg (116 lb)

Lotus Flower Pebble Bowl Fountain
GC143

Includes pump. For optional Pebble Bowl Support, see page 96.

Overall height: 315mm (12³⁄₈")
Bowl width: 720mm (28¹⁄₂")
Total weight: 80kg (176 lb)
Heaviest component: 42kg (93 lb)

Lotus Flower Fountain
GC141 (not illustrated)

Includes pump and X465 Pebble Pool.

Height of stone: 145mm (5³⁄₄")
Width of stone: 500mm (19³⁄₄")
Weight of stone: 32kg (70 lb)

Spiral Egg Pebble Bowl Fountain GC123

Includes pump. For optional Pebble Bowl Support, see page 96.

Overall height: 670mm (26³⁄₈")
Bowl width: 720mm (28¹⁄₂")
Total weight: 130kg (286 lb)
Heaviest component: 80kg (176 lb)

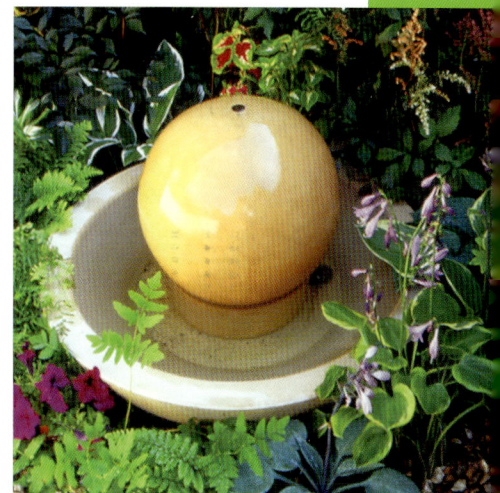

Spiral Egg Fountain
GC121 (not illustrated)

Includes pump and X465 Pebble Pool.

Height of stone: 500mm (19³⁄₄")
Max. width of stone: 380mm (15")
Weight of stone: 80kg (176 lb)

Ball Pebble Bowl Fountain GC163

Includes pump. For optional Pebble Bowl Support, see page 96.

Overall height: 525mm (20⁵⁄₈")
Bowl width: 720mm (28¹⁄₂")
Total weight: 97kg (214 lb)
Heaviest component: 47kg (104 lb)

Ball Fountain
GC161 (not illustrated)

Includes pump and X465 Pebble Pool.

Diameter of stone: 355m (14")
Weight of stone: 47kg (104 lb)

Triple Ball Fountain
GC162

Includes pump, plumbing and X461 Pebble Pool. Glass beads not supplied. Not available as a Pebble Bowl Fountain.

Max height of stone: 355mm (14")
Total weight: 124kg (273 lb)
Heaviest component: 47kg (104 lb)

Ring Maze Fountain
GC181

Includes pump and X465 Pebble Pool. Pebbles not supplied.

Height of stone: 80mm (3⅛")
Max. width of stone: 540mm (21¼")
Weight of stone: 27kg (59 lb)

Ring Maze Pebble Bowl Fountain
GC183 (not illustrated)

Includes pump. For optional Pebble Bowl Support, see page 96.

Overall height: 230mm (9")
Bowl width: 720mm (28½")
Total weight: 76kg (167 lb)
Heaviest component: 42kg (93 lb)

Spiral Tower Pebble Bowl Fountain GC157

Includes pump. For optional Pebble Bowl Support, see page 96.

Overall height: 870mm (34¼")
Bowl width: 720mm (28½")
Total weight: 104kg (229 lb)
Heaviest component: 62kg (137 lb)

Spiral Tower Fountain
GC156 (not illustrated)

Inc. pump and X460 Pebble Pool.

Height of stone: 800mm (31½")
Base width of stone: 200mm (7⅞")
Overall width of stone: 250mm (9⅞")
Weight of stone: 62kg (137 lb)

Arcadian Single Fountain GC131

Includes pump and X460 Pebble Pool. Pebbles not supplied. Not available as a Pebble Bowl Fountain.

Height of stone: 470mm (18½")
Max width of stone: 457mm (18")
Weight of stone: 27kg (59lb)

GARDEN & LANDSCAPE FOUNTAINS - WALL

Haddonstone Wall Fountain HC270

A delightful wall fountain, of neoclassical design. The bowl is supported by a tapered, fluted pedestal with a spiralling ribbon design. Ideal as a wall decoration on a terrace or in a conservatory or hotel foyer. This design can be installed on most existing walls. Includes pump.

Height: 1650mm (65")
Shell projection: 410mm (16⅛")
Width overall: 720mm (28¼")
Weight: 126kg (278 lb)

(Registered Design No. 2046016)

TS Tech Sheet No. F60

Haddonstone Wall Fountain HC271

This delightful wall fountain is a variation on the HC270, see above. It has been designed to allow for face fixing to most existing walls via an ingenious combination of concealed dowels and a wrought iron strap. Includes pump.

Height: 1065mm (42")
Shell projection: 410mm (16⅛")
Width overall: 720mm (28¼")
Weight: 95kg (209 lb)

TS Tech Sheet No. F61

Bayeux Wall Fountain HC135

A self-circulating, wall mounted version of the Bayeux Fountain (see page 93).

Includes pump

Projection from wall: 480mm (18⅞")
Width of bowl: 950mm (37⅜")
Width of base: 572mm (22½")
Overall height: 1525mm (60")
Weight: 134kg (295 lb)
Heaviest component: 48kg (106 lb)

Turn to Specialist Services - Archives for further ornament options

99

GARDEN & LANDSCAPE FOUNTAINS - WALL

Shell Wall Fountain
HC540

A beautiful formalised, scalloped shell forms the bowl of this wall fountain, supported by a boldly voluted console. Illustration shows Shell Wall Fountain HC540 and Console HC550 with Dolphin C170 and Console C160.

Width: 760mm (30")
Shell projection: 650mm (25½")
Height of shell and console: 785mm (31")
Weight: 165kg (363 lb)

Please note that a 215 mm (8½") minimum wall thickness is required for this ensemble. Coping details available on request.

Recommended pump: X220

TS Tech Sheet No. F10 & F11

Grotesque Mask
E340
Grotesque Wall Fountain
C260 (Not illustrated)

A vigorous comic mask.
Height: 265mm (10½")
Width: 230mm (9")
Weight: 8kg (17 lb)

Recommended pump: X210

Lion Wall Fountain
C310
Lion Wall Mask
E470 (Not illustrated)

A handsome lion mask mounted on a square stone. Designed to be built into a wall.

Height of stone: 290mm (11½")
Width of stone: 290mm (11½")
Height of mask: 315mm (12½")
Weight: 15kg (33 lb)

Recommended pump: X210

TS Tech Sheet No. F40 & M59

Also available: Large Lion Mask HE475. Height: 1000mm (39³/₈"), Weight: 570kg (1255 lb)

Large Lion Wall Fountain C315

Designed by Haddonstone in the style of the antique, this robust wall fountain features a lion with a flowing mane.

Width: 452mm (18")
Depth: 170mm (6¾")
Weight: 24kg (53 lb)

Recommended pump: X220

Wood Nymph Wall Fountain C320

Mounted on a square stone, this charming new wall fountain is designed to be built into a wall. As shown, it also provides an alternative to the Lion Wall Fountain when used in conjunction with the C531 Dauphin Fountain.

Width of stone: 295mm (11⁵/₈")
Height of stone: 295mm (11⁵/₈")
Width of mask 320mm (12½")
Height of mask: 480mm (19")
Weight: 24kg (52 lb)

Recommended pump: X210

Dauphin Fountain
C530

Designed in the continental style, this attractive self circulating fountain features a handsome lion mask together with bold scroll details. The half octagonal pool conceals a glass fibre liner. Includes pump. Shown with Swagged Roundel (page 164) and Ionian Jardinieres (page 28).

Width: 1180mm (46½")
Depth: 700mm (27½")
Height: 1460mm (57½")
Weight: 430kg (947 lb)

(Registered Design No. 3002836)

TS Tech Sheet No. F65

Dauphin Fountain
C531 (Not illustrated)

Incorporating the charming Wood Nymph Wall Fountain, see page 100.

GARDEN & LANDSCAPE FOUNTAINS - WALL

Gecko Bowl Fountain
GC531

Incorporating GC750 Bowl & pump.

Height overall: 595mm (23$^1/_2$")
Stone width overall: 350mm (13$^3/_4$")
Total weight: 29kg (64 lb)
Heaviest component: 21kg (46 lb)

Gecko Wall Fountain
GC530A

Stone only. Recom. pump: X190.

Height overall: 345mm (13$^5/_8$")
Width at top: 270mm (10$^5/_8$")
Weight: 7kg (15 lb)

Green Woman Bowl Fountain GC541

Incorporating GC755 Bowl.
Includes pump.

Height overall: 750mm (29$^1/_2$")
Bowl width: 480mm (18$^7/_8$")
Total weight: 54kg 119 lb)
Heaviest component: 34kg (75 lb)

Green Woman Wall Fountain GC540A

Stone only. Recom. pump: X206.

Diameter: 400mm (15$^3/_4$")
Thickness: 100mm (3$^7/_8$")
Weight: 17kg (37 lb)

Registered Design No: 2104236

Tree Frog Bowl Fountain GC551

Incorporating GC755 Bowl.
Includes pump.

Height overall: 750mm (29$^1/_2$")
Bowl width: 480mm (18$^7/_8$")
Total weight: 54kg (119 lb)
Heaviest component: 34kg (75 lb)

Tree Frog Wall Fountain GC550A

Stone only. Recom. pump: X206.

Diameter: 400mm (15$^3/_4$")
Thickness: 100mm (3$^7/_8$")
Weight: 17kg (37 lb)

Medusa Bowl Fountain GC521

Incorporating GC750 Bowl, see
above. Includes pump.

Height overall: 595mm (23$^1/_2$")
Stone width overall:
350mm (13$^3/_4$")
Total weight: 29kg (64 lb)
Heaviest component: 21kg (46 lb)

Medusa Wall Fountain GC520A

Stone only. Recom. pump: X190.

Height overall: 345mm (13$^5/_8$")
Width at top: 270mm (10$^5/_8$")
Weight: 7kg (15 lb)

Green Man Bowl Fountain GC501

Incorporating GC750 Bowl, see
above. Includes pump.

Height overall: 560mm (22")
Stone width overall:
350mm (13$^3/_4$")
Total weight: 28kg (62 lb)
Heaviest component: 21kg (46 lb)

Green Man Wall Fountain GC500A

Stone only. Recom. pump: X190.

Width of stone: 220mm (8$^3/_4$")
Height of stone: 280mm (11")
Weight of stone: 5kg (11 lb)

GARDEN & LANDSCAPE PLAQUES

Griffin Plaque TLQ994

Dating from the late eighteenth century, this replica of a famous Coade design is ideal for enhancing a classical architectural scheme. Built-in version also available.

Width: 1228mm (48⅜")
Height: 890mm (35⅟₁₆")
Depth of block: 65mm (2⁹⁄₁₆")
Weight: 76kg (167 lb)

Tradescant Wall Plaque Q660

Based on an XVII century plaque displayed at the Museum of Garden History. Recarved to depict John Tradescant (1608-1662), gardener to Charles II and famous for bringing numerous plant species to England, including many from America. Up to two letters or numerals may be cast into the stone either side of the figure (i.e. four in total).

Height: 695mm (27⅜")
Width: 555mm (21⅞")
Depth: 135mm (5⁵⁄₁₆")
Weight: 65kg (143 lb)

(Registered Design No. 2061157)

Spring Plaque TLQ990   Summer Plaque TLQ991
Autumn Plaque TLQ992   Winter Plaque TLQ993

The charming Seasons Plaques depict putti with their seasonal attributes: garlands of flowers; sheaves of corn; cornucopia of fruit; and, fire and ice. Built-in versions also available. Faithful reproductions taken from original designs created by the renowned Coade manufactory.

Width: 890mm (35⅟₁₆")   Height: 440mm (17⁵⁄₁₆")   Depth of block: 20mm (¾")   Weight: 22kg (48 lb)

For other plaques see page 164.

GARDEN & LANDSCAPE PLAQUES & ACCENTS

Capturing the majesty of the renowned Parthenon Frieze, this pair of designs is replicated from original carvings which date from c443-438 BC. The originals depict the Panathenaic Procession. These horsemen are from the north frieze. Available individually or as a pair. All dimensions are approximate owing to the shape of the originals. Will require mechanical fixing in most instances.

Parthenon Frieze I TLQ981

Width: 1250mm (49¼")
Depth: 100mm (4")
Height: 1030mm (40½")
Weight: 150kg (330 lb)

Parthenon Frieze II TLQ982

Width: 1250mm (49¼")
Depth: 100mm (4")
Height: 1030mm (40½")
Weight: 150kg (330 lb)

Celtic Stepping Stone - Knotted GN100A

See right (left). Complements Celtic Edging, see page 108.

Diameter: 355mm (14")
Weight: 7.5kg (17 lb)

Celtic Disc GN500A

See right (centre). Can be used with Celtic Stepping Stones, see below. Complements Celtic Edging, see page 108.

Diameter: 600mm (23⅝")
Weight: 25kg (55 lb)

Celtic Stepping Stone - Woven GN200A

See right (right). Complements Celtic Edging, see page 108.

Diameter: 355mm (14")
Weight: 7.5kg (17 lb)

GARDEN & LANDSCAPE ACCENTS

Chimney Pot Planter HA217

Haddonstone replicated this intriguing chimney pot design for a restoration project. Now available as the Chimney Pot Planter, this rustic design should prove a popular addition to both cottage and urban gardens. The Chimney Pot Planter allows roots to reach the underlying soil as the design is produced without a base.

Height: 557mm (21¾")
Length at base: 370mm (14⅝")
Width at base: 298mm (11¾")
Length at top: 343mm (13½")
Width at top: 305mm (12")
Weight: 20kg (44 lb)

Bollard D100

A simple bollard, ideal for contemporary or traditional schemes.

Width at base: 255mm (10")
Height: 610mm (24")
Weight: 50kg (110 lb)

Bollard D110

This bollard surmounted by a fir cone finial may be used with or without connecting chains (not supplied). Hooks available as an optional extra.

Width at base: 165mm (6½")
Height above ground: 650mm (25½")
Depth below ground: 315mm (12½")
Height of fir cone: 180mm (7")
Weight: 33kg (74 lb)

Mini Ammonite GE950

Cast from a genuine ammonite fossil, Mini Ammonites are versatile garden accents. They can be used underwater in a fountain, as a decorative edging or in a paving scheme or garden mosaic. Mini Ammonites are available individually or in packs of 20 (GE951).

Max width: 80mm (3⅛")
Weight: 125g (2oz)

Staddle Stone E900

Staddle stones were originally used to raise grain stores off the ground, thereby stopping vermin from climbing up. Primarily associated with the Cotswolds, staddle stones can be used to flank drives or as garden ornaments. This design was produced in response to requests from clients.

Width at top: 450mm (17¾")
Width at base: 300mm (11¾")
Height: 640mm (25¼")
Weight: 86kg (189 lb)

GARDEN & LANDSCAPE
OBELISKS

EGYPTIAN IN ORIGIN, OBELISKS WERE BROUGHT TO ROME IN THE FIRST CENTURY BC. THE OBELISK THEN ENTERED INTO THE CLASSICAL VOCABULARY, BEING MODIFIED AND DEVELOPED INTO A DECORATIVE FEATURE IN THE ENGLISH LANDSCAPE FROM THE EIGHTEENTH CENTURY ONWARDS.

Ideal for formal or landscape gardens, defining a vista, at the centre of a courtyard or as a balustrade ornament.

Obelisk Finial
HE535

A charming small obelisk for use inside or out. Equally at home on a chimney piece hearth, a window cill, or in the garden.

Width of base: 150mm (6")
Height overall: 700mm (27½")
Weight: 14kg (31 lb)

Balustrade Obelisk
E545

This obelisk has been designed for positioning on a Haddonstone balustrade pier as an interesting alternative to an urn or finial. It may also act as a freestanding obelisk when used in conjunction with a B400, B420 or B440 plinth (see page 49).

Width at base: 152mm (6")
Height: 1005mm (39½")
Weight: 65kg (143 lb)

TS Tech Sheet No. M60

Gothic Obelisk
E540

An obelisk in Gothic style, ideally suited to form a focal point in a small garden.

Width of base: 460mm (18")
Height overall: 1800mm (71")
Weight: 262kg (578 lb)

TS Tech Sheet No. M21

Millennium Obelisk
E555

This imposing structure would make an impressive focal point in any major landscape project aimed at celebrating a unique event. Steps also available, see page 169.

Width of base: 1229mm (48⅜")
Height overall: 6190mm (243¾")
Weight: 3750kg (8260 lb)

TS Tech Sheet No. M22

Obelisk E550

The Obelisk can be used to great effect at the end of a long vista, or in a courtyard or formal garden area.

Width of base: 700mm (27 ½")
Height overall: 2672mm (105 ¼")
Weight: 656kg (1446 lb)

TS Tech Sheet No. M20

GARDEN & LANDSCAPE
LAWN EDGING

Celtic Edging

Inspired by Celtic designs, complementing the Celtic Disc and Stepping Stone, see page 104. Arched below ground for easy installation.

Celtic Edging GN750A
Length: 250mm (9¾")
Width: 30mm (1⅛")
Height above ground: 140mm (5½")
Depth below ground: 100mm (4")
Weight: 3.5kg (8 lb)

Celtic Edging GN750B
Length: 495mm (19½")
Width: 30mm (1⅛")
Height above ground: 140mm (5½")
Depth below ground: 100mm (4")
Weight: 7kg (16 lb)

Celtic Edging Post GN755A
Width: 40mm (1½")
Height above ground: 185mm (7¼")
Depth below ground: 100mm (4")
Weight: 1kg (2 lb 3oz)

Scrolled Edging Stone D220

This edging has a scrolled front and plain back. Left and right-handed terminal lengths are 230mm (9"). Ideal for herbaceous borders.

Length: 457mm (18")
Height above ground: 90mm (3½")
Depth below ground: 140mm (5½")
Weight: 11.5kg (25 lb)

Edging Post D200

For corner or terminal use with Roped or Scrolled Edging.

Width: 75mm (3")
Height above ground: 120mm (4¾")
Depth below ground: 140mm (5½")
Weight: 2.5kg (5½ lb)

Roped Edging Stone D210

This edging, with its attractive rope decoration, is suitable for most situations and should be used with Edging Post D200.

Length: 452mm (17¾")
Height above ground: 90mm (3½")
Depth below ground: 135mm (5¼")
Weight: 9kg (21 lb)

Arcadian Lawn Edging

The unique Arcadian Lawn Edging system can be used as a mowing edge alongside flower borders, around a tree or as a kerb to paths or driveways.

Width: 140mm (5½")   Height: 90mm (3½")

Outside Corner

External Curve

Straight GN700A

Length: 450mm (17¾")   Weight: 8kg (18 lb)

Outside Corner GN700F

Length: 225mm (9")   Weight: 6kg (13 lb)

Inside Corner GN700G

Length: 225mm (9")   Weight: 6kg (13 lb)

Internal Curve GN700H-00500 (not USA)
External Curve GN700I-00500 (not USA)

Radius: 500mm (19¾")   Complete circle 8 sections
Weight per section: 7kg (15 lb)

Internal Curve GN700H-01000 (not USA)
External Curve GN700I-01000 (not USA)

Radius: 1000mm (39¾")   Complete circle: 12 sections
Weight per section: 10kg (22 lb)

External Curve GN700H-00036 (USA only)

Radius: 36"   Complete circle: 14 sections   Weight per section: 18 lb

External Curve GN700H-00072 (USA only)

Radius: 72"   Complete circle: 27 sections   Weight per section: 18 lb

ARCHITECTURAL STONEWORK

The standard range of designs in Haddonstone's Collection offers architects and designers the opportunity to use architectural components true in spirit to the orders of classical architecture. In most circumstances the standard range of designs will satisfy the architect's requirements. Where it cannot, Haddonstone can and do produce custom-made designs to order, as can be seen from the Inspirations images on the following pages.

"Classical architecture is dignified; it is capable of magnificence as well as humility. It can, by the use of its mouldings and vocabulary, express an infinite variety of moods and conditions of man whether it be national, social or historical. It is the expression of civilised man where every person is different."

Quinlan Terry, 1968

With imagination and inspiration, architects and designers can use Haddonstone designs to great effect in a variety of commercial and residential projects, as can be seen by studying the following pages.

Each project has been achieved by using either standard Haddonstone components or custom-made designs created by utilising the company's skilled craftsmen and extensive mould-making facilities. Within reason, the only constraint is your imagination...

Substantial extensions to Malvern College feature custom designs sympathetic to the architectural style of the original buildings.

This imposing neo-classical residence incorporates a Haddonstone portico, pediment and garden ornament.

Custom cladding at Brick Lane Mosque, London.

London's Whittington Hospital features Haddonstone detailing.

The dramatic entranceway to The Rutherford Centre for the Performing Arts at Wimbledon High School utilises custom cladding from Haddonstone.

ARCHITECTURAL STONEWORK INSPIRATIONS

Hospital in Japan makes extensive use of custom and standard Haddonstone.

Façade stonework at Longborough Festival Opera, Gloucestershire.

Japan's Mito Golf Clubhouse features balustrading, columns and window surrounds by Haddonstone.

Client: Mito Golf. Design and Build Contractor: Shimizu Corporation

Dramatic portico and balustraded balcony in Leicestershire.

ARCHITECTURAL STONEWORK
INSPIRATIONS

Custom façades at the Marshes Shopping Centre, Dundalk, Ireland.

Magnificent Surrey residence fully utilising both standard and custom designs.

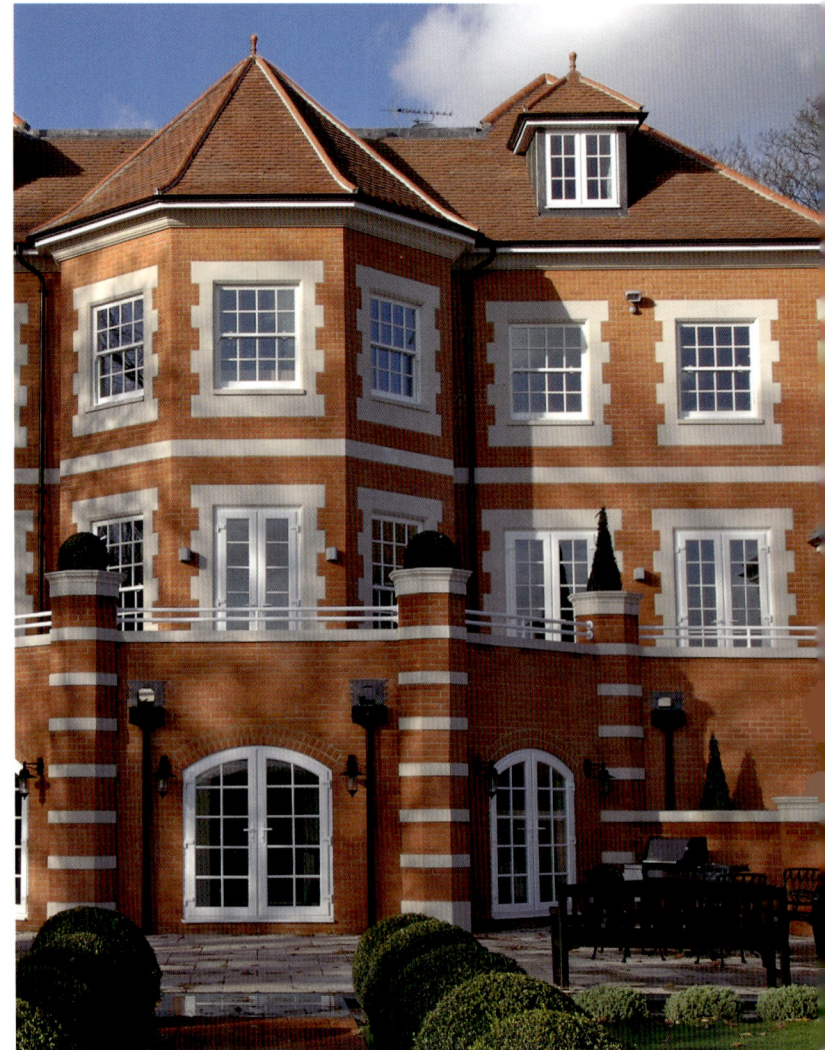

Architects: WRD & RT Taggart   Client: McLaughlin & Harvey   Surveying: Hughes McMichael

Haddonstone has been used extensively in the building and landscape at Coworth Park, Dorchester Collection's luxury country house hotel and spa in Berkshire.

Haddonstone columns, entablature and plinths combine to great effect with natural granite at The Academy Shopping Centre, Aberdeen.

This stunning property in Leicestershire combines standard and custom-made architectural stonework in Haddonstone, TecLite and TecStone.

Developer: Alpha Homes

ARCHITECTURAL STONEWORK INSPIRATIONS

Custom entrances created for Camberley's Main Square shopping area.

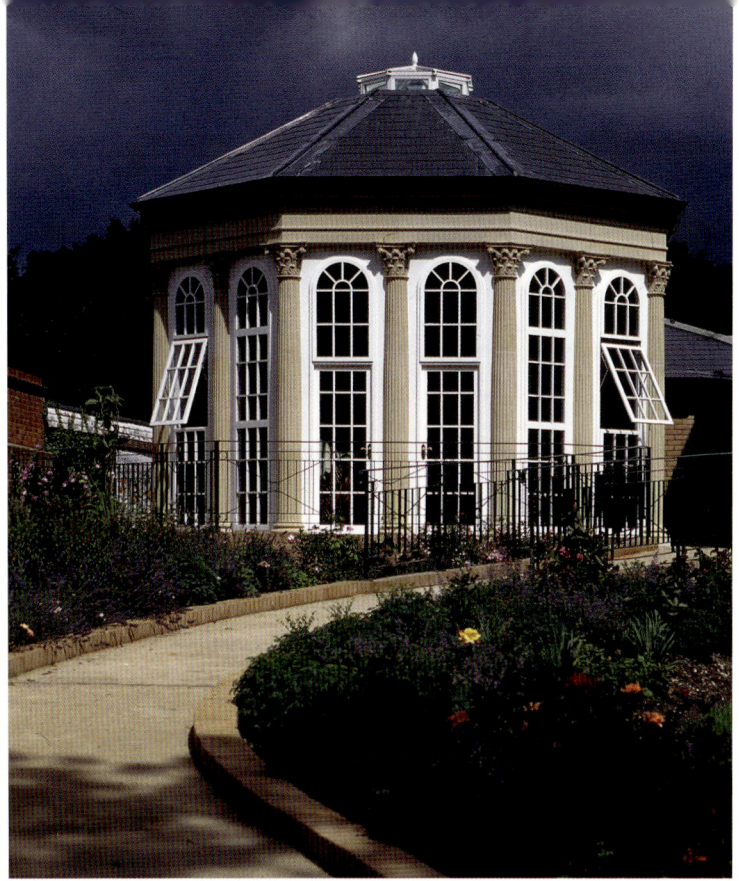

Unique Orangery at Thamesfield Nursing Home, Henley-on-Thames.

Design & Build: Simon Barnett.

Bespoke gate piers at Swinfen Hall Hotel in Staffordshire.

This inspirational Surrey home makes full use of Haddonstone's capabilities - from collonaded entrance portico and balustraded parapet to window surrounds and band courses.

ARCHITECTURAL STONEWORK INSPIRATIONS

Development in Berkshire featuring a wide range of Haddonstone designs.

Spectacular private residence in Middlesex incorporating custom portico.

Haddonstone's standard and custom-made stonework in Bedfordshire.

Architects: Robert H Robertson & Associates

Omni Shoreham Hotel in Washington DC features Haddonstone designs.

Private house in Staffordshire incorporating window and door surrounds.

Custom and standard designs combine at this Ohio residence.

A private residence in West Yorkshire featuring a curved Haddonstone portico with balustraded balcony and a Mount Edgcumbe Finial in the foreground.

Langdale Chase Hotel in Cumbria contrasts local stone with Haddonstone.

Extension to St Mary's Church, Loughton, Essex incorporating slender custom columns with dramatic effect.

Stonework installation: Les Simblet.

Haddonstone supplied the bay window and TecLite quoins, strings and cladding panels for this development in Leicester.

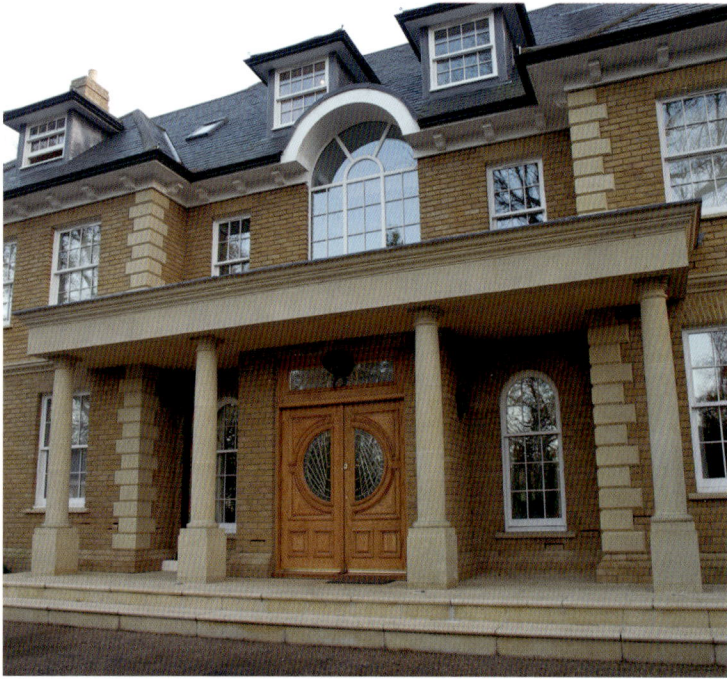
Significant Surrey residence incorporating Haddonstone extensively.

The entrance to the Atlantic Hotel, Jersey features Haddonstone columns.

London residence transformed by incorporating Haddonstone architectural features including custom portico, window heads and cills, quoins, copings and balls.

ARCHITECTURAL STONEWORK
INSPIRATIONS

Architect/Designer: Sampson Associates

The Castle public house, Woodford Green, Essex was transformed by
the imaginative use of stonework - including columns, parapet screening,
statuary, finials, door surrounds, chimney pieces and a Venetian Folly façade.

Original Design: Michael Rosenauer, Tonnet & Associates

The Sheraton Heathrow Hotel features Haddonstone balustrading.

Client: Ragdale Hall Health Hydro, Leicestershire.

Stylish jacuzzi featuring Haddonstone Columns and entablature at a prestige
Health Hydro in Leicestershire.

Haddonstone can be painted and gilded to great effect, as seen at this grand
residence in Northamptonshire.

THERE ARE FOUR TYPES OF BALUSTRADING:

The Standard Range

Illustrated on pages 125, 126 and 127, the standard range is available in six styles: Flat, Part-Weathered or Weathered, each available to suit central or side run-in situations, with a choice of standard balusters. If balustrading is to be used as a parapet wall or a raised terrace edge, we have several optional under-copings that can be used below plinth course to increase the height of the balustrade, or to cope a substructure.

The 1100 Balustrade

Shown on page 128, this is a heavier balustrade designed to comply with the Building Regulation height of 1100mm (43⁵⁄₁₆") required in certain instances. It comprises a weathered rail, weathered plinth, Georgian-style baluster and rectangular pier.

The Kensington Balustrade (USA only)

Shown on page 128, this is an imposing balustrade of handsome proportions.

It comprises weathered rail, upper and lower plinths, Regency-style K610B square balusters and rectangular piers. The plinth moulding is used to frame the inset panel of the pier shaft.

The Spiral Balustrade

Shown on page 129, the Spiral Balustrade is available only with flat rail, K533G-style baluster, standard style of plinth and optional T920 style of under-coping to the radii and falls indicated.

The Standard Range
Style FC: Flat Central Run-in

See page 132 for balusters.

See page 132 for balusters.

TS Tech Sheet No.B10 & B70

Plans below show Pier Caps.
For component weights see page 131

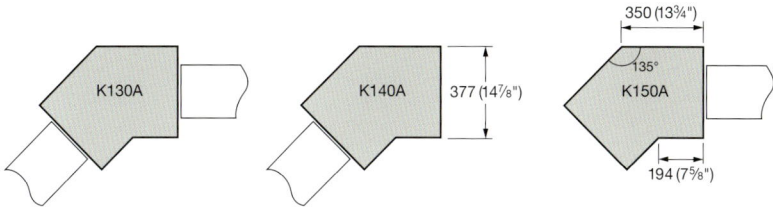

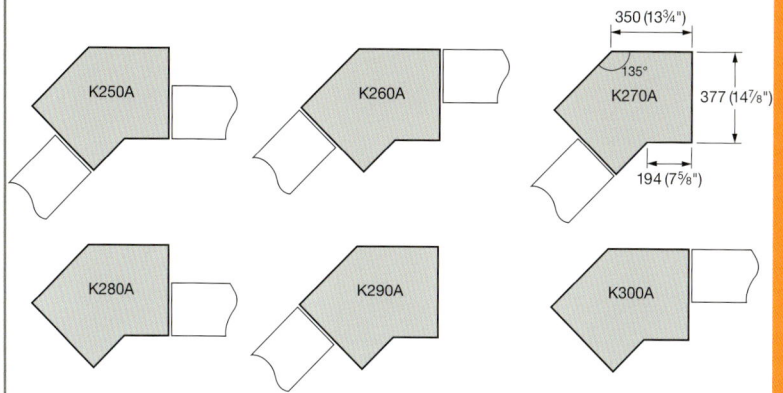

K130A   K140A   350 (13¾")
                              135°
                              K150A   377 (14⅞")
                              194 (7⅝")

FC style with K533G Balusters / T930 Under Copings

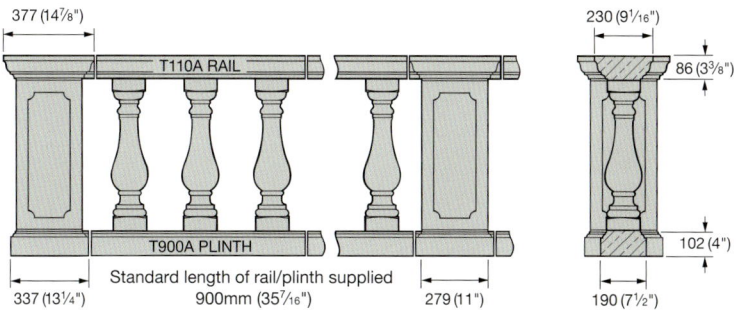

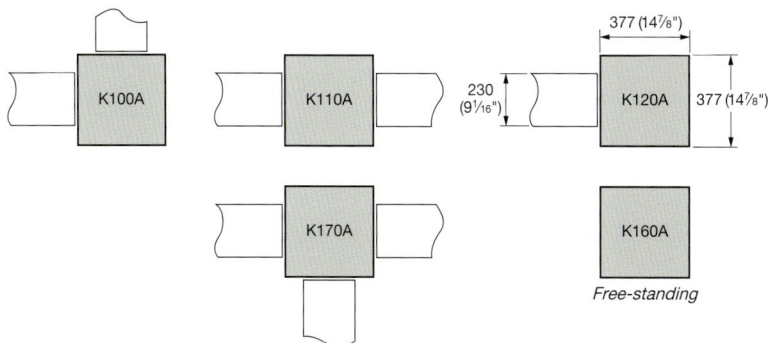

377 (14⅞")   230 (9¹/₁₆")
         T110A RAIL   86 (3⅜")
         T900A PLINTH   102 (4")
Standard length of rail/plinth supplied
337 (13¼")   900mm (35⁷/₁₆")   279 (11")   190 (7½")

K100A   K110A   230   377 (14⅞")
                              (9¹/₁₆")   K120A   377 (14⅞")

               K170A   K160A

                              Free-standing

The Standard Range
Style FS: Flat Side Run-in

See page 132 for balusters.

TS Tech Sheet No. B15 & B70

Plans below show Pier Caps.
For component weights see page 131.

K250A   K260A   350 (13¾")
                              135°
                              K270A   377 (14⅞")
                              194 (7⅝")

K280A   K290A   K300A

FS style with K533G Balusters / T925 Under Copings

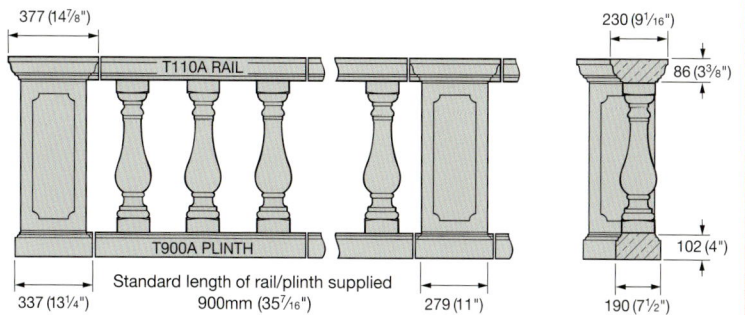

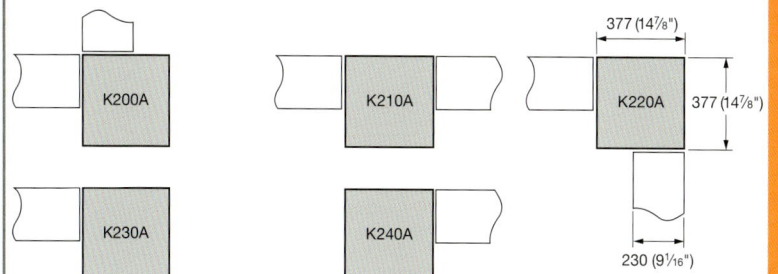

377 (14⅞")   230 (9¹/₁₆")
         T110A RAIL   86 (3⅜")
         T900A PLINTH   102 (4")
Standard length of rail/plinth supplied
337 (13¼")   900mm (35⁷/₁₆")   279 (11")   190 (7½")

K200A   K210A   377 (14⅞")
                              K220A   377 (14⅞")

K230A   K240A

                              230 (9¹/₁₆")

Custom-made products are available on request. 125

The Standard Range
Style PC: Part-Weathered Central Run-in

See page 132 for balusters.

TS Tech Sheet No.B20

Plans below show Pier Caps.
For component weights see page 131.

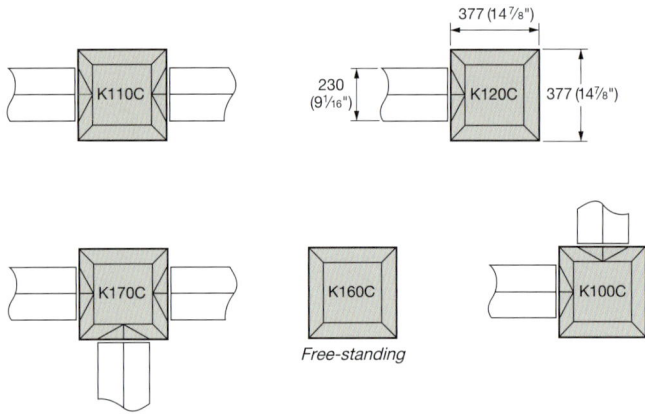

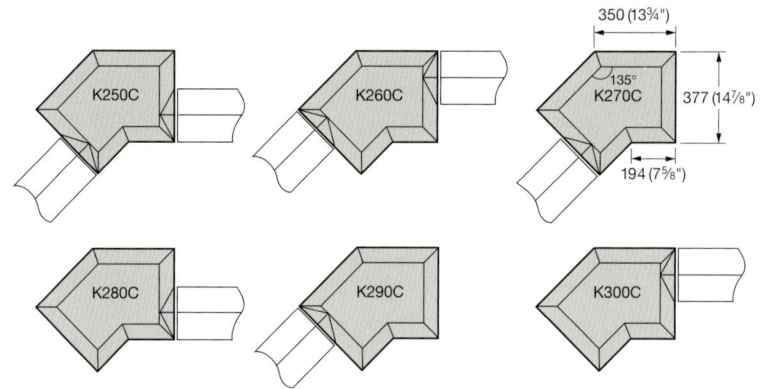

K110C

377 (14⁷⁄₈")
377 (14⁷⁄₈")
230 (9¹⁄₁₆")
K120C

K170C

K160C
Free-standing

K100C

PC style with K457G Balusters / Q560 Plinth (custom piers)

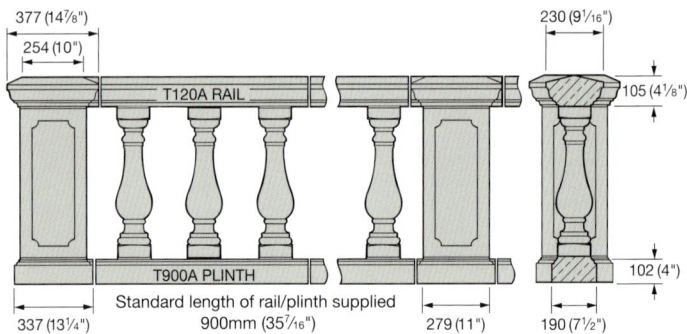

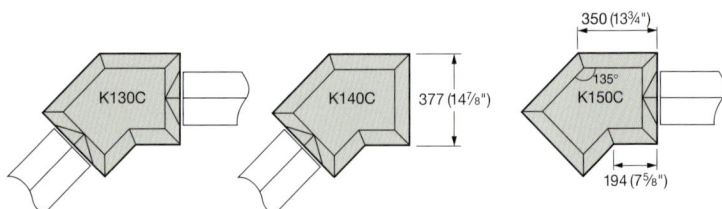

377 (14⁷⁄₈")
254 (10")
230 (9¹⁄₁₆")
105 (4¹⁄₈")
T120A RAIL
T900A PLINTH
102 (4")
337 (13¼")
Standard length of rail/plinth supplied
900mm (35⁷⁄₁₆")
279 (11")
190 (7½")

350 (13¾")
377 (14⁷⁄₈")
K130C
K140C
135°
K150C
194 (7⁵⁄₈")

The Standard Range
Style PS: Part-Weathered Side Run-in

See page 132 for balusters.

TS Tech Sheet No. B25

Plans below show Pier Caps.
For component weights see page 131.

350 (13¾")
377 (14⁷⁄₈")
135°
K250C
K260C
K270C
194 (7⁵⁄₈")

K280C
K290C
K300C

PS style with K533G Balusters

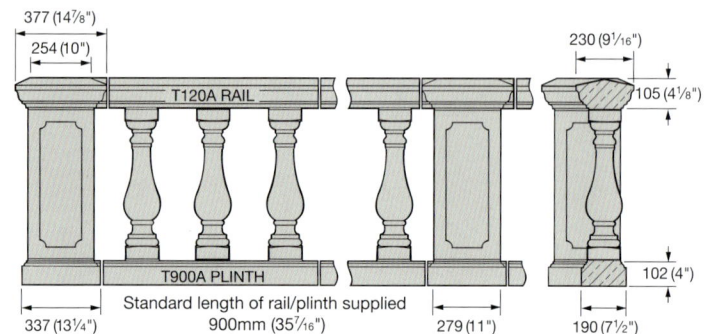

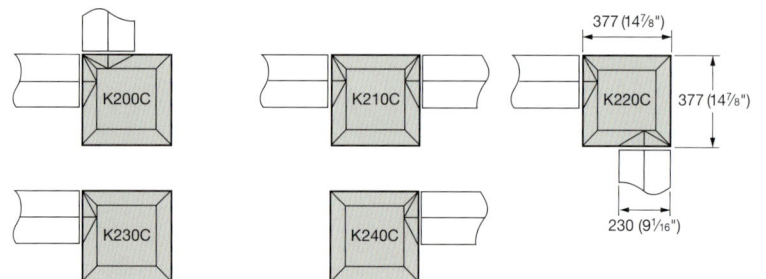

377 (14⁷⁄₈")
254 (10")
230 (9¹⁄₁₆")
105 (4¹⁄₈")
T120A RAIL
T900A PLINTH
102 (4")
337 (13¼")
Standard length of rail/plinth supplied
900mm (35⁷⁄₁₆")
279 (11")
190 (7½")

377 (14⁷⁄₈")
377 (14⁷⁄₈")
K200C
K210C
K220C

K230C
K240C
230 (9¹⁄₁₆")

Custom-made products are available on request.

The Standard Range
Style WC: Weathered Central Run-in

See page 132 for balusters.

TS Tech Sheet No.B35

Plans below show Pier Caps.
For component weights see page 131.

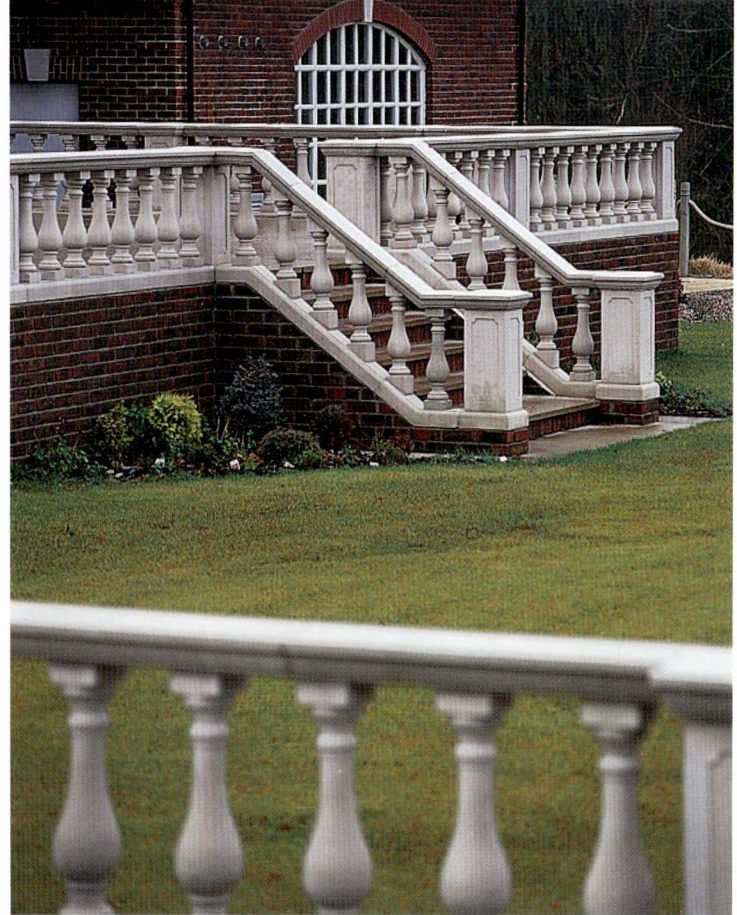

WC style with K610G Balusters

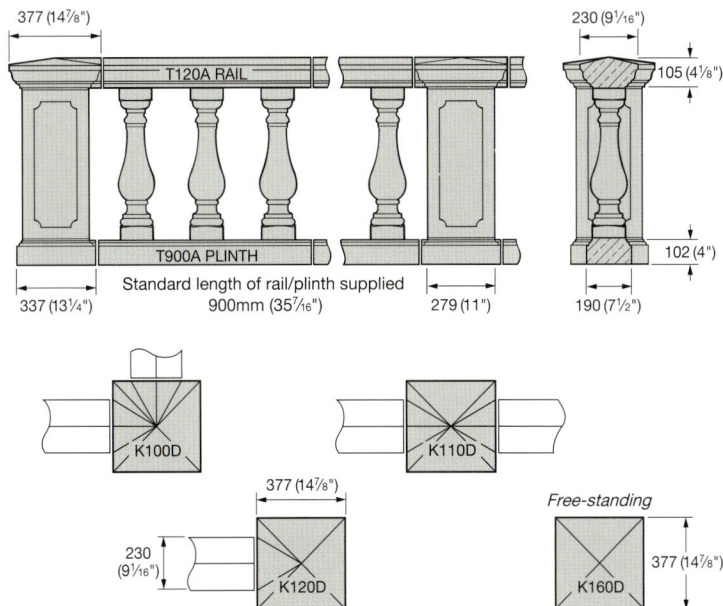

T120A RAIL

T900A PLINTH

377 (14⁷⁄₈")
230 (9¹⁄₁₆")
105 (4¹⁄₈")
102 (4")
337 (13¼")
Standard length of rail/plinth supplied
900mm (35⁷⁄₁₆")
279 (11")
190 (7½")

K100D
K110D
K120D
377 (14⁷⁄₈")
230 (9¹⁄₁₆")
Free-standing
K160D
377 (14⁷⁄₈")

The Standard Range
Style WS: Weathered Side Run-in

See page 132 for balusters.

TS Tech Sheet No. B35

Plans below show Pier Caps.
For component weights see page 131.

WS style with K533G Balusters

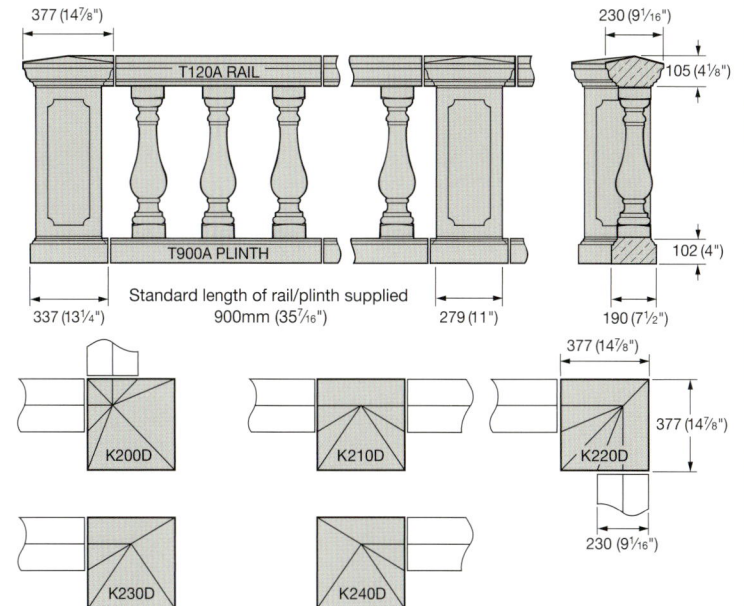

T120A RAIL

T900A PLINTH

377 (14⁷⁄₈")
230 (9¹⁄₁₆")
105 (4¹⁄₈")
102 (4")
337 (13¼")
Standard length of rail/plinth supplied
900mm (35⁷⁄₁₆")
279 (11")
190 (7½")

K200D
K210D
K220D
377 (14⁷⁄₈")
377 (14⁷⁄₈")
230 (9¹⁄₁₆")
K230D
K240D

127

The 1100 Balustrade

The 1100 Balustrade is offered as an alternative to the Standard Range should you require a heavier design of balustrading. It also complies with the Building Regulation height of 1100mm (43⁵⁄₁₆"), which is required in certain instances, without the need to use additional under-copings or to construct upstands.

TS Tech Sheet No. B40

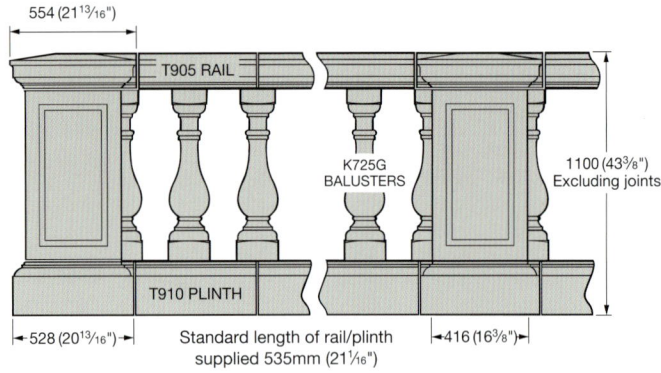

554 (21¹³⁄₁₆")
T905 RAIL
K725G BALUSTERS
1100 (43³⁄₈") Excluding joints
T910 PLINTH
528 (20¹³⁄₁₆")
416 (16³⁄₈")
Standard length of rail/plinth supplied 535mm (21¹⁄₁₆")

K725G Baluster - 20kg (44 lb)
Standard Pier (complete) - 212kg (466 lb)
Corner Pier (complete) - 296kg (651 lb)
T905 Rail - 67kg/m (45 lb/ft)
T910 Plinth - 121kg/m (81 lb/ft)

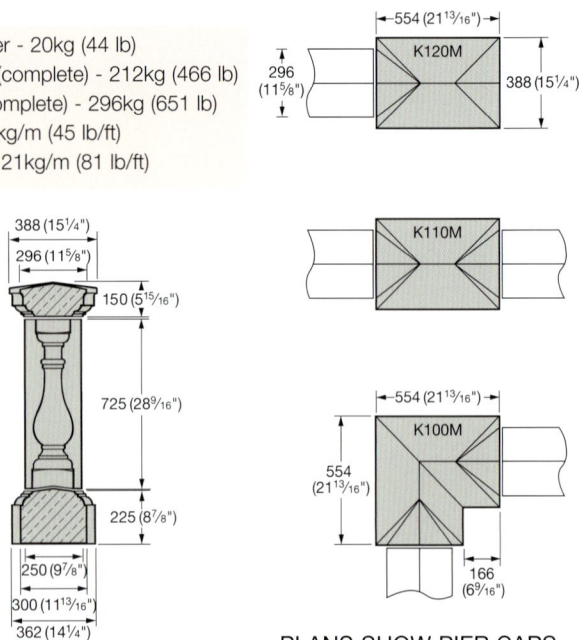

554 (21¹³⁄₁₆")
K120M
296 (11⁵⁄₈")
388 (15¹⁄₄")

388 (15¹⁄₄")
296 (11⁵⁄₈")
150 (5¹⁵⁄₁₆")
725 (28⁹⁄₁₆")
225 (8⁷⁄₈")
250 (9⁷⁄₈")
300 (11¹³⁄₁₆")
362 (14¹⁄₄")

K110M

554 (21¹³⁄₁₆")
K100M
554 (21¹³⁄₁₆")
166 (6⁹⁄₁₆")

PLANS SHOW PIER CAPS

The Kensington Balustrade (USA only)

The Kensington Balustrade is an imposing balustrade of handsome proportions. It comprises weathered rail, upper and lower plinths, unique K610B square balusters and rectangular piers. The plinth moulding is used to frame the inset panel of the pier shaft.

TS Tech Sheet No. B45

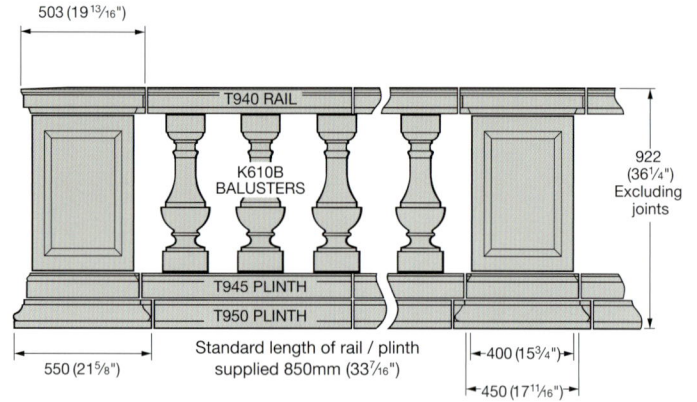

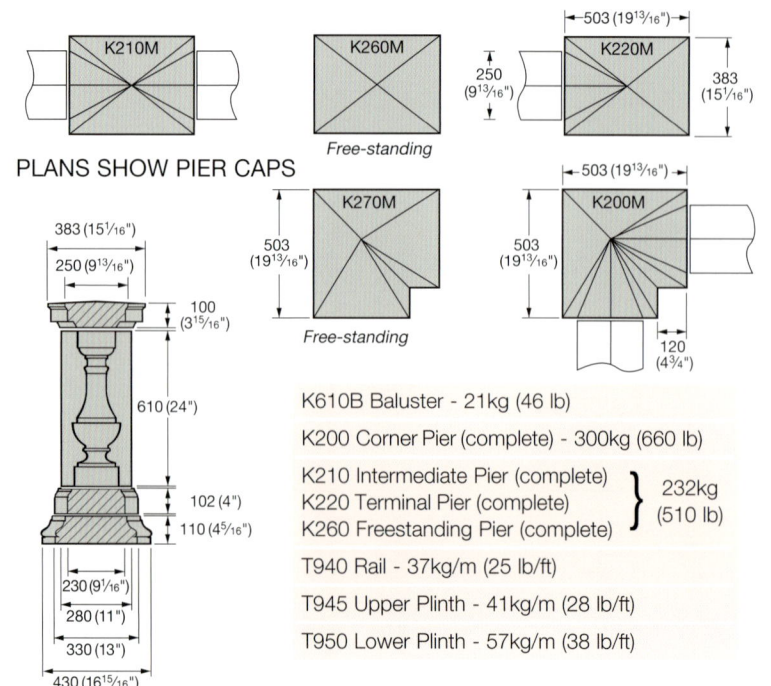

503 (19¹³⁄₁₆")
T940 RAIL
K610B BALUSTERS
922 (36¹⁄₄") Excluding joints
T945 PLINTH
T950 PLINTH
550 (21⁵⁄₈")
400 (15³⁄₄")
450 (17¹¹⁄₁₆")
Standard length of rail / plinth supplied 850mm (33⁷⁄₁₆")

K210M
K260M Free-standing
503 (19¹³⁄₁₆")
K220M
250 (9¹³⁄₁₆")
383 (15¹⁄₁₆")

PLANS SHOW PIER CAPS

K270M Free-standing
503 (19¹³⁄₁₆")
K200M
503 (19¹³⁄₁₆")
120 (4³⁄₄")

383 (15¹⁄₁₆")
250 (9¹³⁄₁₆")
100 (3¹⁵⁄₁₆")
610 (24")
102 (4")
110 (4⁵⁄₁₆")
230 (9¹⁄₁₆")
280 (11")
330 (13")
430 (16¹⁵⁄₁₆")

K610B Baluster - 21kg (46 lb)

K200 Corner Pier (complete) - 300kg (660 lb)

K210 Intermediate Pier (complete)
K220 Terminal Pier (complete) } 232kg (510 lb)
K260 Freestanding Pier (complete)

T940 Rail - 37kg/m (25 lb/ft)

T945 Upper Plinth - 41kg/m (28 lb/ft)

T950 Lower Plinth - 57kg/m (38 lb/ft)

Custom-made products are available on request.

ARCHITECTURAL STONEWORK BALUSTRADING

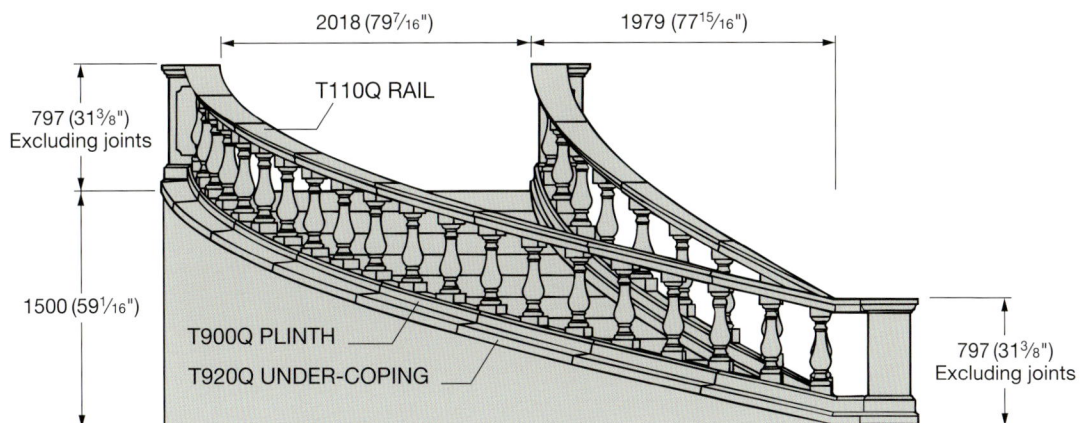

2018 (79⁷⁄₁₆")   1979 (77¹⁵⁄₁₆")

797 (31³⁄₈")
Excluding joints

T110Q RAIL

1500 (59¹⁄₁₆")

T900Q PLINTH
T920Q UNDER-COPING

797 (31³⁄₈")
Excluding joints

Left hand Spiral Balustrade illustrated above.

The Spiral Balustrade

This is a very special type of balustrade and can be offered, as standard, only in the components and dimensions indicated in the table below.

TS Tech Sheet No. B60

Dimensions
Left and Right-handed 90° sweeps:
Total Rise: 1500mm (59¹⁄₁₆")
Outer c/l Radius: 4112mm (161⁷⁄₈")
Inner c/l Radius: 1865mm (73⁷⁄₁₆")
Width of Staircase: 2018mm (79⁷⁄₁₆")

Components
FS-style balustrading comprising:
T110-style Rail
T900-style Plinth
KG533-style Baluster
T920-style Under-Coping (optional)

ARCHITECTURAL STONEWORK BALUSTRADING

Installation Details

We recommend that non-ferrous fixings (available as part of the Balustrading Fixing Pack X950 - UK only) be incorporated at all rail joints and in horizontal beddings in all cases. All balusters are supplied with stainless steel dowels for installing to rails and plinths. All rails, plinths and under-copings are supplied in standard lengths, cutting and drilling to final specification to be undertaken by your installation contractor.

Professional advice should be taken particularly where Building Regulations / Codes and local bye-laws need to be complied with. It is recommended that, if pier shafts are in-filled with concrete, the shaft section should be lined with polystyrene (Styrofoam) or similar to act as an isolating medium.

Haddoncraft Forge has a range of wrought iron Baluster Bars for use in conjunction with Haddonstone balustrading, see image below. The bars can be used to meet Building Regulation spacing requirements.

PS style with K610G Balusters and T920 Under-Copings

FS style with K724G Balusters

Haddoncraft Forge Baluster Bar

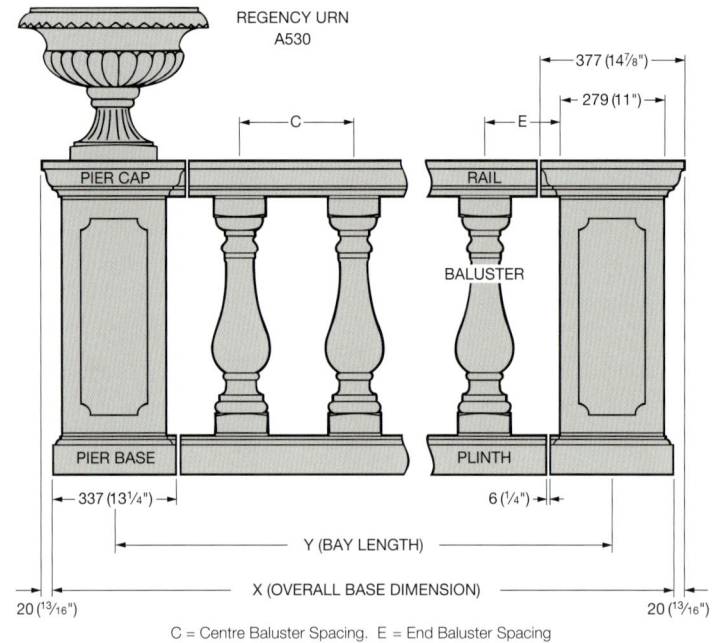

REGENCY URN
A530

377 (14⁷⁄₈")
279 (11")

PIER CAP

RAIL

BALUSTER

PIER BASE

PLINTH

337 (13¼")

6 (¼")

Y (BAY LENGTH)

X (OVERALL BASE DIMENSION)

20 (¹³⁄₁₆")   20 (¹³⁄₁₆")

C = Centre Baluster Spacing. E = End Baluster Spacing

It is most important to refer to Tech Sheet GAR1 to ensure correct installation. Standard assembly recommendations and typical details are available on request. Please ask for the relevant Tech Sheet.

Cutting Recommendations:

TS Tech Sheet No. B50

General Assembly:

TS Tech Sheet No. GAR1

TABLE A

For normal baluster spacing: approx. 305mm (12") centres
Select highest band available unless there are other overriding factors

Band	Bay Lengths (centreline to centreline of piers) in mm	Bay Lengths (centreline to centreline of piers) in inches	Rails/Plinths No. of 900mm (35⁷⁄₁₆") long rails/plinths and under-copings where applicable)	Balusters
1	-829	-32⁵⁄₈"	1	1
2	830-1129	32¹¹⁄₁₆"-44⁷⁄₁₆"	1	2
3	1130-1249	44½"-49³⁄₁₆"	1	3
4	1250-1429	49¼"-56¼"	2	3
5	1430-1729	56⁵⁄₁₆"-68¹⁄₁₆"	2	4
6	1730-2029	68¹⁄₈"-79⁷⁄₈"	2	5
7	2030-2155	79¹⁵⁄₁₆"-84¹³⁄₁₆"	2	6
8	2156-2329	84⁷⁄₈"-91¹¹⁄₁₆"	3	6
9	2330-2629	91³⁄₄"-103½"	3	7
10	2630-2929	103⁹⁄₁₆"-115⁵⁄₁₆"	3	8
11	2930-3061	115³⁄₈"-120½"	3	9
12	3062-3229	120⁹⁄₁₆"-127¹⁄₈"	4	9
13	3230-3529	127³⁄₁₆"-138¹⁵⁄₁₆"	4	10
14	3530-3829	139"-150¾"	4	11
15	3830-3967	150¹³⁄₁₆"-156¹⁄₈"	4	12

This table has been compiled to give an approximate Centre Baluster Spacing (see diagram) of 305mm (12") and a fixed End Baluster Spacing of 200mm (8").

The Standard Range

Tables A, B, C, D and E have been compiled to simplify the ordering of the STANDARD RANGE of balustrade components and enable you to design and price your own balustrade. Alternatively, approximate guide prices can be obtained from the price list.

You will also find below tables of the many horizontal curves and ramps available in the STANDARD RANGE – these are shown in Tables C and D.

The terms Weathered and Part-Weathered refer to the style of the balustrading rails and caps and not to the maturity of the stonework. For standard colours and finishes see page 194.

Haddonstone (USA) Ltd offers additional Balustrading and Parapet Screening designs to comply with specific Building Codes. For further details, refer to the Architectural Supplement or view:

www.haddonstone.com/view-catalogue

HOW TO USE TABLES A and B
By following this simple procedure you will be able to design, price and order your own balustrading from the STANDARD RANGE:

1. Choose type of baluster (see page 132) and style of balustrade (see pages 125, 126 and 127).

2. Measure the overall base dimension of each run of balustrading giving consideration to the fact that, particularly where balustrading abuts a wall, the cap oversails the base by 20mm ($^{13}/_{16}$"), see diagram opposite.

3. Divide each run into suitable bays, generally incorporating piers at ends and corners.

4. When determining bay lengths, as a guideline, the highest band should be selected, but other overriding factors may need to be taken into account, such as achieving aesthetic balance, correlating with other architectural elements, relating bays to the height of the balustrade and the overall scale of the surroundings.

5. To calculate bay lengths, first deduct 337mm (13¼") from the overall base dimension to determine the distance between the centres of the end piers, then divide this figure by the number of bays required. Then refer to Tables A and B.

6. Should extra height be required or coping to a substructure, select appropriate under-coping to suit balustrading (see page 133).

7. Choose piers to suit balustrading layout, i.e. number of end piers, number of intermediate piers, number of corner piers.

8. ORDER CHECKLIST
The order should comprise total number of balusters, total number of rails, total number of plinths, total number of piers incorporating end piers, intermediate piers and corner piers as required.

TABLE B
For close baluster spacing: approx. 225mm (9") centres
Select highest band available unless there are other overriding factors

Band	Bay Lengths (centreline to centreline of piers) in mm	(centreline to centreline of piers) in inches	Rails/Plinths No. of 900mm (35 ⁷/₁₆") long rails/plinths (and under-copings where applicable)	Balusters
16	-691	-27³/₁₆"	1	1
17	692-916	27¹/₄"-36¹/₁₆"	1	2
18	917-1141	36¹/₈"-44¹⁵/₁₆"	1	3
19	1142-1249	45"-49³/₁₆"	1	4
20	1250-1366	49¹/₄"-53³/₄"	2	4
21	1367-1591	53¹³/₁₆"-62⅝"	2	5
22	1592-1816	62¹¹/₁₆"-71½"	2	6
23	1817-2041	71⁹/₁₆"-80⅜"	2	7
24	2042-2155	80⁷/₁₆"-84¹³/₁₆"	2	8
25	2156-2266	84⁷/₈"-89³/₁₆"	3	8
26	2267-2491	89¹/₄"-98¹/₁₆"	3	9
27	2492-2716	98¹/₈"-106¹⁵/₁₆"	3	10
28	2717-2941	107"-115¹³/₁₆"	3	11
29	2942-3061	115⁷/₈"-120½"	3	12
30	3062-3166	120⁹/₁₆"-124⅝"	4	12
31	3167-3391	124¹¹/₁₆"-133½"	4	13
32	3392-3616	133⁹/₁₆"-142⅜"	4	14
33	3617-3841	142⁷/₁₆"-151¼"	4	15
34	3842-3967	151⁵/₁₆"-156¹/₈"	4	16

This table has been compiled to give an approximate Centre Baluster Spacing (see diagram) of 225mm (9") and a fixed End Baluster Spacing of 150mm (6").

TABLE C
Horizontal Curved Balustrade Rails and Plinths

Available in both Flat and Weathered configurations in the following radii:

500mm (19¹¹/₁₆")
1000mm (39³/₈")
1500mm (59¹/₁₆")
2000mm (78³/₄")
2500mm (98⁷/₁₆")
3000mm (118¹/₈")
3500mm (137¹³/₁₆")
4000mm (157½")
4500mm (177³/₁₆")
5000mm (196⁷/₈")
6000mm (236¼")
7000mm (275⁹/₁₆")
8000mm (314¹⁵/₁₆")
9000mm (354⁵/₁₆")
10000mm (393¹¹/₁₆")

All radii to centrelines of plinth/rail.

TABLE D
Ramped Balusters

KG311	16° 18° 27°
KG356	20° 27°
KG430	13°
KG457	13° 20° 27° 30° 33° 40°
KG464	16° 23°
KG520	23°
KG533	13° 16° 20° 21° 27° 30° 36°
KB609	27° 33° 42°
KG609	30°
KG610	13° 16° 20° 21° 23° 27° 30° 33° 36°
KJ610	27° 30° 36°
KG629	20° 27° 29° 31° 33°
KG724	13° 16° 20° 23° 26° 27° 29° 30° 33°
KG725	34° 1100 Balustrade

The ramp angle is the angle of rise/pitch measured from the horizontal.

TABLE E
Typical Component Weights

Baluster Type:	K724G	K610G	K533G	K457G	K356G
	15kg (33 lb)	11kg (24 lb)	10kg (22 lb)	8kg (18 lb)	4.5kg (10 lb)
Standard pier to suit (complete):	105kg (231 lb)	97kg (214 lb)	87kg (191 lb)	81kg (178 lb)	75kg (165 lb)
135° pier to suit (complete):	154kg (339 lb)	147kg (323 lb)	134kg (295 lb)	121kg (266 lb)	120kg (264 lb)

T120A 900mm Standard Rail 31kg (68 lb)

T900A 900mm Standard Plinth 30kg (66 lb)

ARCHITECTURAL STONEWORK BALUSTRADING

Standard Balusters These balusters are circular in section except top and bottom blocks which are square.

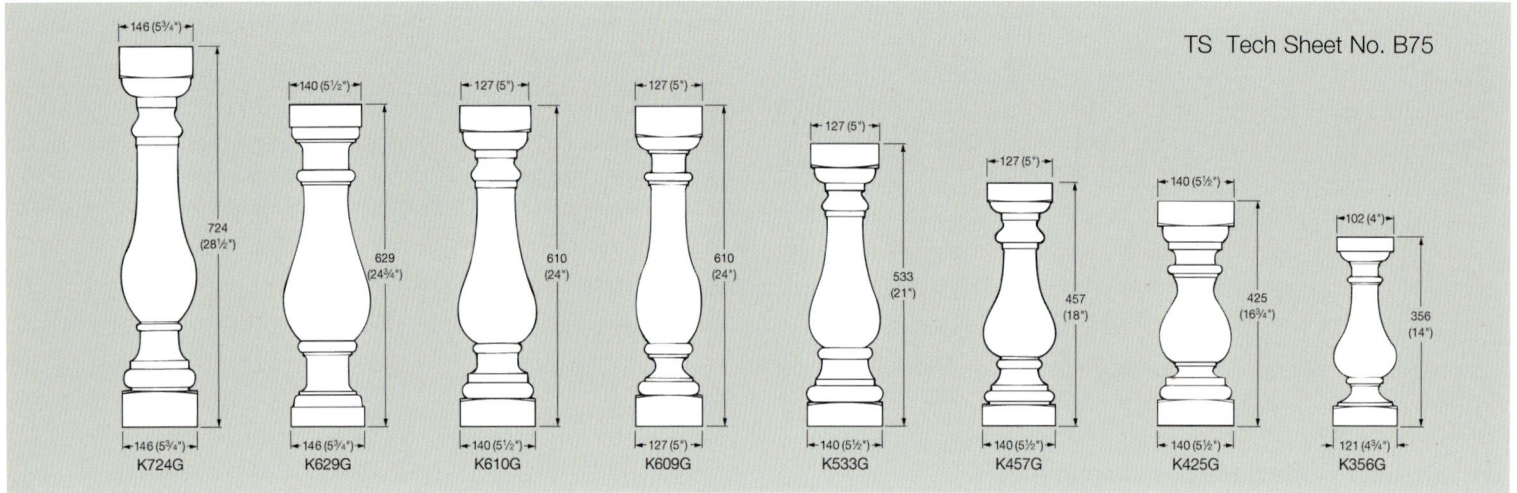

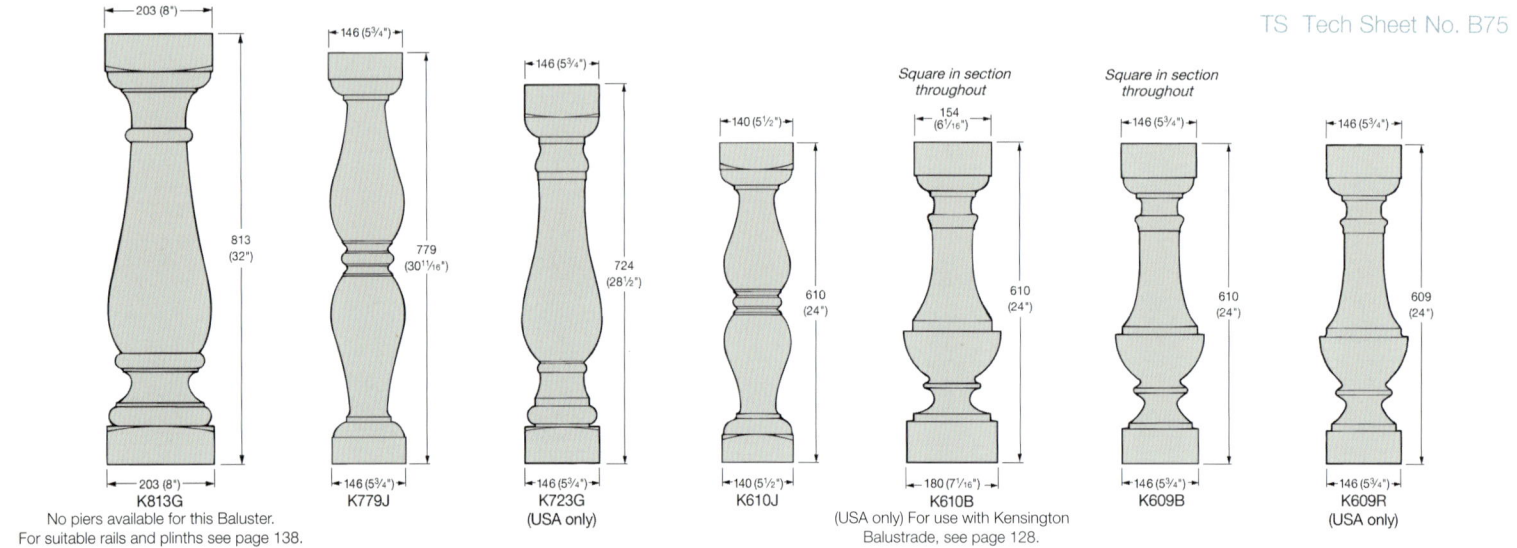

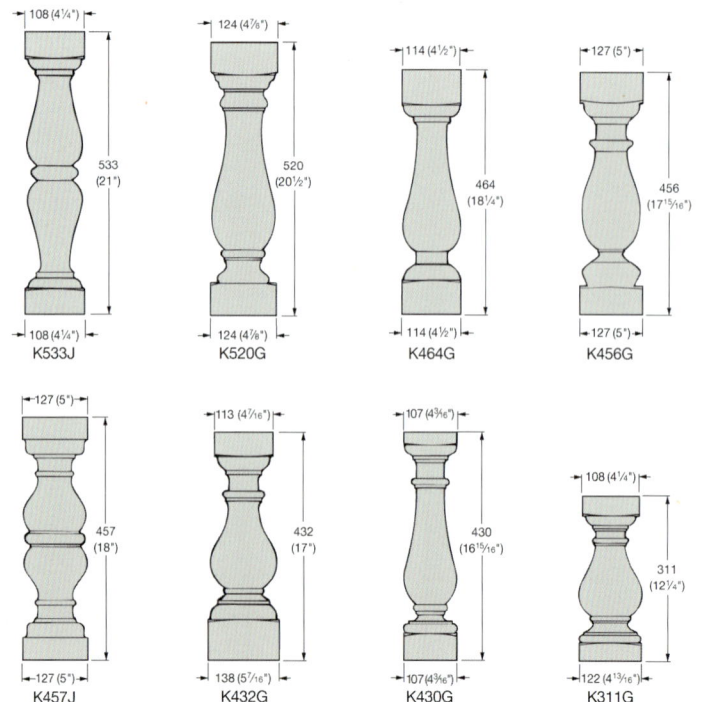

TS Tech Sheet No. B75

146 (5¾")	140 (5½")	127 (5")	127 (5")	127 (5")	127 (5")	140 (5½")	102 (4")
724 (28½")	629 (24¾")	610 (24")	610 (24")	533 (21")	457 (18")	425 (16¾")	356 (14")
146 (5¾")	146 (5¾")	140 (5½")	127 (5")	140 (5½")	140 (5½")	140 (5½")	121 (4¾")
K724G	K629G	K610G	K609G	K533G	K457G	K425G	K356G

Non Standard Balusters Unless otherwise stated, these balusters are circular in section except top and bottom blocks which are square.

TS Tech Sheet No. B75

				Square in section throughout	Square in section throughout		
203 (8")	146 (5¾")	146 (5¾")	140 (5½")	154 (6¹/₁₆")		146 (5¾")	146 (5¾")
813 (32")	779 (30¹¹/₁₆")	724 (28½")	610 (24")	610 (24")		610 (24")	609 (24")
203 (8")	146 (5¾")	146 (5¾")	140 (5½")	180 (7¹/₁₆")		146 (5¾")	146 (5¾")
K813G	K779J	K723G (USA only)	K610J	K610B (USA only) For use with Kensington Balustrade, see page 128.		K609B	K609R (USA only)

K813G — No piers available for this Baluster. For suitable rails and plinths see page 138.

108 (4¼")	124 (4⅞")	114 (4½")	127 (5")
533 (21")	520 (20½")	464 (18¼")	456 (17¹⁵/₁₆")
108 (4¼")	124 (4⅞")	114 (4½")	127 (5")
K533J	K520G	K464G	K456G

127 (5")	113 (4⁷/₁₆")	107 (4³/₁₆")	108 (4¼")
457 (18")	432 (17")	430 (16¹⁵/₁₆")	311 (12¼")
127 (5")	138 (5⁷/₁₆")	107 (4³/₁₆")	122 (4¹³/₁₆")
K457J	K432G	K430G	K311G

FS style with KG533 Ramped Balusters and T920 Wide Under-Copings

BALUSTRADE UNDER-COPINGS Optional, for use with the standard balustrading range. Available in 900mm (35⁷⁄₁₆") lengths only.
Pier Under-Coping 20kg (44 lb)   135° Pier Under-Coping 29kg (64 lb)

Narrow Central Run-In Under Copings

TS Tech Sheet No. B90

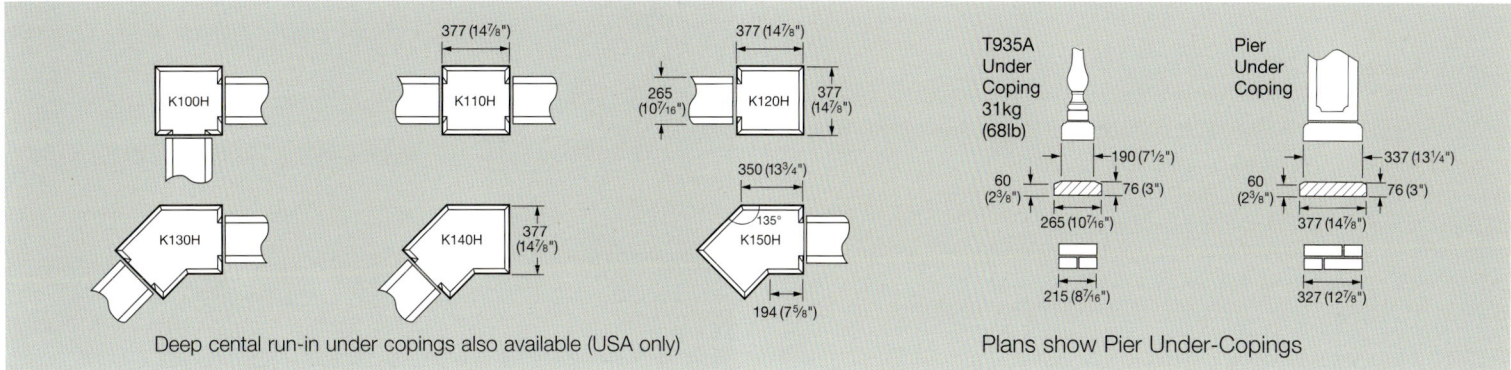

Deep cental run-in under copings also available (USA only)

Plans show Pier Under-Copings

Narrow Side Run-In Under Copings

TS Tech Sheet No. B91

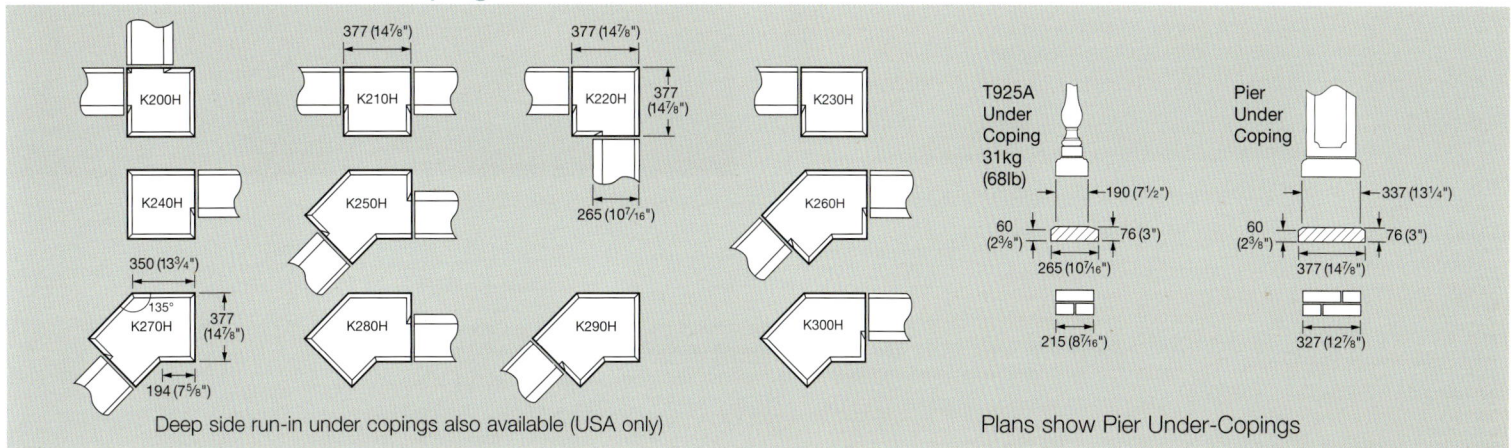

Deep side run-in under copings also available (USA only)

Plans show Pier Under-Copings

Wide Central Run-In Under Copings

TS Tech Sheet No. B92

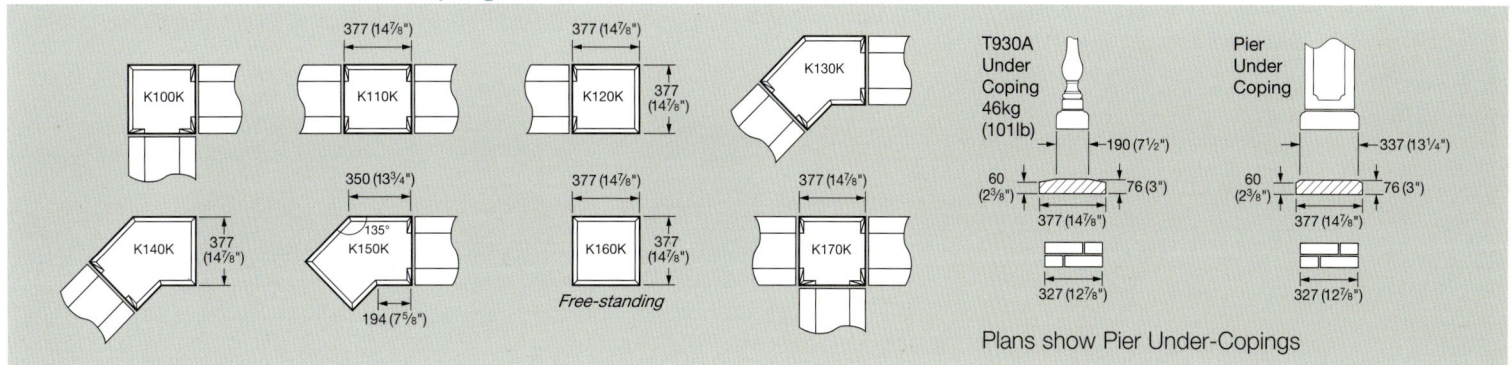

Free-standing

Plans show Pier Under-Copings

Wide Side Run-In Under Copings

TS Tech Sheet No. B93

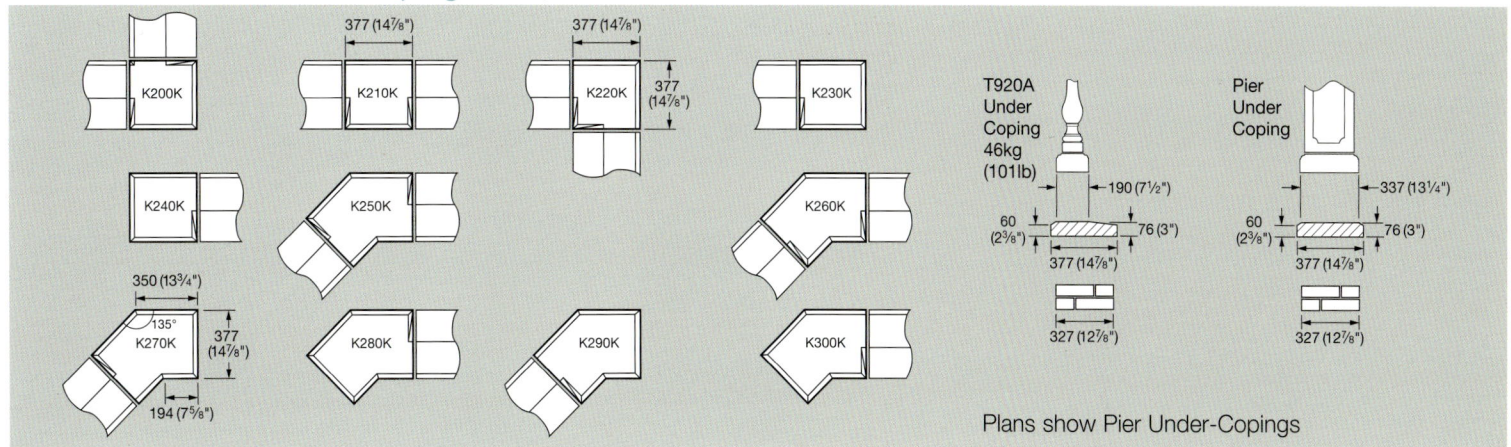

Plans show Pier Under-Copings

ARCHITECTURAL STONEWORK PARAPET SCREENING

For a less formal and more decorative alternative to balustrading, parapet screening provides an effective solution.

As shown in the drawings, the length of parapet unit can be varied by using different combinations of the two basic panels J248 and J362. We show six of the most commonly used bays (TYPES A-F). The bay dimensions shown are from centreline to centreline of pier.

The piers are specially designed and produced for end, centre and corner use as well as for 135° angles; so when ordering please state clearly the number and reference of each type required.

All rails and plinths are supplied in standard lengths as indicated, cutting to final specification to be undertaken by your installation contractor.

TS Tech Sheet No. PS10

Parapet Screening (showing TYPE F bay)

Typical Component Weights

J400A Rail: 16kg (35 lb)
J400F Plinth: 25kg (55 lb)
J248 End Panel: 9kg (20 lb)
J362 Centre Panel: 13kg (29 lb)
Standard Pier (complete): 76kg (167 lb)
135° Pier (complete): 151kg (332 lb)

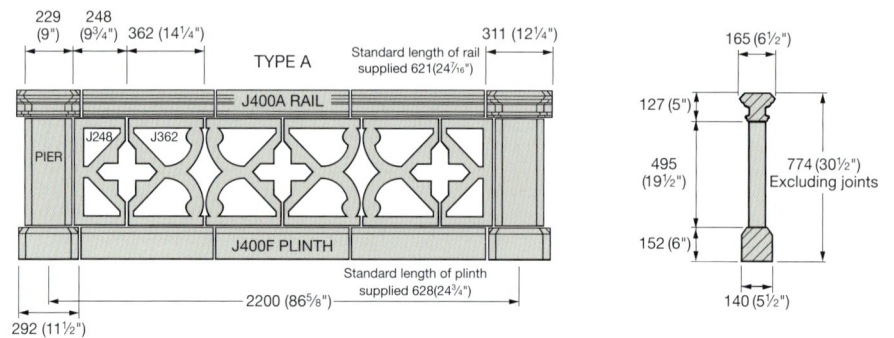

Plans showing Pier Caps

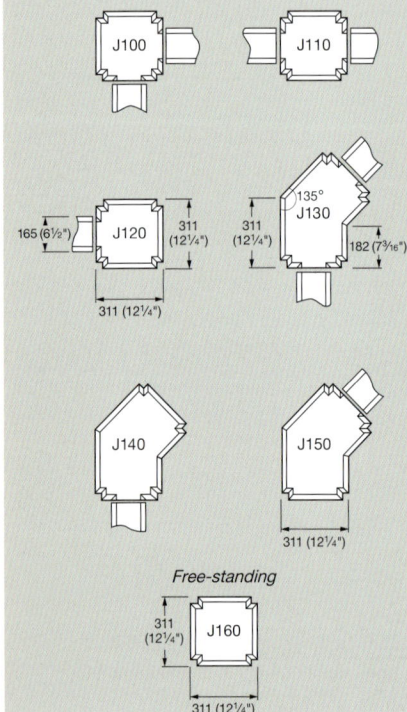

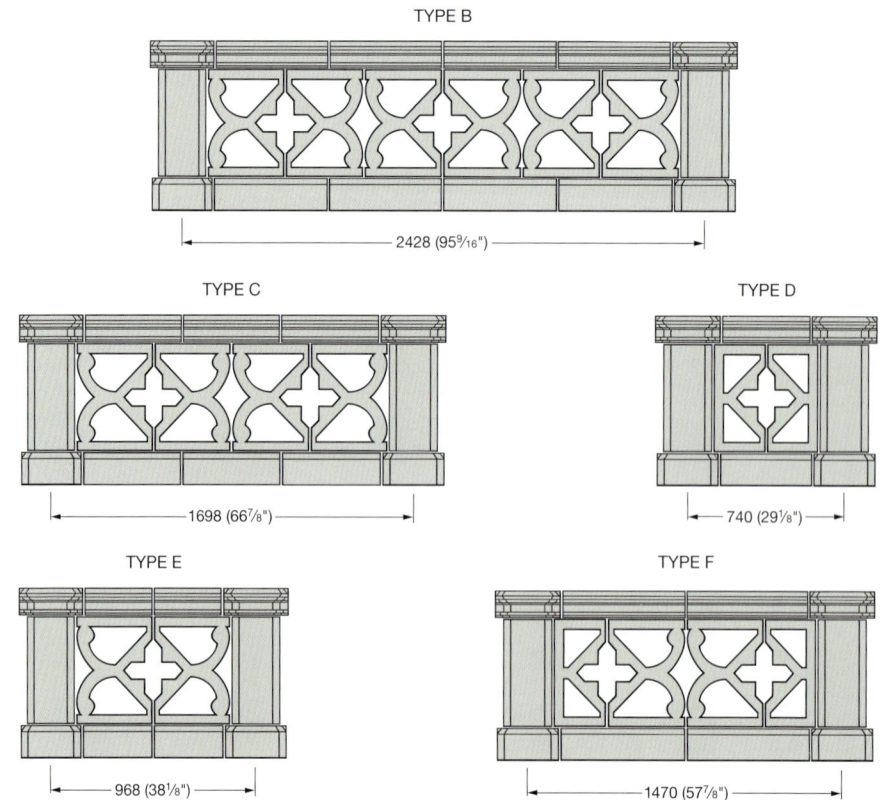

J100

J110

J120   165 (6½")   311 (12¼")

135° J130   311 (12¼")   182 (7³⁄₁₆")

311 (12¼")

J140   J150   311 (12¼")

Free-standing

311 (12¼")   J160

311 (12¼")

229 (9")   248 (9¾")   362 (14¼")   311 (12¼")

TYPE A   Standard length of rail supplied 621(24⁷⁄₁₆")

165 (6½")

J400A RAIL

127 (5")

PIER   J248   J362

495 (19½")   774 (30½") Excluding joints

152 (6")

J400F PLINTH

Standard length of plinth supplied 628(24¾")

140 (5½")

2200 (86⁵⁄₈")

292 (11½")

TYPE B

2428 (95⁹⁄₁₆")

TYPE C

1698 (66⁷⁄₈")

TYPE D

740 (29⅛")

TYPE E

968 (38⅛")

TYPE F

1470 (57⁷⁄₈")

Gate Pier S120

This gate pier is a standard item in the Haddonstone collection. Heights can be varied according to the number of centre shaft units used. When ordering please note that each course is supplied in two halves. Both halves need to be ordered. Custom-made products are available on request.

If the gate piers are to be infilled with concrete the shaft sections should be lined with 25mm (1") polystyrene (Styrofoam) or similar to act as an isolating medium. It is most important to refer to the relevant Tech Sheet to ensure correct installation.

Haddoncraft Forge is able to supply gates and railings to individual specifications for use in conjunction with these Gate Piers, see page 183.

TS Tech Sheet No. M40

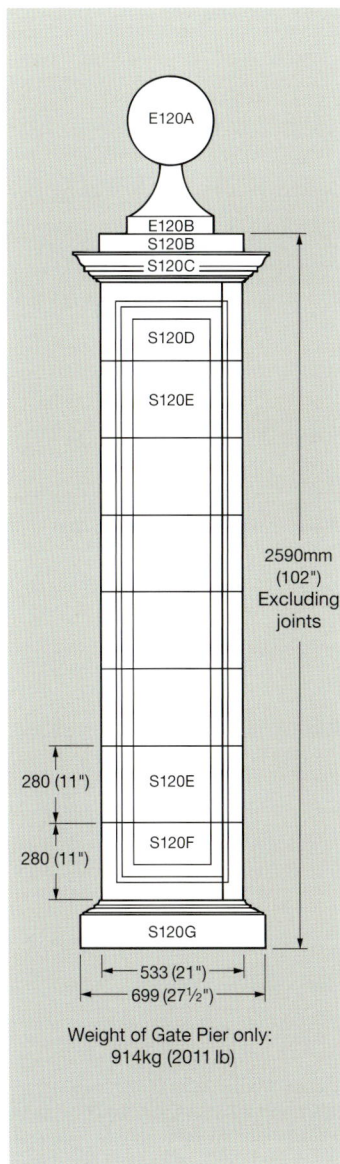

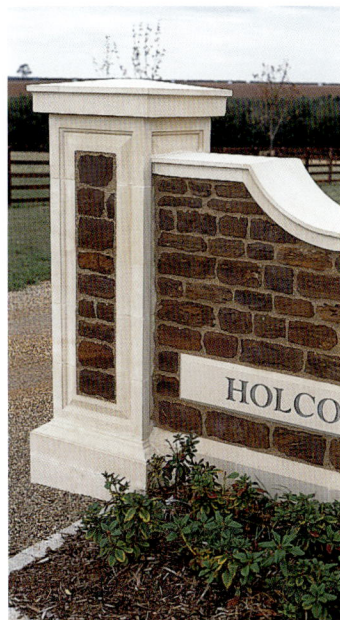

E120A

E120B
S120B
S120C

S120D

S120E

2590mm
(102")
Excluding
joints

280 (11")   S120E

280 (11")   S120F

S120G

533 (21")
699 (27½")

Weight of Gate Pier only:
914kg (2011 lb)

Custom gate pier.

Custom gate pier.

ARCHITECTURAL STONEWORK PIER CAPS

Haddonstone has a large selection of Pier Cap designs in a range of sizes. If your requirements are not featured we can produce custom designs to your specifications.

For Finials and Balls & Bases to complement our range of Pier Caps refer to pages 71-74.

TS Tech Sheet No. PC10 & PC11

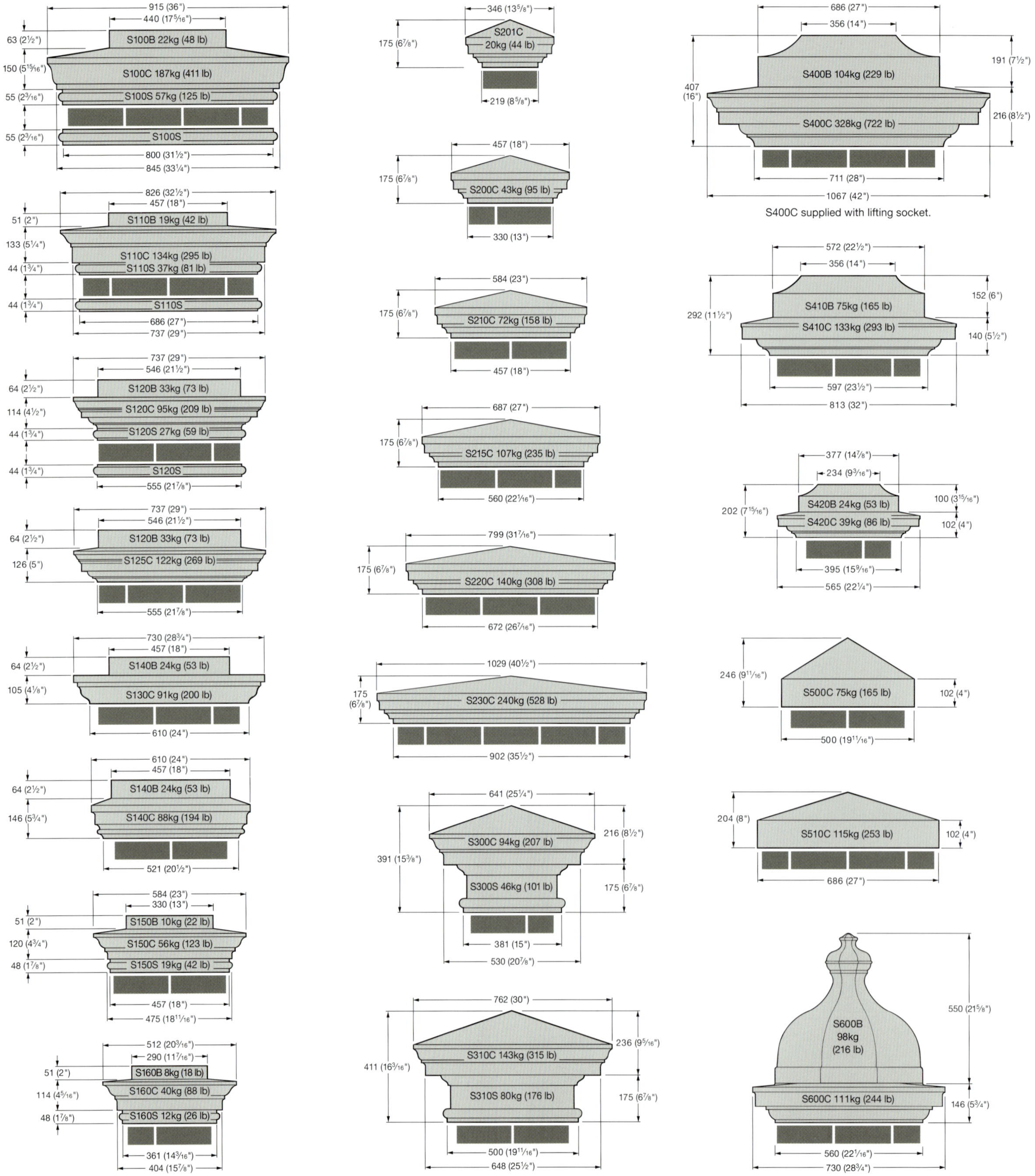
915 (36")
440 (17 5/16")
63 (2½")
S100B 22kg (48 lb)
150 (5 15/16")
S100C 187kg (411 lb)
55 (2 3/16")
S100S 57kg (125 lb)
55 (2 3/16")
S100S
800 (31½")
845 (33¼")
826 (32½")
457 (18")
51 (2")
S110B 19kg (42 lb)
133 (5¼")
S110C 134kg (295 lb)
44 (1¾")
S110S 37kg (81 lb)
44 (1¾")
S110S
686 (27")
737 (29")
737 (29")
546 (21½")
64 (2½")
S120B 33kg (73 lb)
114 (4½")
S120C 95kg (209 lb)
44 (1¾")
S120S 27kg (59 lb)
44 (1¾")
S120S
555 (21⅞")
737 (29")
546 (21½")
64 (2½")
S120B 33kg (73 lb)
126 (5")
S125C 122kg (269 lb)
555 (21⅞")
730 (28¾")
457 (18")
64 (2½")
S140B 24kg (53 lb)
105 (4⅛")
S130C 91kg (200 lb)
610 (24")
610 (24")
457 (18")
64 (2½")
S140B 24kg (53 lb)
146 (5¾")
S140C 88kg (194 lb)
521 (20½")
584 (23")
330 (13")
51 (2")
S150B 10kg (22 lb)
120 (4¾")
S150C 56kg (123 lb)
48 (1⅞")
S150S 19kg (42 lb)
457 (18")
475 (18 11/16")
512 (20 3/16")
290 (11 7/16")
51 (2")
S160B 8kg (18 lb)
114 (4 5/16")
S160C 40kg (88 lb)
48 (1⅞")
S160S 12kg (26 lb)
361 (14 3/16")
404 (15⅞")
346 (13⅝")
175 (6⅞")
S201C 20kg (44 lb)
219 (8⅝")
457 (18")
175 (6⅞")
S200C 43kg (95 lb)
330 (13")
584 (23")
175 (6⅞")
S210C 72kg (158 lb)
457 (18")
687 (27")
175 (6⅞")
S215C 107kg (235 lb)
560 (22 1/16")
799 (31 7/16")
175 (6⅞")
S220C 140kg (308 lb)
672 (26 7/16")
1029 (40½")
175 (6⅞")
S230C 240kg (528 lb)
902 (35½")
641 (25¼")
391 (15⅜")
216 (8½")
S300C 94kg (207 lb)
175 (6⅞")
S300S 46kg (101 lb)
381 (15")
530 (20⅞")
762 (30")
411 (16 3/16")
236 (9 5/16")
S310C 143kg (315 lb)
175 (6⅞")
S310S 80kg (176 lb)
500 (19 11/16")
648 (25½")
686 (27")
356 (14")
407 (16")
191 (7½")
S400B 104kg (229 lb)
216 (8½")
S400C 328kg (722 lb)
711 (28")
1067 (42")
S400C supplied with lifting socket.
572 (22½")
356 (14")
292 (11½")
152 (6")
S410B 75kg (165 lb)
S410C 133kg (293 lb)
140 (5½")
597 (23½")
813 (32")
377 (14⅞")
234 (9 3/16")
202 (7 15/16")
100 (3 15/16")
S420B 24kg (53 lb)
S420C 39kg (86 lb)
102 (4")
395 (15 9/16")
565 (22¼")
246 (9 11/16")
S500C 75kg (165 lb)
102 (4")
500 (19 11/16")
204 (8")
S510C 115kg (253 lb)
102 (4")
686 (27")
550 (21⅝")
S600B 98kg (216 lb)
S600C 111kg (244 lb)
146 (5¾")
560 (22 1/16")
730 (28¾")

Custom-made products are available on request.

For Finials and Balls & Bases see pages 71-74.

S620C
325 (12¾")
600 (23⅝")
S620C
150kg (331 lb)

S715C
403 (15⅞")
75 (2¹⁵⁄₁₆")
S715C 20kg (44 lb)

S720C
515 (20⁵⁄₁₆")
75 (2¹⁵⁄₁₆")
S720C 32kg (70 lb)

S800C
800 (31½")
142 (5⁹⁄₁₆")
S800C 127kg (279 lb)
760 (29¹⁵⁄₁₆")

S840C
430 (16¹⁵⁄₁₆")
80 (3⅛")
S840C 20kg (44 lb)
400 (15¾")

S850C
403 (15⅞")
85 (3⅜")
S850C 20kg (44 lb)
363 (14⁵⁄₁₆")

S890C
329 (12¹⁵⁄₁₆")
89 (3½")
S890C 14kg (31 lb)
240 (9⁷⁄₁₆")

S900C
419 (16½")
102 (4")
S900C 25kg (55 lb)
330 (13")

S910C
419 (16½")
89 (3½")
S910C 24kg (53 lb)
330 (13")

S950C
565 (22¼")
108 (4¼")
S950C 49kg (108 lb)
476 (18¾")

S955C
609 (24")
89 (3½")
S955C 51kg (112 lb)
520 (20½")

S956C
609 (24")
108 (4¼")
S956C 57kg (125 lb)
520 (20½")

S960C
670 (26⅜")
108 (4¼")
S960C 65kg (143 lb)
580 (22¹³⁄₁₆")

S961C
670 (26⅜")
89 (3½")
S961C 65kg (143 lb)
580 (22¹³⁄₁₆")

S810C
675 (26⁹⁄₁₆")
142 (5⁹⁄₁₆")
S810C 100kg (220 lb)
635 (25")

S820C
550 (21⅝")
110 (4⁵⁄₁₆")
S820C 45kg (99 lb)
520 (20½")

S830C
518 (20⅜")
85 (3⅜")
S830C 34kg (75 lb)
478 (18¹³⁄₁₆")

S920C
500 (19¹¹⁄₁₆")
105 (4⅛")
S920C 40kg (88 lb)
417 (16⁷⁄₁₆")

S930C
550 (21⅝")
108 (4¼")
S930C 45kg (99 lb)
460 (18⅛")

S940C
565 (22¼")
89 (3½")
S940C 44kg (97 lb)
476 (18¾")

S970C
705 (27¾")
108 (4¼")
S970C 74kg (163 lb)
615 (24³⁄₁₆")

S980C
760 (29¹⁵⁄₁₆")
108 (4¼")
S980C 90kg (198 lb)
670 (26⅜")

S990C
820 (32⁵⁄₁₆")
108 (4¼")
S990C 101kg (222 lb)
730 (28¾")

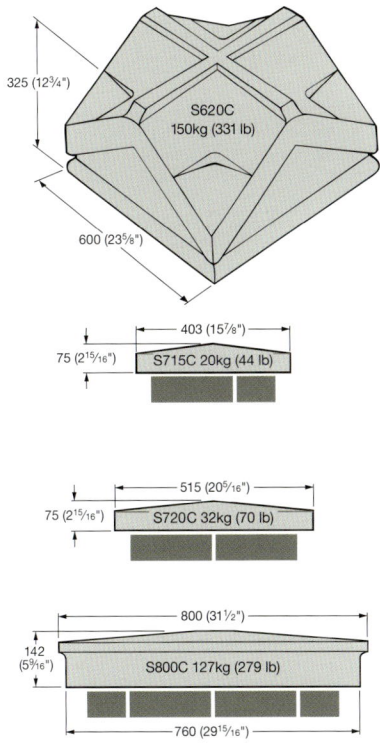

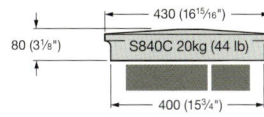

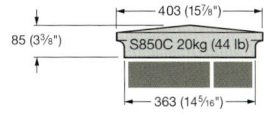

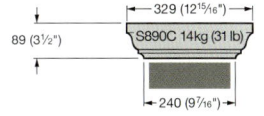

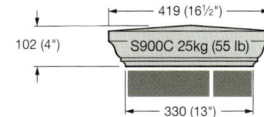

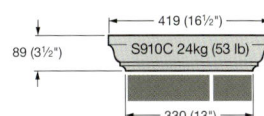

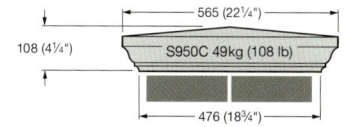

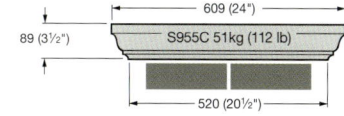

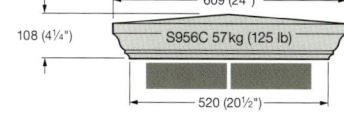

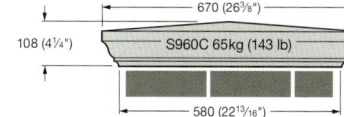

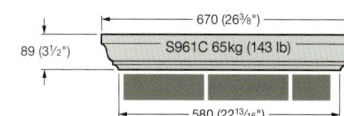

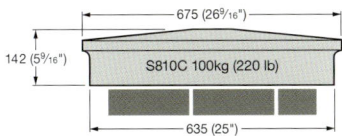

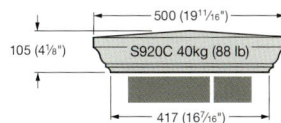

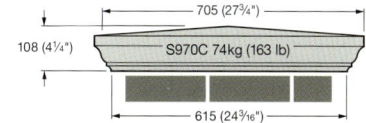

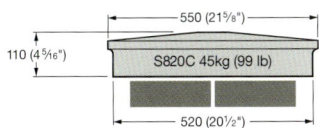

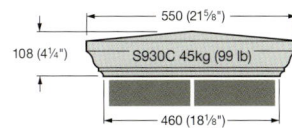

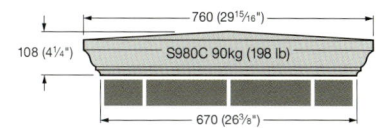

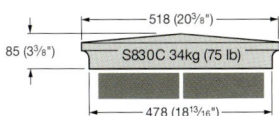

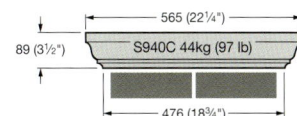

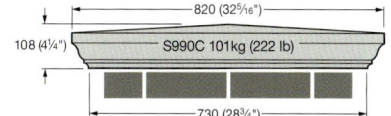

S995C - 32" underside version of S990C. (USA only)
S997C - 36" underside version of S990C. (USA only)

ARCHITECTURAL STONEWORK
COPINGS & CAPPINGS

The Haddonstone collection includes copings and cappings in many designs. Most requirements for straight flat runs of wall, curved wall sections, ramped walls, serpentine walls and stepped walls can be met from our standard range.

We would be pleased to discuss your special requirements.

For standard lengths, please refer to the price list. Custom-made Copings and Cappings are available on request.

All copings and cappings are supplied throated, although not necessarily to BS 5642: 1983 in certain applications. **We strongly recommend that you refer to Eurocode 6 and PD 6697: 2010.**

TS Tech Sheet No. WC10, WC20 & WC30

13" Ball & Collared Base (see p74), Block S140B, Cap S130 & Coping T150.

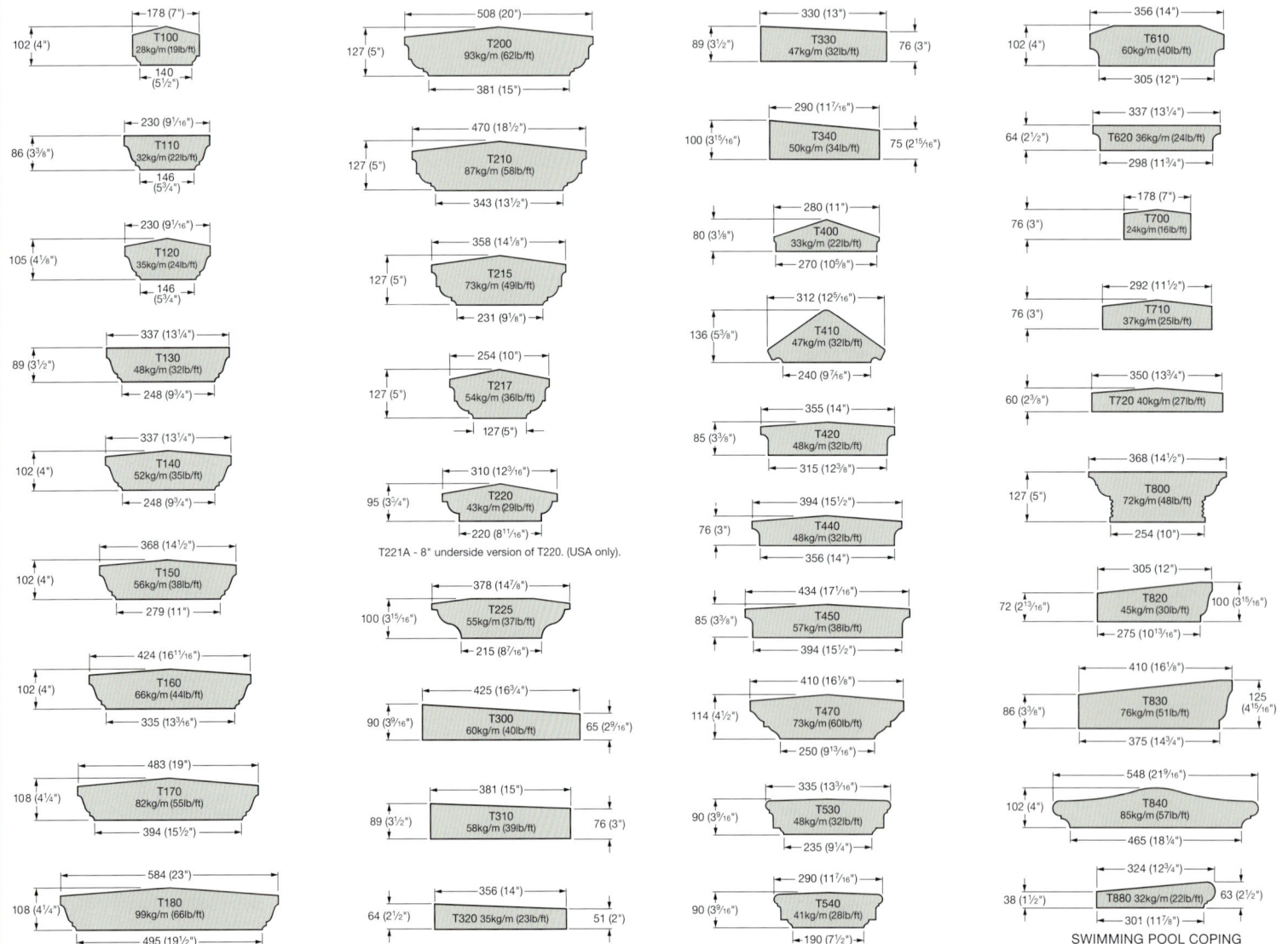

T100 28kg/m (19lb/ft) — 178 (7") / 102 (4") / 140 (5½")	**T200** 93kg/m (62lb/ft) — 508 (20") / 127 (5") / 381 (15")	**T330** 47kg/m (32lb/ft) — 330 (13") / 89 (3½") / 76 (3")	**T610** 60kg/m (40lb/ft) — 356 (14") / 102 (4") / 305 (12")
T110 32kg/m (22lb/ft) — 230 (9¹/₁₆") / 86 (3⅜") / 146 (5¾")	**T210** 87kg/m (58lb/ft) — 470 (18½") / 127 (5") / 343 (13½")	**T340** 50kg/m (34lb/ft) — 290 (11⁷/₁₆") / 100 (3¹⁵/₁₆") / 75 (2¹⁵/₁₆")	**T620** 36kg/m (24lb/ft) — 337 (13¼") / 64 (2½") / 298 (11¾")
T120 35kg/m (24lb/ft) — 230 (9¹/₁₆") / 105 (4⅛") / 146 (5¾")	**T215** 73kg/m (49lb/ft) — 358 (14⅛") / 127 (5") / 231 (9⅛")	**T400** 33kg/m (22lb/ft) — 280 (11") / 80 (3⅛") / 270 (10⅝")	**T700** 24kg/m (16lb/ft) — 178 (7") / 76 (3")
T130 48kg/m (32lb/ft) — 337 (13¼") / 89 (3½") / 248 (9¾")	**T217** 54kg/m (36lb/ft) — 254 (10") / 127 (5") / 127 (5")	**T410** 47kg/m (32lb/ft) — 312 (12⁵/₁₆") / 136 (5⅜") / 240 (9⁷/₁₆")	**T710** 37kg/m (25lb/ft) — 292 (11½") / 76 (3")
T140 52kg/m (35lb/ft) — 337 (13¼") / 102 (4") / 248 (9¾")	**T220** 43kg/m (29lb/ft) — 310 (12³/₁₆") / 95 (3¾") / 220 (8¹¹/₁₆") T221A - 8" underside version of T220. (USA only).	**T420** 48kg/m (32lb/ft) — 355 (14") / 85 (3⅜") / 315 (12⅜")	**T720** 40kg/m (27lb/ft) — 350 (13¾") / 60 (2⅜")
T150 56kg/m (38lb/ft) — 368 (14½") / 102 (4") / 279 (11")	**T225** 55kg/m (37lb/ft) — 378 (14⅞") / 100 (3¹⁵/₁₆") / 215 (8⁷/₁₆")	**T440** 48kg/m (32lb/ft) — 394 (15½") / 76 (3") / 356 (14")	**T800** 72kg/m (48lb/ft) — 368 (14½") / 127 (5") / 254 (10")
T160 66kg/m (44lb/ft) — 424 (16¹¹/₁₆") / 102 (4") / 335 (13³/₁₆")	**T300** 60kg/m (40lb/ft) — 425 (16¾") / 90 (3⁹/₁₆") / 65 (2⁹/₁₆")	**T450** 57kg/m (38lb/ft) — 434 (17¹/₁₆") / 85 (3⅜") / 394 (15½")	**T820** 45kg/m (30lb/ft) — 305 (12") / 72 (2¹³/₁₆") / 100 (3¹⁵/₁₆") / 275 (10¹³/₁₆")
T170 82kg/m (55lb/ft) — 483 (19") / 108 (4¼") / 394 (15½")	**T310** 58kg/m (39lb/ft) — 381 (15") / 89 (3½") / 76 (3")	**T470** 73kg/m (60lb/ft) — 410 (16⅛") / 114 (4½") / 250 (9¹³/₁₆")	**T830** 76kg/m (51lb/ft) — 410 (16⅛") / 86 (3⅜") / 125 (4¹⁵/₁₆") / 375 (14¾")
T180 99kg/m (66lb/ft) — 584 (23") / 108 (4¼") / 495 (19½")	**T320** 35kg/m (23lb/ft) — 356 (14") / 64 (2½") / 51 (2")	**T530** 48kg/m (32lb/ft) — 335 (13³/₁₆") / 90 (3⁹/₁₆") / 235 (9¼")	**T840** 85kg/m (57lb/ft) — 548 (21⁹/₁₆") / 102 (4") / 465 (18¼")
		T540 41kg/m (28lb/ft) — 290 (11⁷/₁₆") / 90 (3⁹/₁₆") / 190 (7½")	**T880** 32kg/m (22lb/ft) — 324 (12¾") / 38 (1½") / 63 (2½") / 301 (11⅞") SWIMMING POOL COPING

Refer to the Architectural Supplement for specific US designs.   For TecLite cappings see page 171.

To assist our private and professional clients with the ordering of Haddonstone copings and cappings, we have introduced this new page to the catalogue containing all the relevant terminology required.

For further details relating to coping and capping terminology, please either contact your nearest Haddonstone office or refer to:

TS Tech Sheet No. WC10, WC20 & WC30

Pier Caps S600B/C and S960C with Coping T150.

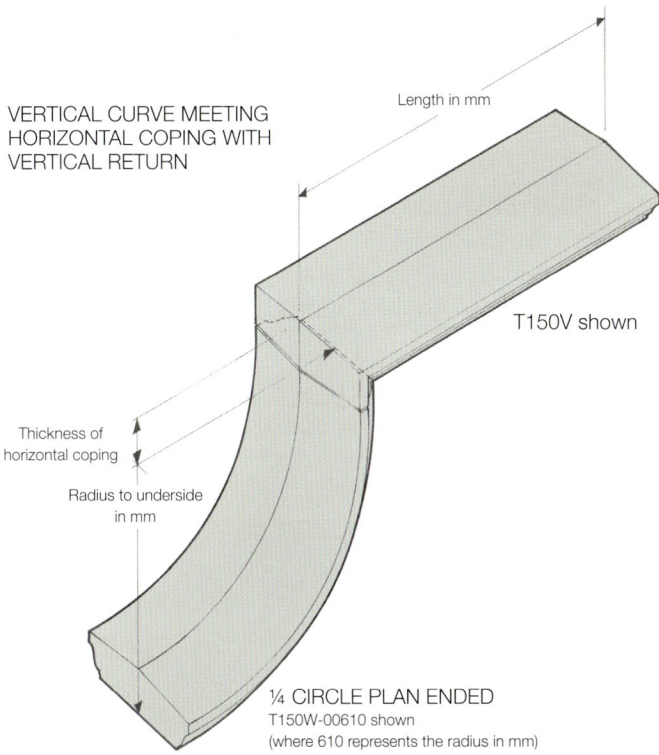

VERTICAL CURVE MEETING HORIZONTAL COPING WITH VERTICAL RETURN

Length in mm

T150V shown

Thickness of horizontal coping

Radius to underside in mm

¼ CIRCLE PLAN ENDED
T150W-00610 shown
(where 610 represents the radius in mm)

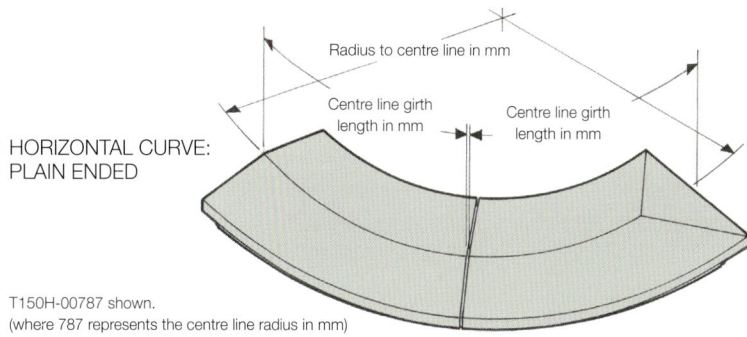

HORIZONTAL CURVE: PLAIN ENDED

Radius to centre line in mm

Centre line girth length in mm

Centre line girth length in mm

T150H-00787 shown.
(where 787 represents the centre line radius in mm)

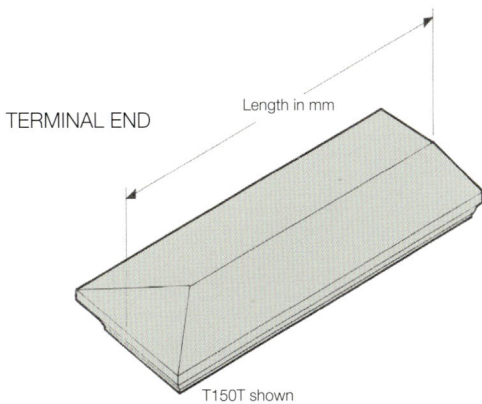

TERMINAL END

Length in mm

T150T shown

PLAIN ENDED

Length in mm

T150A shown

CORNER STONE
(Symmetrical coping only)

T150E shown

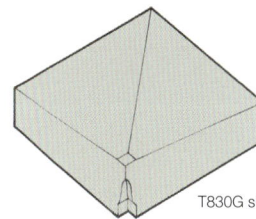

INSIDE CORNER STONE
(Asymmetrical coping only)

T830G shown

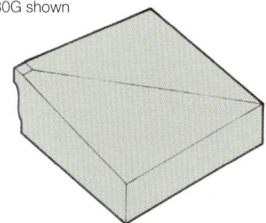

OUTSIDE CORNER STONE
(Asymmetrical coping only)

T830F shown

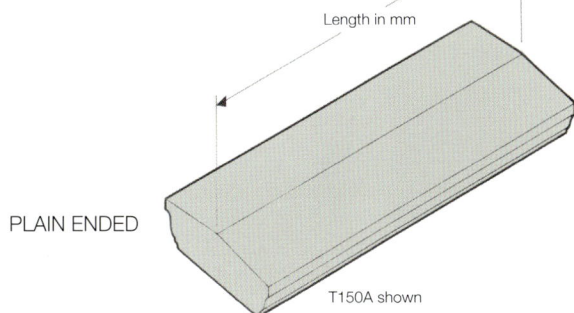

Our range of columns and pilasters are derived from the architectural vocabulary of the ancient world.

A column will usually have an entablature of some kind to support, for example as part of a portico, temple, pavilion or classical facade.

Our columns are designed to be non-structural elements and so are provided with hollow cores. These, if filled with reinforced concrete or used to sleeve a structural steel member, can then be used in structural situations. They are supplied in component form, as indicated, and should be erected on suitable foundations designed by a structural engineer to suit loadings and ground conditions.

The shaft sections should be lined with polystyrene (Styrofoam) or similar to act as an isolating medium when column cores are infilled.

We strongly recommend that professional advice is taken to ensure that any proposal is designed to be structurally sound. It is most important to refer to Tech Sheet CAD1 to ensure correct installation.

M1 Columns with Corinthian Capitals

TS Tech Sheet No. C50 for M1
TS Tech Sheet No. C40 for M2
TS Tech Sheet No. C30 for M3
TS Tech Sheet No. C10 for M4 & M5
TS Tech Sheet No. C20 for M7 & M8
TS Tech Sheet No. C60 for M9
TS CAD1 Column Assembly Details

TUSCAN
COLUMN
M5
355kg (781 lb)
Core 160mm (6$^5/_{16}$")

CAPITAL OPTIONS

TUSCAN COLUMN M8 — 136kg (299 lb) — Core 110 mm (4$^5/_{16}$") — Half column also available

TUSCAN PILASTER M8 — 69kg (152 lb)

TUSCAN COLUMN M7 — 247kg (543 lb) — Core 110 mm (4$^5/_{16}$") — Half column also available

TUSCAN PILASTER M7 — 95kg (209 lb)

TUSCAN COLUMN M7 — 258kg (568 lb) — Core 110 mm (4$^5/_{16}$") — Half column also available

TUSCAN PILASTER M7 — 101kg (222 lb)

TUSCAN COLUMN M7 — 352kg (775 lb) — Core 110 mm (4$^5/_{16}$") — Square in section (Shaft has no diminution)

TUSCAN PILASTER M5 — 145kg (319 lb)

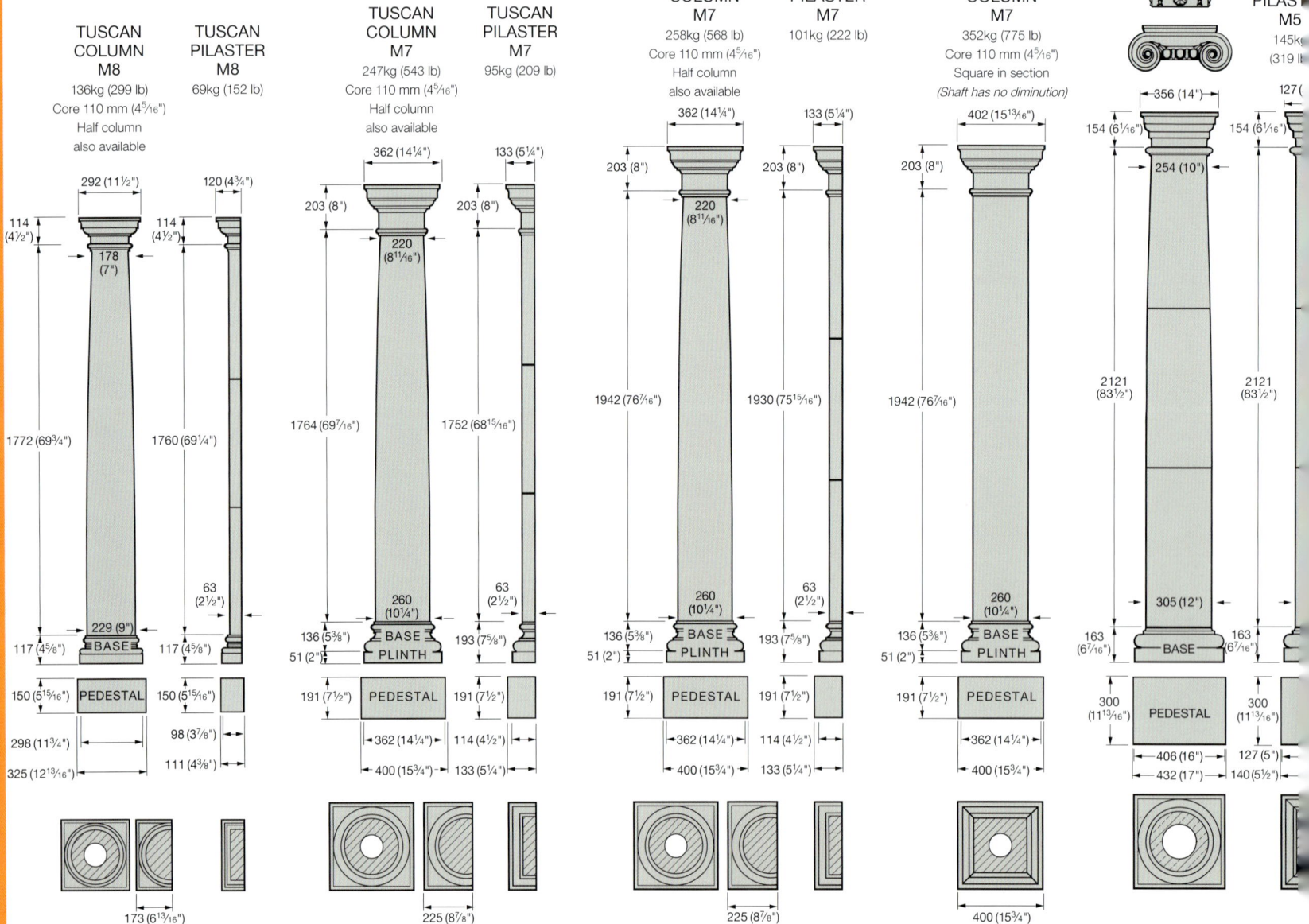

Custom-made products are available on request.

General note: Column dimensions exclude joints. Allow 6mm (¼") for joints.

CORINTHIAN COLUMN M1
2361 kg (5194 lb)
Core 300-400mm (11¹³⁄₁₆"-15¾")

CAPITAL OPTIONS

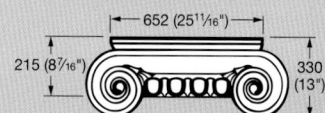

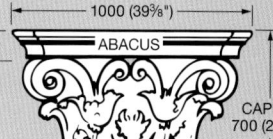

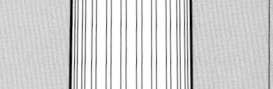

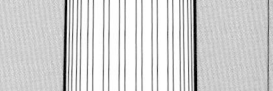

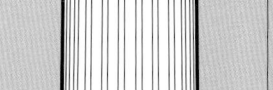

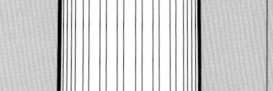

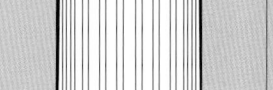

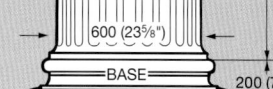

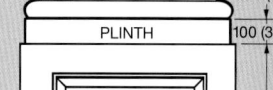

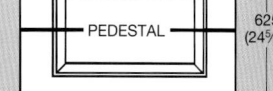

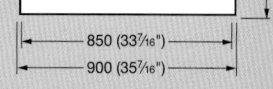

652 (25¹¹⁄₁₆")
215 (8⁷⁄₁₆")
330 (13")

900 (35⁷⁄₁₆")
ABACUS
450 (17¹¹⁄₁₆")

1000 (39⅜")
ABACUS
100 (3¹⁵⁄₁₆")

CAPITAL
700 (27⁹⁄₁₆")

500 (19¹¹⁄₁₆")

SHAFT
5200 (204¾")

600 (23⅝")

BASE
200 (7⅞")

PLINTH
100 (3¹⁵⁄₁₆")

PEDESTAL
625 (24⅝")

850 (33⁷⁄₁₆")
900 (35⁷⁄₁₆")

TUSCAN COLUMN M3
1680 kg (3696 lb)
Core 225-310mm
(8⁷⁄₈"-12³⁄₁₆")

CAPITAL OPTIONS

255 (10¹⁄₁₆")

175 (6⁷⁄₈")

650 (25⁹⁄₁₆")

255 (10¹⁄₁₆")

425 (16¾")

4491 (176¹³⁄₁₆")

510 (20¹⁄₁₆")

165 (6½")

BASE
PLINTH
123 (4¹³⁄₁₆")

PEDESTAL
500 (19¹¹⁄₁₆")

680 (26¾")
720 (28⅜")

CORINTHIAN CAPITAL
59kg (130 lb)

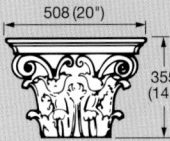

508 (20")
355 (14")

DORIC CAPITAL
29kg (64 lb)

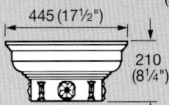

445 (17½")
210 (8¼")

IONIC CAPITAL
25kg (55 lb)

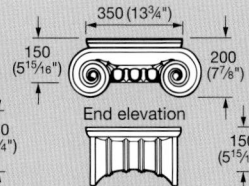

350 (13¾")
150 (5⁵⁄₁₆")
200 (7⅞")

End elevation

TUSCAN CAPITAL
24kg (53 lb)

382 (15¹⁄₁₆")
150 (5¹⁵⁄₁₆")

CAPITALS FOR M2, M4 AND M5 COLUMNS (Interchangeable)

COLUMN M9
1116kg (2458 lb)
Core 200mm (7⅞")

CAPITAL OPTIONS

625 (24⅝")

175 (6⅞")

255 (10¹⁄₁₆")

655 (25¾")

255 (10¹⁄₁₆")

425 (16¾")

4968 (195⅝")

425 (16¾")

BASE

155 (6⅛")

PLINTH
75 (3")

570 (22⁷⁄₁₆")

TUSCAN COLUMN M4
365kg (887 lb)
Core 160mm (6⁵⁄₁₆")
Half column also available

CAPITAL OPTIONS

TUSCAN PILASTER M4
139kg (337 lb)

130 (5⅛")

382 (15¹⁄₁₆")
150 (5¹⁵⁄₁₆")
250 (9¹³⁄₁₆")

136 (5⅜")
150 (5¹⁵⁄₁₆")

2388 (94")

2388 (94")

300 (11¹³⁄₁₆")

70 (2¾")

190 (7½")

BASE

190 (7½")

PEDESTAL

300 (11¹³⁄₁₆")

400 (15¾")
424 (16¹¹⁄₁₆")

120 (4¾")
132 (5³⁄₁₆")

CORINTHIAN COLUMN M2
396kg (871 lb)
Core 160mm (6⁵⁄₁₆")

CAPITAL OPTIONS

CORINTHIAN PILASTER M2
155kg (341 lb)
(Shaft has no diminution)

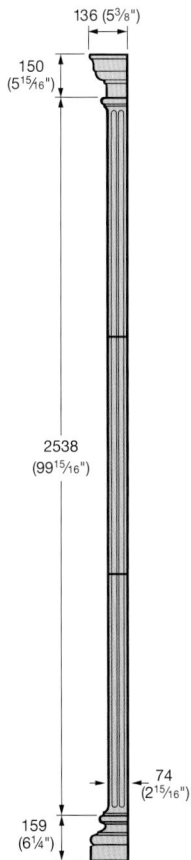

508 (20")
355 (14")

254 (10")

136 (5⅜")
150 (5¹⁵⁄₁₆")

2782 (109½") as shown, or
2538 (99¹⁵⁄₁₆")

2538 (99¹⁵⁄₁₆")

305 (12")

74 (2¹⁵⁄₁₆")

102 (4")
51 (2")

BASE
PLINTH

159 (6¼")

279 (11")
PEDESTAL

279 (11")

445 (17½")
457 (18")

144 (5¹¹⁄₁₆")
150 (5¹⁵⁄₁₆")

402 (15¹³⁄₁₆")

250 (9¹³⁄₁₆")

237 (9⁵⁄₁₆")

ARCHITECTURAL STONEWORK PORTICOS

In the XIX century, porticos were a frequent feature of houses for both aesthetic and practical reasons. Whilst providing welcome shelter from the elements, they also offered architects the opportunity to embellish an otherwise perhaps rather dull entrance, uplifting it to much grander proportions.

Today, the benefits and opportunities provided by utilising these architectural features are again being appreciated, for both public and private buildings.

The Haddonstone collection of porticos includes five designs using standard Haddonstone architectural elements. As can be seen from the photographs, it is often possible to combine individual elements to create a completely new design. An additional four components are also offered for use as individual entablature pieces.

Haddonstone also specialises in the manufacture of custom-made porticos to individual designs and requirements.

Note: The architrave will, in most cases, require backing with an in-situ reinforced concrete beam sufficient to carry the weight of the structure. Please ask for relevant Tech Sheet number for assembly recommendations.

For column details see pages 140-141.

TS CAD1 Column Assembly Details

Portico A

Portico A with M4 Columns, HN1 Steps and HN3 Risers

Octagonal Portico A with HN1 Steps and HN3 Risers

Portico A with M4 Columns, additional Plinth Block and Plain Parapet, HN1 Steps and HN3 Risers

Portico B with M4 Columns and Half Columns featuring Ionic Capitals, HN1 Steps and HN3 Risers

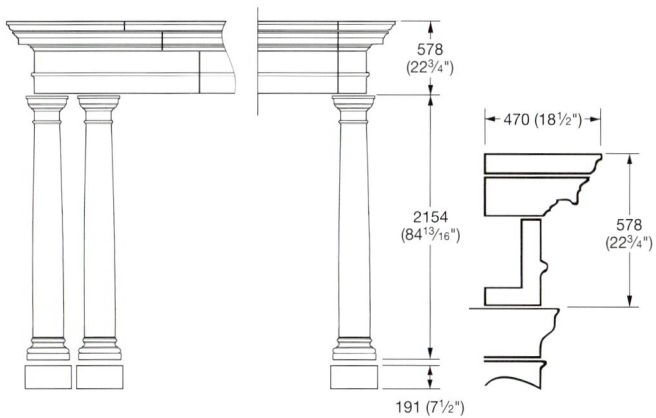

FRONT ELEVATION   SIDE ELEVATION   ENTABLATURE

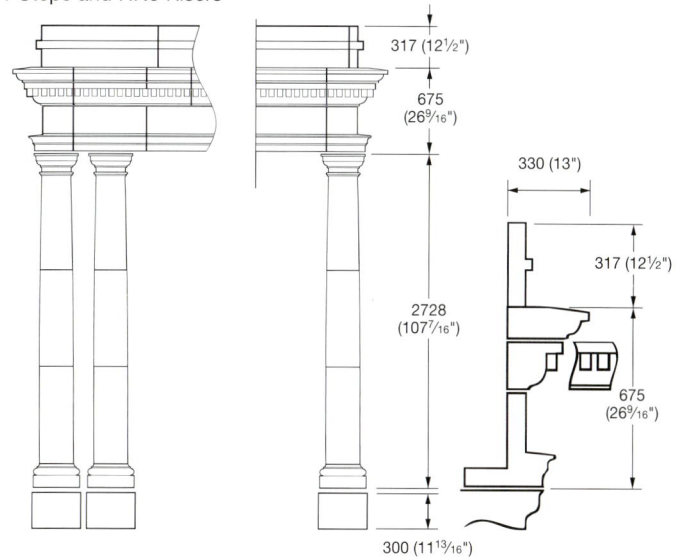

FRONT ELEVATION   SIDE ELEVATION   ENTABLATURE

Portico A Components

L110   Upper Cornice
L120   Lower Cornice
L130   Architrave
M7   Column

TS Tech Sheet No. PT10 for Portico A

TS Tech Sheet No. PT11 for Portico A detail

Portico B Components

L200   Blocking (optional)
L210   Upper Cornice
L220   Lower Cornice (with dentils)
L230   Architrave
M4   Column (shown with Tuscan Capital)

TS Tech Sheet No. PT20 for Portico B

TS Tech Sheet No. PT21 for Portico B detail

Portico E with L330 Architrave

Portico D with HN1 Steps and HN3 Risers

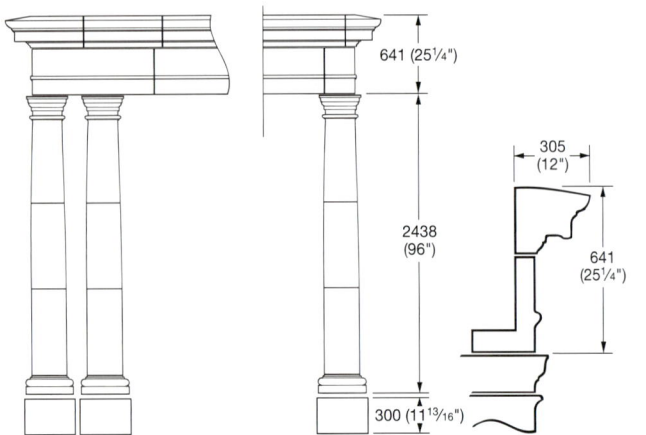

FRONT ELEVATION   SIDE ELEVATION   ENTABLATURE

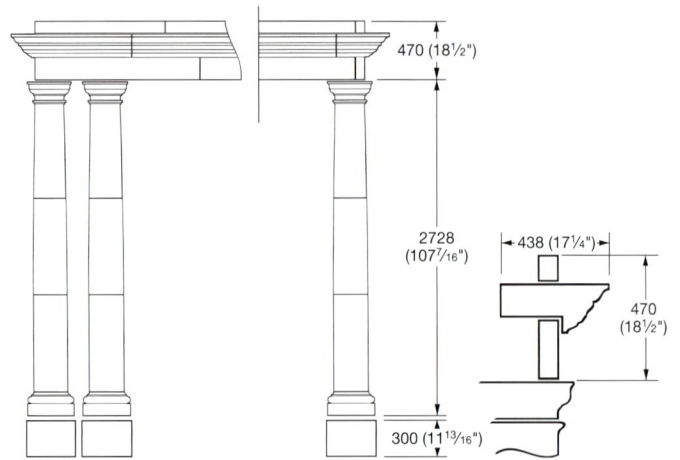

FRONT ELEVATION   SIDE ELEVATION   ENTABLATURE

Portico C Components

L310   Cornice
L330   Architrave
M5   Column (shown with Tuscan Capital)

TS Tech Sheet No. PT30 for Portico C

TS Tech Sheet No. PT31 for Portico C detail

Portico D Components

L400   Blocking
L410   Cornice
L430   Architrave
M4   Column (shown with Tuscan Capital)

TS Tech Sheet No. PT40 for Portico D

TS Tech Sheet No. PT41 for Portico D detail

Custom-made products are available on request.   Dimensions exclude joints. Allow 6mm (¼") for joints.

Portico A with M2 Columns.

Custom Portico A with HN1 Steps and HN3 Risers.

Portico D, M7 Columns and Balustrading.

Portico A with square M7 Columns.

Portico C with M4 Columns.

Custom portico with special square columns and balustrading.

Custom portico with M4 Columns with HN1 Steps and HN3 Risers.

145

Portico E with additional Blocking Course and M2 Columns

M7 Columns with L130 Architrave, L120 Lower Cornice,
L220 Dentilled Cornice and L110 Upper Cornice with HN1 Steps and
HN3 Risers

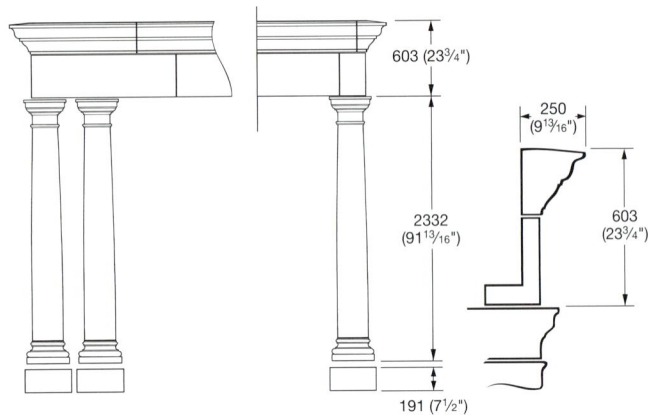

FRONT ELEVATION   **SIDE ELEVATION**   **ENTABLATURE**

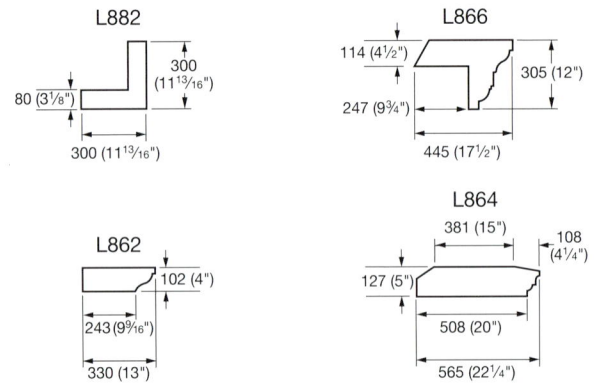

603 (23¾")

2332 (91¹³⁄₁₆")

603 (23¾")

250 (9¹³⁄₁₆")

191 (7½")

L882

300 (11¹³⁄₁₆")
80 (3⅛")
300 (11¹³⁄₁₆")

L866

114 (4½")
305 (12")
247 (9¾")
445 (17½")

L862

102 (4")
243 (9⁹⁄₁₆")
330 (13")

L864

381 (15")
108 (4¼")
127 (5")
508 (20")
565 (22¼")

Portico E Components

L510   Cornice
L530   Architrave
M7   Column

TS Tech Sheet No. PT50 for Portico E

TS Tech Sheet No. PT51 for Portico E detail

Note: L864 Cornice is suitable for carrying the Haddonstone
Standard Balustrading Range (see pages 124 to 132).

Note: Haddonstone supply Steps and Risers for all Portico
and Door Surround designs. For Steps and Risers, see
page 169 for further information.

M4 Columns on special Piers with L210 Upper Cornice, L220 Lower Cornice
and L330 Architrave

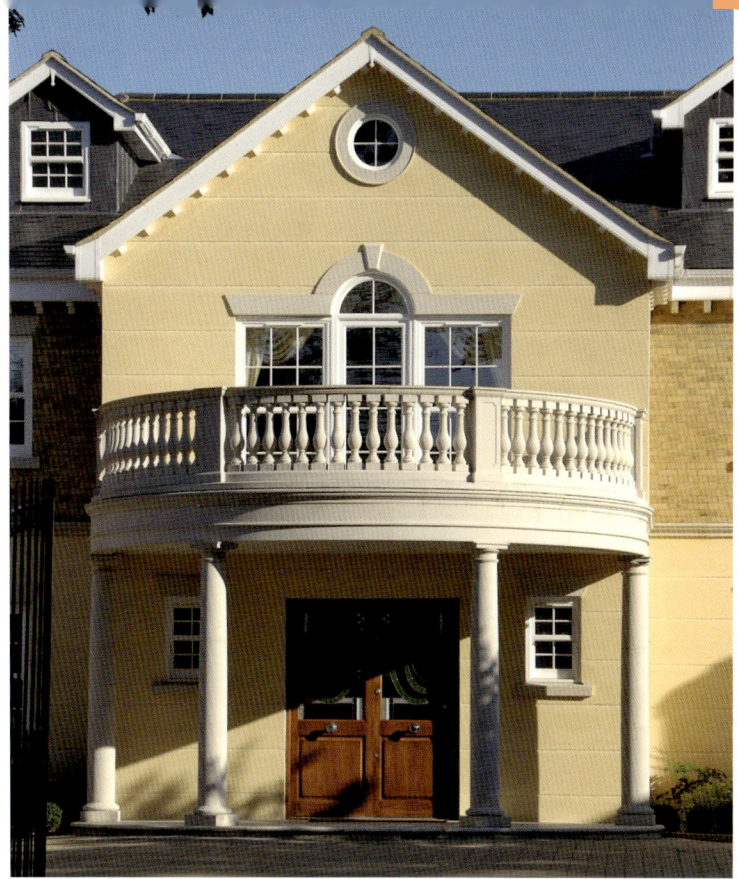

ORMONDE COURT

Custom portico with FC balustrading, HN1 Steps and HN3 Risers

Portico A, HN1 Steps and HN3 Risers

Special M4 Columns and Curved Entablature

Half M7 Columns, L330/L410 Entablature

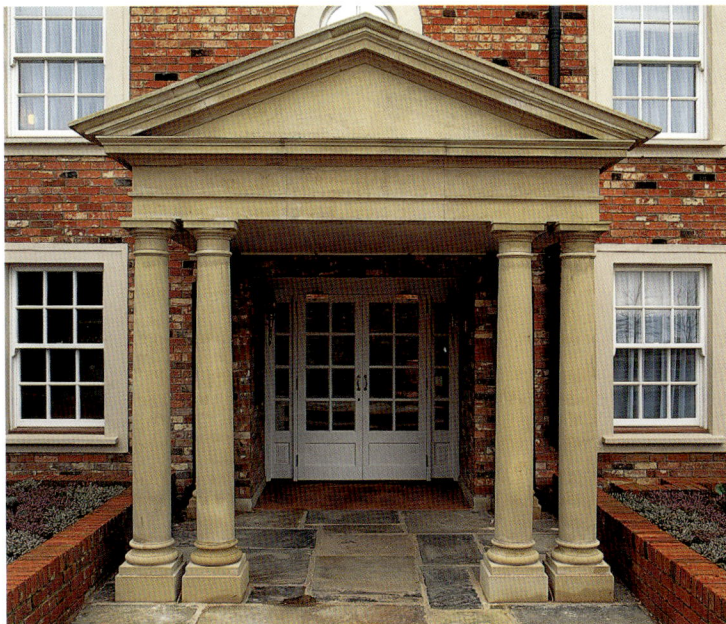

Pedimented Portico

Portico E

ARCHITECTURAL STONEWORK DOOR SURROUNDS

Haddonstone can create a wide variety of door surrounds from standard architectural components including half columns, pilasters and entablatures. These designs are suitable for both interior and exterior applications. Please contact your nearest Haddonstone Technical Department to discuss your precise requirements.

Special door surrounds can be created using standard Haddonstone components

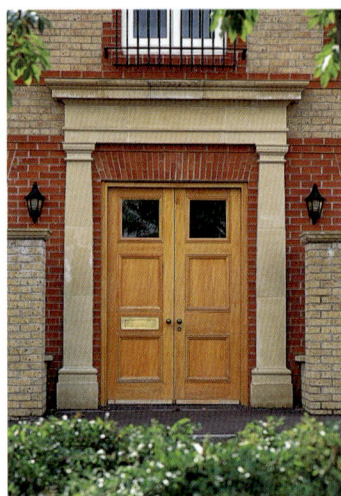

William Kent Door Surround Q200 with HN1 Step

William Kent Door Surround
Q200

William Kent Door Surround (with pediment)
Q210

These designs by Haddonstone are in the style of the prolific early XVIII century architect William Kent, a great admirer of Inigo Jones and a protege of the architect Lord Burlington. William Kent's sumptuous designs derived partly from the Italian Baroque and partly from Palladio.

Height overall (without pediment): 2640mm (104")
Height overall (with pediment): 3072mm (121")
Maximum width (without pediment): 2000mm (78¾")
Maximum width (with pediment): 2024mm (79¾")
Height of opening: 2038mm (80¼")
Width of opening: 924mm (36½")
Weight (without pediment): 583kg (1285 lb)
Weight (with pediment): 712kg (1570 lb)

TS Tech Sheet No. DS10

William Kent Door Surround Q210

For TecLite door surrounds see pages 172-173.

Refer to the Architectural Supplement for specific US designs.

Belvedere L9500

The Belvedere, inspired by the designs of Sir Charles Barry (1795-1860) for Queens Park, Brighton and Trentham Hall in Staffordshire, utilises standard Haddonstone architectural components including balustrading, columns, architrave and cornice. Square in plan, this impressive structure was first created for the 1998 Chelsea Flower Show.

Overall height: 3205mm (126¼")
Base width: 2193mm (86⅜")

TS Tech Sheet No. T60 & T61

ARCHITECTURAL STONEWORK ORANGERIES

Orangeries built from cast stone are an exciting and original concept. Since launching at the Chelsea Flower Show in 2001, Haddonstone has created a range of half columns and pilasters in Doric, Ionic, Tuscan and Gothic styles specifically for this project.

The unique and refined architectural language of the orangery allows for the creation of buildings with great presence and style that are simply unavailable elsewhere.

Traditionally used to over-winter citrus fruits for grand county houses, today orangeries are seen as versatile structures functioning as pool houses, dining rooms, or simply as elegant living spaces. They can be either freestanding or connected to an existing property.

Haddonstone can also source joinery and glazing for all your conservatory and orangery requirements. For further information please contact your nearest Haddonstone office.

Custom-made products are available on request.

Orangeries can be designed to meet your needs, with: five types of capital; three types of column and pilaster; numerous patterns of glazed joinery; and, perhaps most importantly, any size.

Half Column Capitals

Tuscan

Ionic

Doric

Half Octagonal Capital

Gothic

Pilaster Capital

Tuscan

Columns

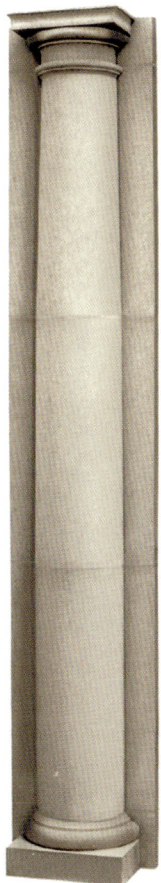
Half Column

Half Octagon

Tuscan Pilaster

"... at the ends and extremities of a park are beautiful pavilions of masonry, which the French call belvederes, or pavilions of Aurora, which are as pleasant to rest oneself in, after a long walk, as they are to the eye, for the handsome prospect they yield; they serve also to retire into for shelter when it rains."

Anon, XVIII century

Venetian Folly
L9400

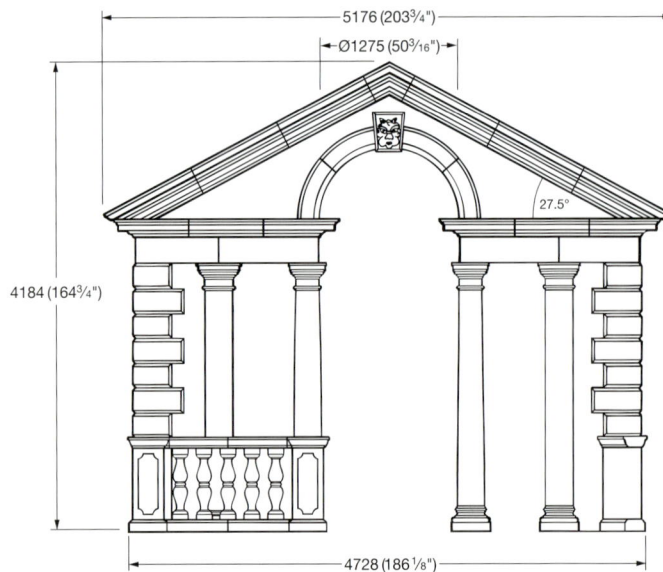

The Venetian Folly, unveiled at the Chelsea Flower Show in 1990, has the classical proportions of a Serlian window, combining the use of Tuscan columns, pedimented arch, quoins and optional balustrading.

TS Tech Sheet No. T50 for L9400

TS Tech Sheet No. T51 for L9400 Detail

TS Tech Sheet No. T52 for L9400 Detail

TS CAD1 Column Assembly Details

Venetian Folly L9400

5176 (203¾")
Ø1275 (50³⁄₁₆")
4184 (164¾")
27.5°
4728 (186⅛")

FRONT ELEVATION

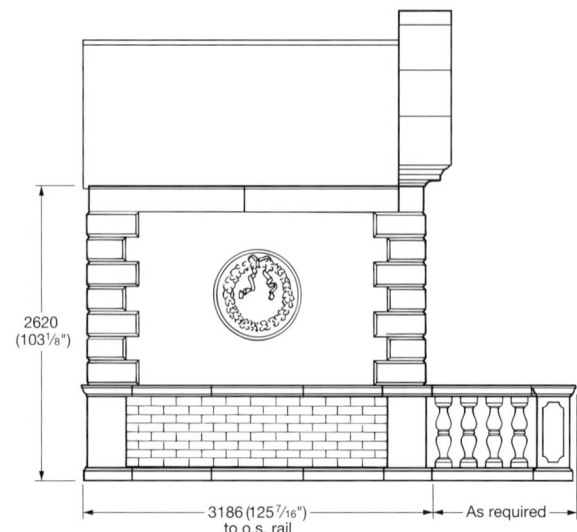

2620 (103⅛")
3186 (125⁷⁄₁₆") to o.s. rail
As required

SIDE ELEVATION

Pavilion L9300

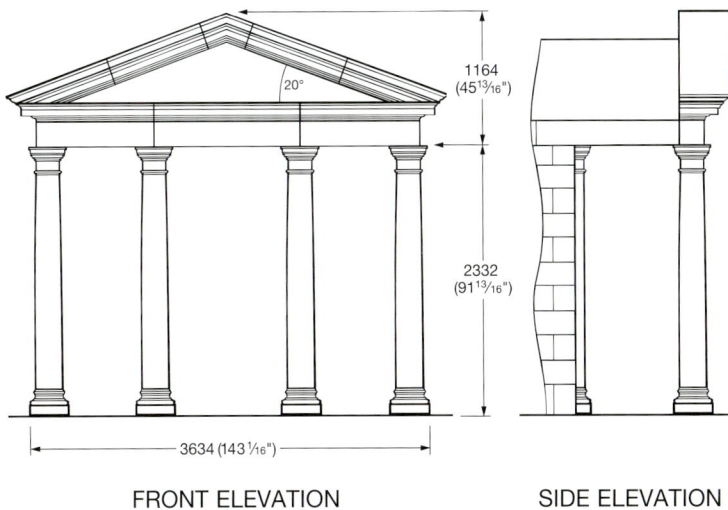

The pavilion is based on our M7 Tuscan Column series and can easily be adapted for use as a portico. Please note that the pediment can be supplied in the standard 20°, 27½° or 30° pitch. Flooring and steps can be supplied to individual requirements. See pages 166 to 169.

TS Tech Sheet No. T40 for L9300

TS Tech Sheet No. T41 for L9300 Detail

TS Tech Sheet No. T42 for L9300 Detail

TS CAD1 Column Assembly Details

Pavilion L9300

20°

1164
(45¹³⁄₁₆")

2332
(91¹³⁄₁₆")

3634 (143¹⁄₁₆")

FRONT ELEVATION

SIDE ELEVATION

Dimensions exclude joints. Allow 6mm (¼") for joints.

ARCHITECTURAL STONEWORK TEMPLES

Glass fibre domes are available in a lead-effect finish for L9000 (X510A), L9100 (X510B), L9250 and L9200 (X510C) temples. These are supplied in sections for assembly on site.

WX5150 Wrought Iron Dome for L9000 Temple. Other sizes also available.

Large Classical Temple L9100 with non-standard dome and HN6006 floor.

Balustraded Temple L9000 with Dome X510A and custom floor.

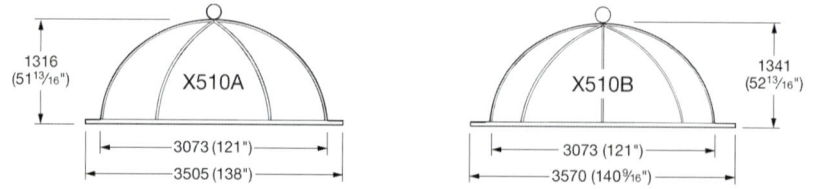

X510A

1316 (51¹³/₁₆")

3073 (121")
3505 (138")

BALUSTRADED TEMPLE L9000

For Temple Flooring, see page 156.

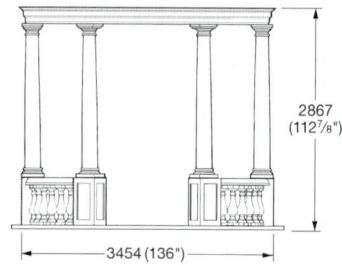

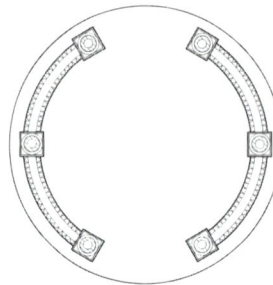

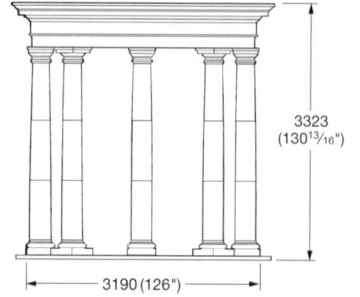

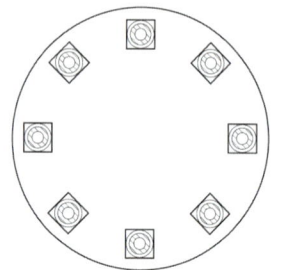

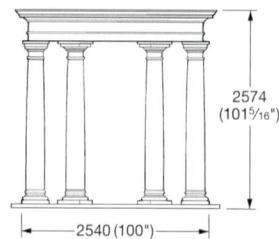

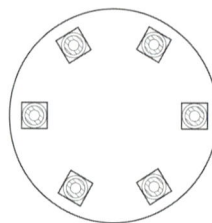

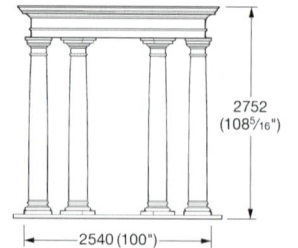

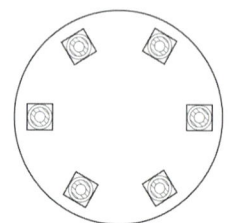

2867 (112⁷/₈")

3454 (136")

TS Tech Sheet No. T10 & T11
TS CAD1 Column Assembly Details

X510B

1341 (52¹³/₁₆")

3073 (121")
3570 (140⁹/₁₆")

LARGE CLASSICAL TEMPLE L9100

For Temple Flooring, see page 156.

3323 (130¹³/₁₆")

3190 (126")

TS Tech Sheet No. T20 & T21
TS CAD1 Column Assembly Details

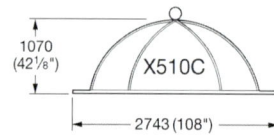

X510C

1070 (42⅛")

2743 (108")

SMALL CLASSICAL TEMPLE L9250

For Temple Flooring, see page 156.

2574 (101⁵/₁₆")

2540 (100")

TS Tech Sheet No. T30 & T31
TS CAD1 Column Assembly Details

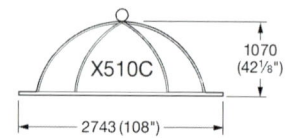

X510C

1070 (42⅛")

2743 (108")

SMALL CLASSICAL TEMPLE L9200

For Temple Flooring, see page 156.

2752 (108⁵/₁₆")

2540 (100")

TS Tech Sheet No. T30 & T31
TS CAD1 Column Assembly Details

Custom-made products are available on request.

Dimensions exclude joints. Allow 6mm (¼") for joints.

Temples should not be regarded as mere buildings but as classical ornaments, best viewed from afar at the end of a vista or cresting a rise. They are essentially frivolous and mood-evoking, often intended for no other purpose than to enliven the senses. Wherever one finds them, temples should be just this, or more.

Small Classical Temple L9250 with X510C Dome and HN6005 Floor. For Piper Statue, see page 66.

155

Temple Flooring

Available for Balustraded, Small Classical and Large Classical Temples. Stepped Temple Floors are available for Small and Large Classical Temples. Produced in TecStone cast stone as standard.

TS Tech Sheet No. T25 for Stepped Flooring

TS Tech Sheet No. T35 for Flooring

ARCHITECTURAL STONEWORK PERGOLA

Pergola L900

Designed for the M7 Tuscan Column range. Can be supplied for column spacings of up to 1829mm (72") centres.

TS Tech Sheet No. PG10

TS CAD1 Column Assembly Details

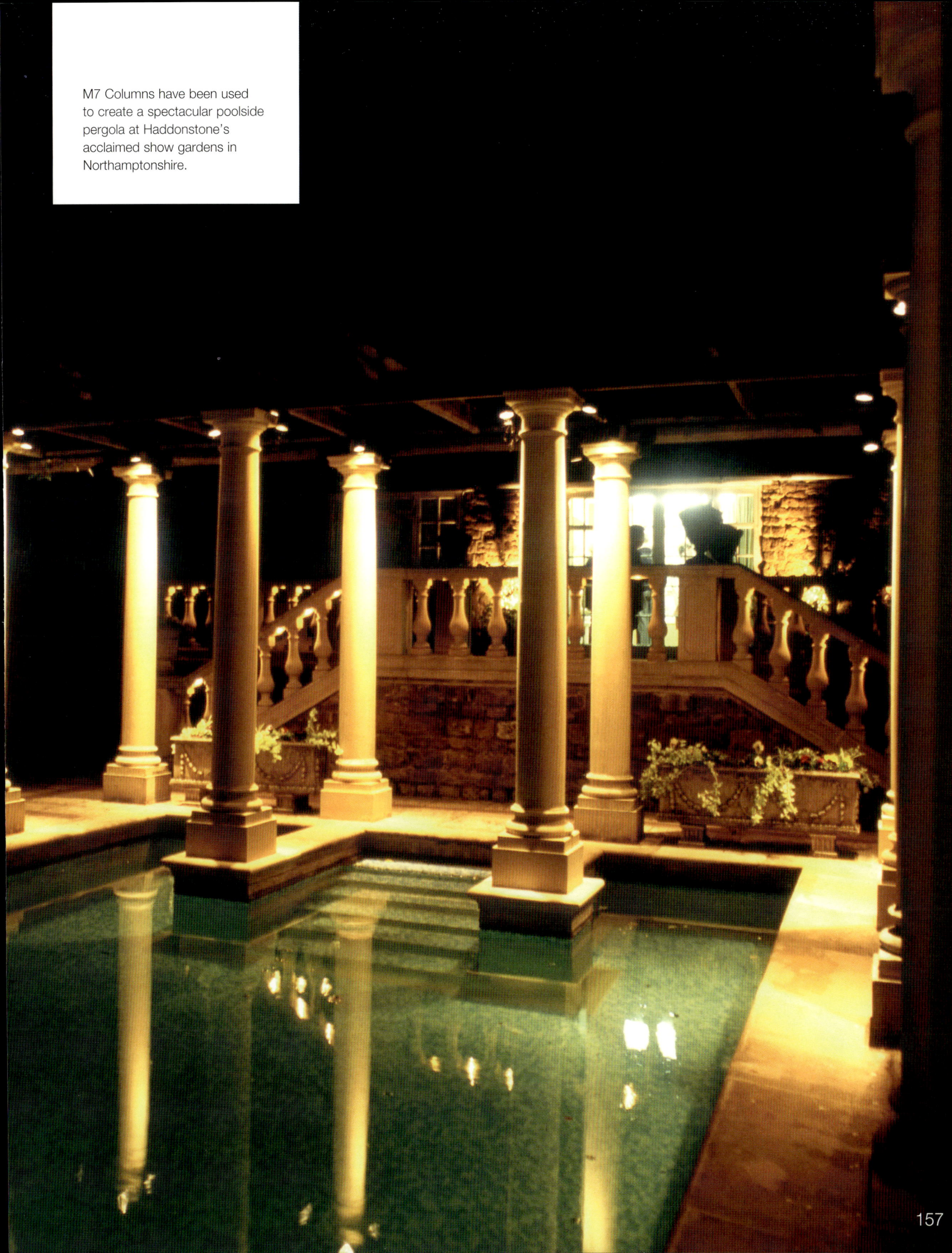

"Mood, association, magic:
these are indeed the essence of follies"

Gervase Jackson-Stops, 1989

Ruins, follies and grottoes were in vogue for a considerable period of the XVIII and XIX centuries: valued for their aesthetic, emotional and romantic qualities.

Using standard architectural and ornamental components from the Haddonstone collection it is possible – with flair and imagination – to design and construct picturesque structures in the style of the antique.

Based on the L9300 Pavilion, this ruinous folly has been constructed in the City of Westminster, Colorado, USA.

Folly from Haddonstone's 1995 Chelsea exhibit rebuilt in a London garden.

A private garden in the West Midlands features this ruinous Venetian Folly.

Landscaping by Notcutts

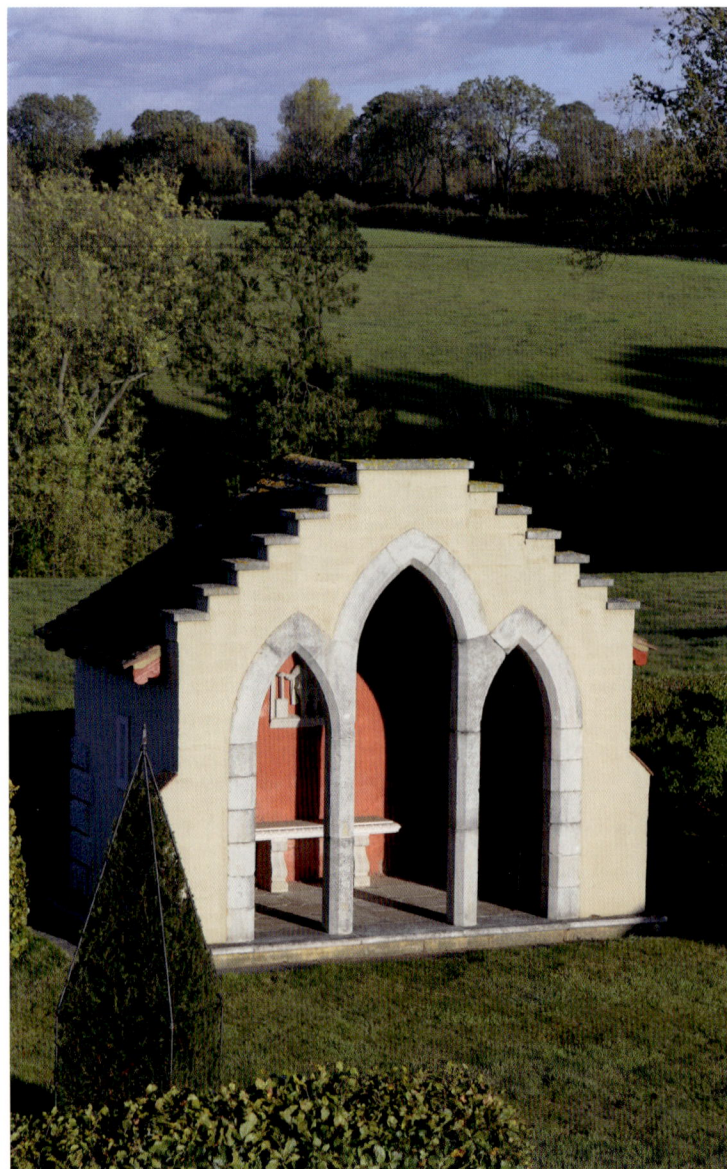

Folly featuring L9605 Gothic Arch at a private Northamptonshire home.

Custom-made products are available on request.

Inspired by the works of Piranesi, Haddonstone's 2003 Chelsea Show Garden used standard designs to recreate an evocative scene of Roman antiquity.

Haddonstone's Northamptonshire showgarden features this Gothic Grotto.

Triumphal arch created for Nanatsudo Park in Mito City, Japan.

This Gothic folly enhances the grounds of a private residence in Suffolk.

Intriguing water feature with Grotesque Masks and Fontainebleau Fountain.

HEADS, CILLS, KEYSTONES & WINDOW SURROUNDS

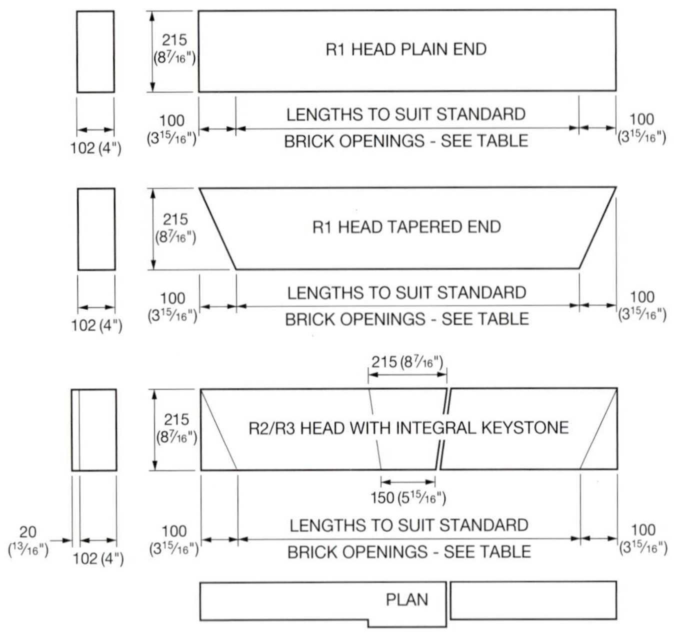
215 (8 7/16")
R1 HEAD PLAIN END
102 (4")
100 (3 15/16")
LENGTHS TO SUIT STANDARD
BRICK OPENINGS - SEE TABLE
100 (3 15/16")
215 (8 7/16")
R1 HEAD TAPERED END
102 (4")
100 (3 15/16")
LENGTHS TO SUIT STANDARD
BRICK OPENINGS - SEE TABLE
100 (3 15/16")
215 (8 7/16")
215 (8 7/16")
R2/R3 HEAD WITH INTEGRAL KEYSTONE
150 (5 15/16")
20 (13/16")
102 (4")
100 (3 15/16")
LENGTHS TO SUIT STANDARD
BRICK OPENINGS - SEE TABLE
100 (3 15/16")
PLAN

Window Heads

Our standard designs – R1, plain-ended or tapered; R2, plain-ended with integral keystone; and R3, tapered with integral keystone – suit a three-brick course height in a normal cavity-wall situation. They are available to suit the following British Standard brick openings:

R1, R2, R3

460mm (18 1/8")	910mm (35 13/16")	1248mm (49 1/8")	1585mm (62 3/8")*
685mm (26 15/16")	1135mm (44 11/16")	1360mm (53 9/16")	1810mm (71 1/4")*

*Only supplied as a two-piece head, left-hand end of R2 and R3 incorporating keystone.

Please note that other head sizes can be manufactured to order.

Supporting lintels must be used as these window heads are not structural members.

We strongly recommend that you refer to Eurocode 6 and PD 6697: 2010.

R3 Head with P2 Cill

Q920 Keystone

Window Cills

Our three standard designs suit one or two-brick course heights in a normal cavity-wall situation. They are available in the following lengths to suit British Standard brick openings:

P1		P2/P9	
460mm (18 1/8")	1248mm (49 1/8")*	460mm (18 1/8")	1248mm (49 1/8")
685mm (26 15/16")	1360mm (53 9/16")*	685mm (26 15/16")	1360mm (53 9/16")*
910mm (35 13/16")	1585mm (62 3/8")*	910mm (35 13/16")	1585mm (62 3/8")*
1135mm (44 11/16")**	1810mm (71 1/4")*	1135mm (44 11/16")	1810mm (71 1/4")*

Note: Dimensions exclude stooling - maximum 100mm (3 15/16") at each end.

*Only supplied as a two-piece cill.

**One-piece only when supplied without stools.

Please note that other cill sizes can be manufactured to order.

We strongly recommend that you refer to Eurocode 6 and PD 6697: 2010, and our Tech Sheet M90/TS for installation recommendations.

TS Tech Sheet No. M90

Keystones

We have three standard designs: Q900A, Q910A and Q920A. Please note that other keystones can be manufactured to individual requirements.

KEYSTONES

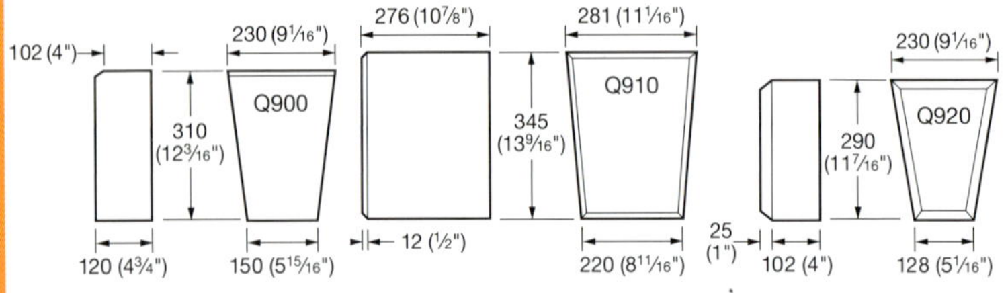
102 (4")
230 (9 1/16")
Q900
310 (12 3/16")
120 (4 3/4")
150 (5 15/16")
276 (10 7/8")
345 (13 9/16")
12 (1/2")
281 (11 1/16")
Q910
220 (8 11/16")
25 (1")
102 (4")
290 (11 7/16")
230 (9 1/16")
Q920
128 (5 1/16")

TecLite Quoin TLQ920 also available. Thickness 25mm (1").

WINDOW CILLS

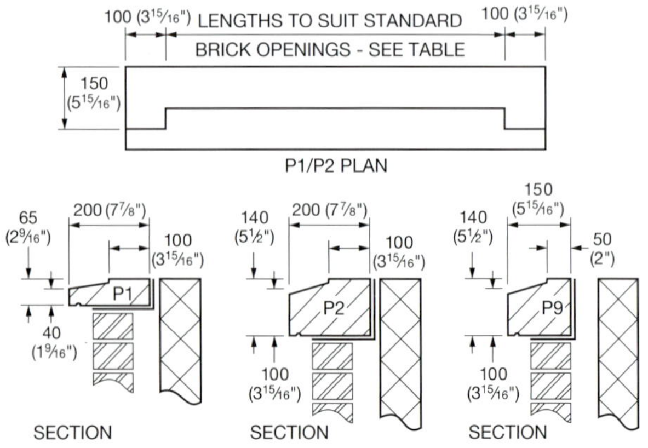
100 (3 15/16") LENGTHS TO SUIT STANDARD 100 (3 15/16")
BRICK OPENINGS - SEE TABLE
150 (5 15/16")
P1/P2 PLAN
65 (2 9/16")
200 (7 7/8")
100 (3 15/16")
P1
40 (1 9/16")
SECTION
140 (5 1/2")
200 (7 7/8")
100 (3 15/16")
P2
100 (3 15/16")
SECTION
150 (5 15/16")
140 (5 1/2")
50 (2")
P9
100 (3 15/16")
SECTION

Custom-made products are available on request.

TecLite Heads and Cills also available, see page 171

Window Surrounds

Haddonstone has a range of classical window surrounds which can be tailored to suit individual requirements. These surrounds, based on the Tuscan style, can be used for new build or refurbishment.

Haddonstone will always continue to create custom-made surrounds, either to an architect's drawing or to match an existing design. Please contact your nearest Technical Department for further information.

We strongly recommend that you refer to Eurocode 6 and PD 6697: 2010.

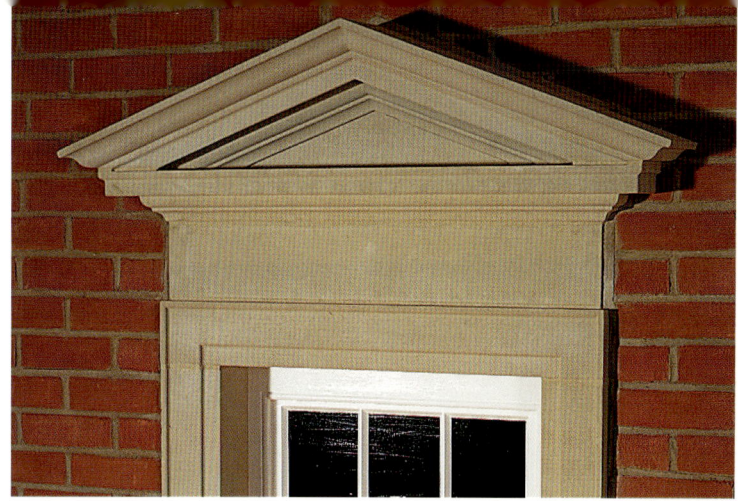

WS6 (SECTION)

272 (10¹¹/₁₆")

230 (9¹/₁₆")

WS3/6

WS4/7

WS2/5

WS5/6/7

WS1

WS6 Window Surround

WS2 Window Surround

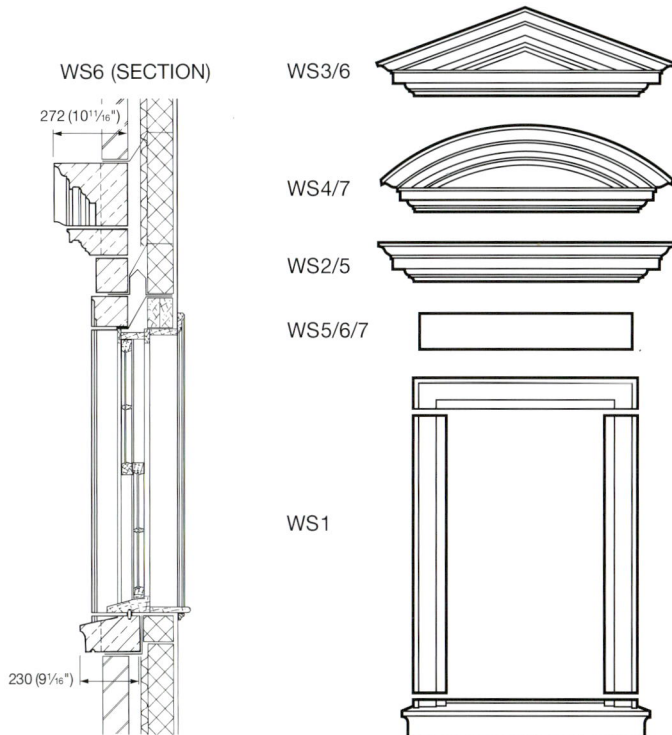

Bull's-Eye Window Surrounds

Offered in addition to Haddonstone's standard range of surrounds, Bull's-Eye windows are available in three standard styles, as illustrated below:

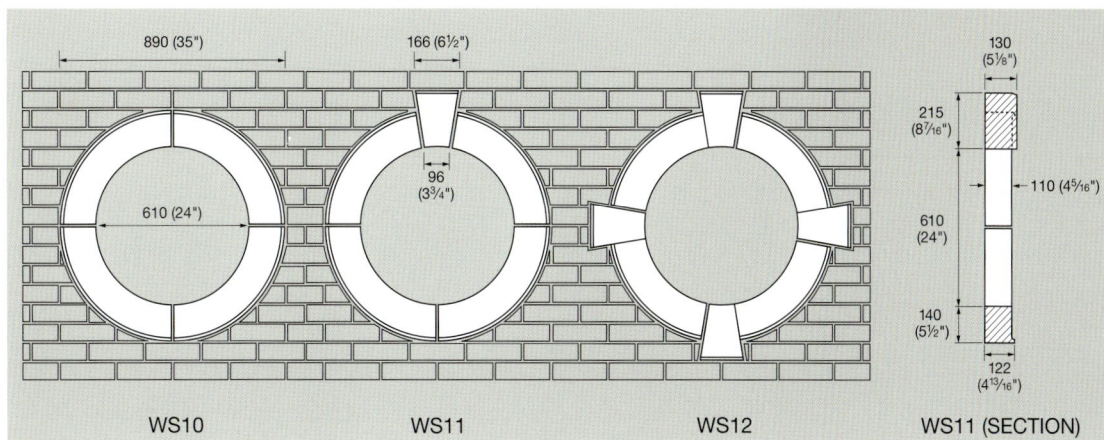

890 (35")

166 (6½")

96 (3¾")

610 (24")

WS10

WS11

WS12

130 (5⅛")

215 (8⁷/₁₆")

110 (4⁵/₁₆")

610 (24")

140 (5½")

122 (4¹⁵/₁₆")

WS11 (SECTION)

TecLite Window Surrounds also available, see page 171.

Refer to the Architectural Supplement for specific US designs.
Custom-made products are available on request.

ARCHITECTURAL STONEWORK
PLINTHS, STRING COURSES & DETAILS

Plinth Courses

The five standard designs illustrated are available in lengths shown in the price list. Plinth courses can also be produced to individual requirements. The Q540 plinth course matches the S120G pier base.

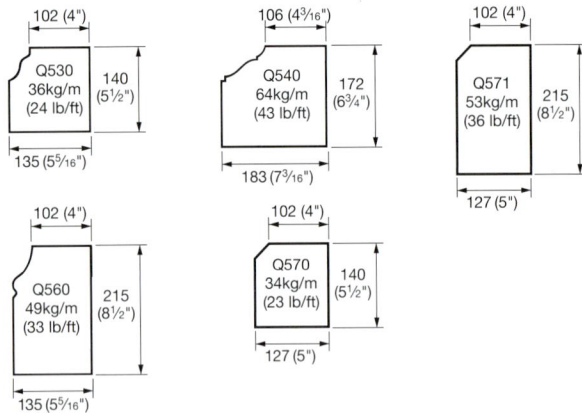

Q530 36kg/m (24 lb/ft) — 102 (4"), 140 (5½"), 135 (5⁵⁄₁₆")

Q540 64kg/m (43 lb/ft) — 106 (4³⁄₁₆"), 172 (6¾"), 183 (7³⁄₁₆")

Q571 53kg/m (36 lb/ft) — 102 (4"), 215 (8½"), 127 (5")

Q560 49kg/m (33 lb/ft) — 102 (4"), 215 (8½"), 135 (5⁵⁄₁₆")

Q570 34kg/m (23 lb/ft) — 102 (4"), 140 (5½"), 127 (5")

String Courses

Five standard designs are available in lengths shown in the price list. String courses can also be produced to individual requirements.

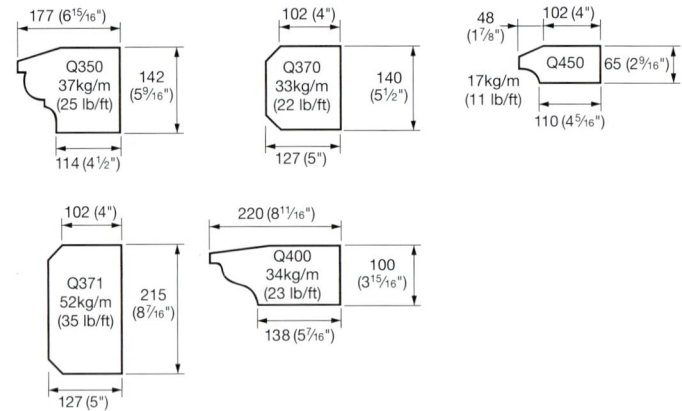

Q350 37kg/m (25 lb/ft) — 177 (6¹⁵⁄₁₆"), 142 (5⁹⁄₁₆"), 114 (4½")

Q370 33kg/m (22 lb/ft) — 102 (4"), 140 (5½"), 127 (5")

Q450 17kg/m (11 lb/ft) — 48 (1⅞"), 102 (4"), 65 (2⁹⁄₁₆"), 110 (4⁵⁄₁₆")

Q371 52kg/m (35 lb/ft) — 102 (4"), 215 (8⁷⁄₁₆"), 127 (5")

Q400 34kg/m (23 lb/ft) — 220 (8¹¹⁄₁₆"), 100 (3¹⁵⁄₁₆"), 138 (5⁷⁄₁₆")

Hood Mould Q250

Hood moulds can be made for both new and restoration work. This hood mould has been designed to suit British Standard nominal brick size including joint of 225mm x 112.5mm x 75mm (8⅞" x 4⁷⁄₁₆" x 2¹⁵⁄₁₆") and can be supplied in maximum 865mm (34¹⁄₁₆") lengths to fit any structural opening.

Supporting lintels must be used as these hood moulds are not structural members.

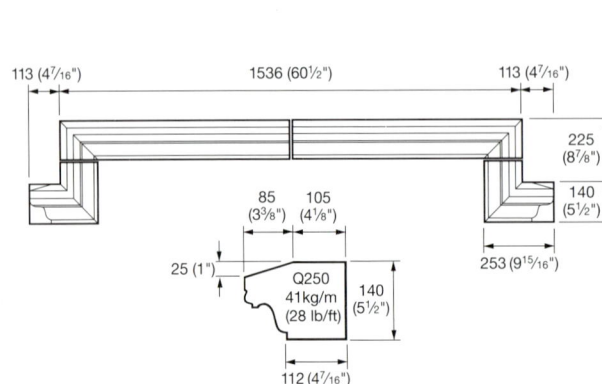

113 (4⁷⁄₁₆"), 1536 (60½"), 113 (4⁷⁄₁₆"), 225 (8⅞"), 85 (3⅜"), 105 (4⅛"), 140 (5½"), 253 (9¹⁵⁄₁₆"), 25 (1")

Q250 41kg/m (28 lb/ft) — 140 (5½"), 112 (4⁷⁄₁₆")

House gable showing special vent, corbels and copings.

Gable Vent Q680

This architectural feature is normally used in the gable end of a house.

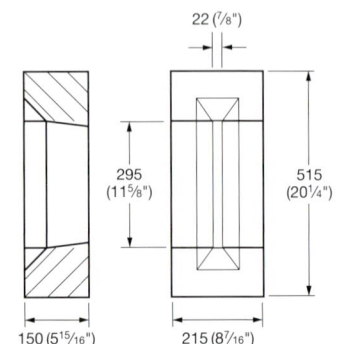

22 (⅞"), 295 (11⅝"), 515 (20¼"), 150 (5¹⁵⁄₁₆"), 215 (8⁷⁄₁₆")

Weight: 31kg (68 lb)

ARCHITECTURAL STONEWORK
BRACKETS, CORBELS & QUOINS

Brackets & Corbels

Haddonstone's range of standard brackets and corbels can be applied as decorative features below cills, ledges, balconies, parapets and any other projecting element. Where our standard designs do not match your requirements, we can produce custom-made stonework to order.

Please note that attention must be given to the damp-proofing detail where a bracket or corbel bridges a cavity wall.

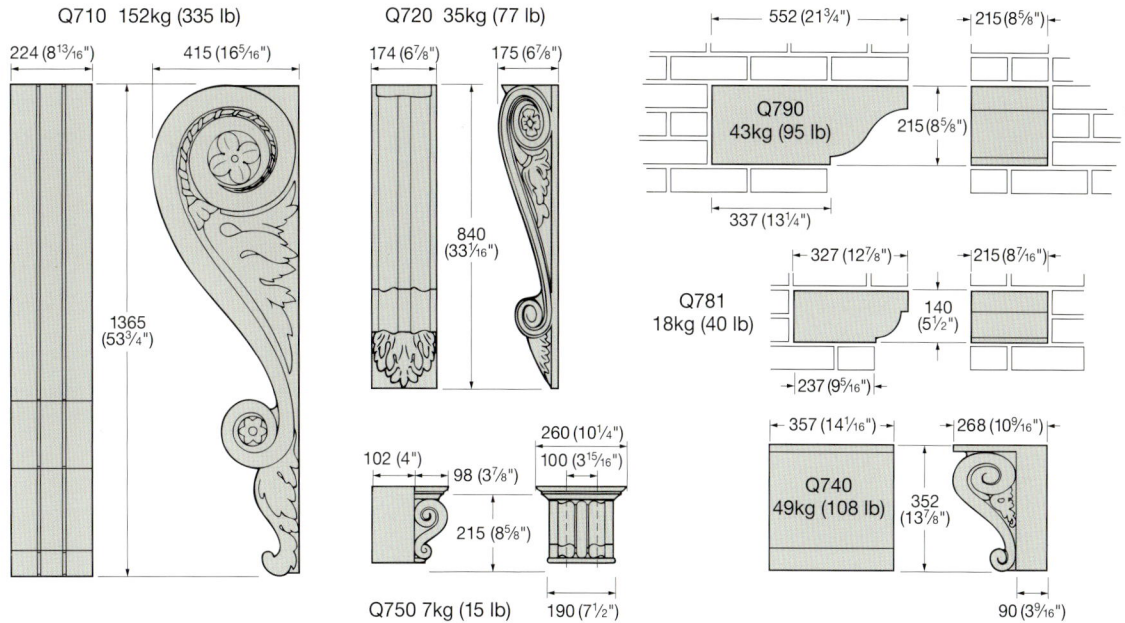

Q710 152kg (335 lb)

Q720 35kg (77 lb)

Q790 43kg (95 lb)

Q781 18kg (40 lb)

Q750 7kg (15 lb)

Q740 49kg (108 lb)

Q100 Quoins

Q110 Quoins

Q180 Quoins

Q790 Corbel

Quoins

Haddonstone has a range of standard designs to suit most applications. Custom-made designs available on request.   Q110 weight: 37kg (81 lb)

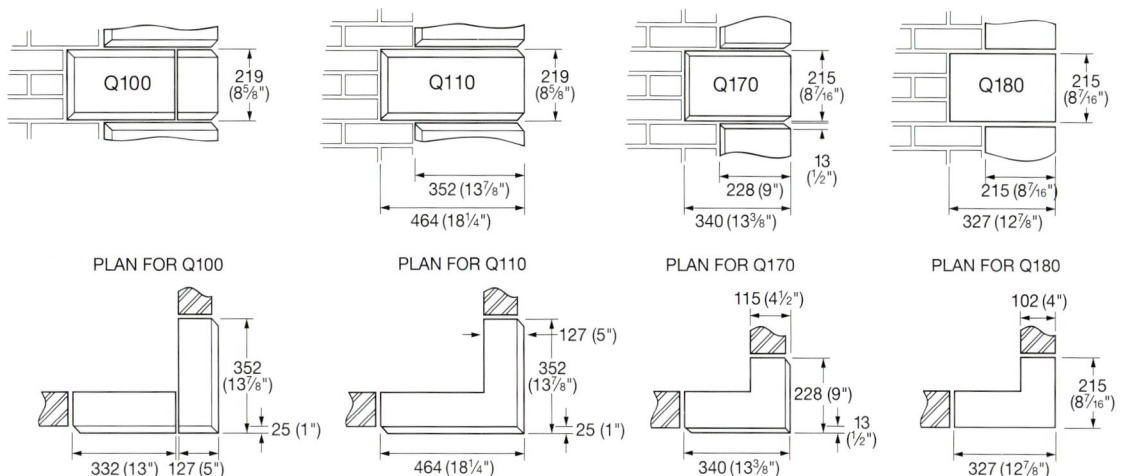

PLAN FOR Q100

PLAN FOR Q110

PLAN FOR Q170

PLAN FOR Q180

TecLite Quoin also available, see page 171.

Refer to the Architectural Supplement for specific US designs.

Custom-made products are available on request.

ARCHITECTURAL STONEWORK
ROUNDELS & PLAQUES

The roundels and plaques illustrated have been specially commissioned by clients. We would be pleased to quote for your individual requirements.

Gothic Roundel Q620

Diameter: 432mm (17")
Thickness: 115mm (4½")
Weight: 31kg (68 lb)

Surround Q621

Internal diameter: 445mm (17 ½")
External diameter: 625mm (24½")
Thickness: 200mm (7⅞")
Weight: 21kg (46 lb)

Image above shows Q620/Q621

Rose Roundel Q640

Diameter: 595mm (23½")
Thickness: 100mm (3¹⁵⁄₁₆")
Weight: 36kg (79 lb)

Swagged Q650

A date can be incorporated within this design at additional cost.

Diameter: 785mm (31")
Thickness: 110mm (4½")
Weight: 84kg (185 lb)

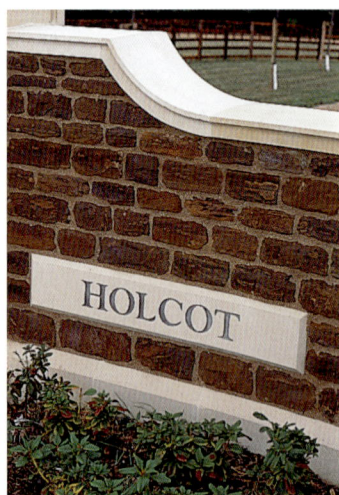

Custom-made name plaque.

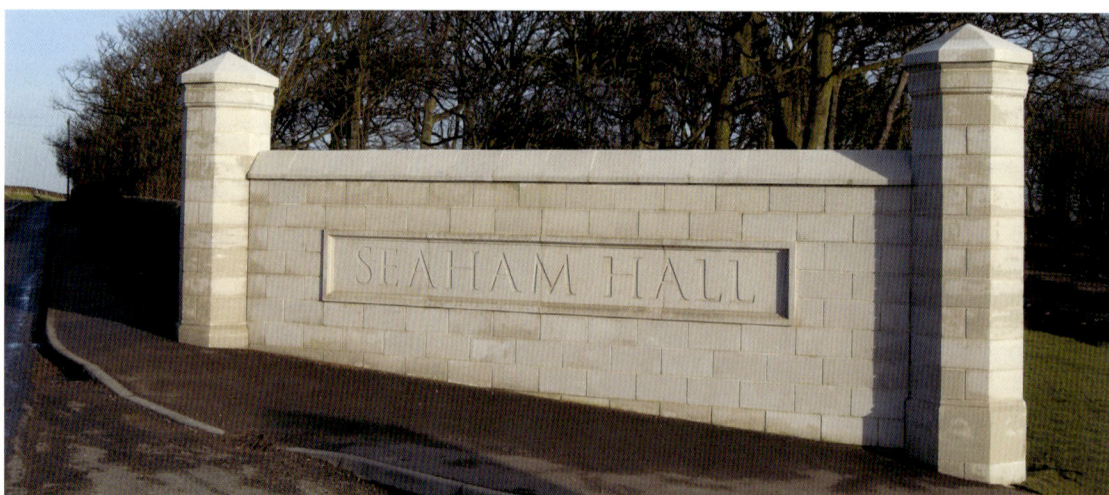

Custom-made name plaque for the entrance to Seaham Hall Hotel in County Durham

Circular Q625

A date or letters can be incorporated within this design.

Diameter: 432mm (17")
Thickness: 102mm (4")
Weight: 30kg (66 lb).

Surround Q621

Internal diameter: 445mm (17½")
External diameter: 625mm (24½")
Thickness: 200mm (7⅞")
Weight: 21kg (46 lb).

Image below shows Q625/Q621

Rectangular Q630

Date or letters can be cast in.

Length: 440mm (17⁵⁄₁₆")
Height: 290mm (11⁷⁄₁₆")
Thickness: 102mm (4")
Weight: 26kg (57 lb)

Plaque TLQ635

Haddonstone is now able to offer retro-fit house number plaques.

Length: 200mm (7⅞")
Height: 120mm (4¾")
Thickness: 16mm (⅝")
Weight: 650g (1½ lb)

For ornamental plaques see page 103-104.
Custom-made products are available on request.

CLADDING &
RAIN SCREEN CLADDING

In recent years, Haddonstone has gained an increasing reputation for the custom-manufacture of blocks for cladding and rain screen cladding. Examples can be seen on this page. Designers, developers and private clients are encouraged to contact their nearest Haddonstone office to discuss any appropriate projects.

Londonderry city centre features extensive cladding by Haddonstone.

Cladding with cast-in quotations at Wimbledon High School Rutherford Centre.

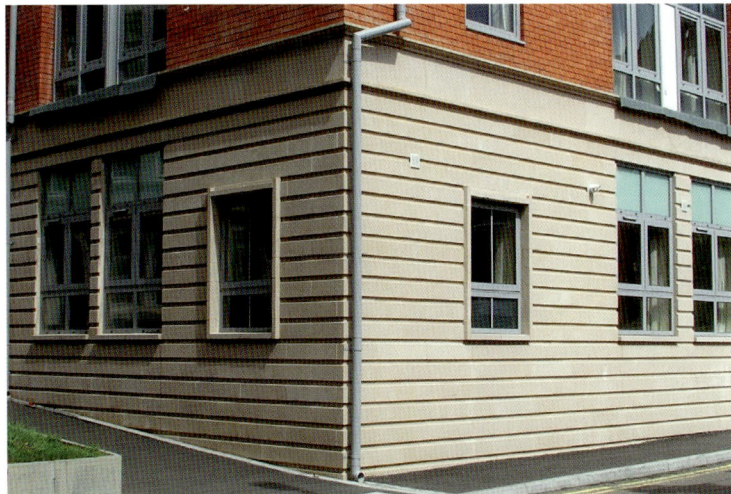
Apartments in Northampton town centre featuring Haddonstone cladding.

Rain screen cladding at Seaham Hall Hotel and Serenity Spa.

Cladding in Nottingham City centre.

Extensive use of custom cladding for prominent fast-food outlet in Bridlington.

Cladding on a New York Development.

ARCHITECTURAL STONEWORK
FLOORING & PAVING

Haddonstone offers a range of flooring and paving designs for interior and exterior use. Weight: 89kg per m² (18 lb per ft²)

For interior use, the conservatory and orangery flooring ranges are etched and a seal applied at our manufactory before dispatch. Both then require sealing by the client after installation.

Like quarried stone, Haddonstone can exhibit slight shade variations from piece to piece, reflecting the colour of the natural materials used in the production process.

Conservatory Flooring

Suitable for indoor use. Standard sizes can be combined to create many different patterns.

HN722A: 300 x 300 x 25mm (11¹³/₁₆" x 11¹³/₁₆" x 1")
HN725A: 450 x 450 x 25mm (17³/₄" x 17³/₄" x 1")
HN726A: 450 x 225 x 25mm (17³/₄" x 8⁷/₈" x 1")

For exterior applications, see Smooth Paving on page 167.

Orangery Flooring

Suitable for indoor use. A traditional Victorian-style flooring system which can be seen to best effect if ordered in contrasting colours as shown above.

HN750A / HN755A: 394 x 394 x 38mm (15¹/₂" x 15¹/₂" x 1¹/₂")
HN750B: 102 x 102 x 38mm (4" x 4" x 1¹/₂")

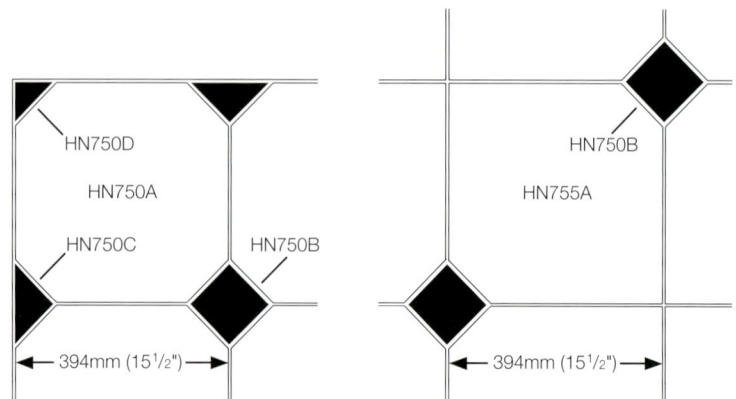

Textured Paving HN800/HN801/HN805

Haddonstone manufactures a range of paving with a subtle texture which is available in the following sizes:

HN800A: 600 x 600 x 38mm
(23⅝" x 23⅝" x 1½")

HN801A: 600 x 300 x 38mm
(23⅝" x 11¹³/₁₆" x 1½")

HN802A: 300 x 300 x 38mm
(11¹³/₁₆" x 11¹³/₁₆" x 1½")

HN805A: 450 x 450 x 38mm
(17¾" x 17¾" x 1½")

Riven Paving HN855

Customers can achieve a random effect by alternating the grain direction. In addition to the standard colours, Riven Paving is also available in York colour as shown above. Available in one size only:

Size: 450 x 450 x 38mm (17¾" x 17¾" x 1½")

Smooth Paving

Suitable for exterior use. Standard sizes can be combined to create many different patterns, see photograph page 168.
For interior applications, see Conservatory Paving on page 166.

HN700A: 600 x 600 x 38mm (23⅝" x 23⅝" x 1½")
HN701A: 600 x 300 x 38mm (23⅝" x 11¹³/₁₆" x 1½")
HN702A: 300 x 300 x 38mm (11¹³/₁₆" x 11¹³/₁₆" x 1½")
HN705A: 450 x 450 x 38mm (17¾" x 17¾" x 1½")
HN706A: 450 x 225 x 38mm (17¾" x 8⅞" x 1½")

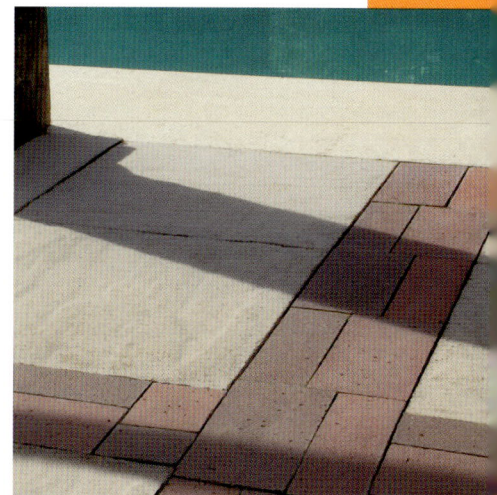

Haddon Pavers HN870/HN871

Haddonstone offers simple paver-style blocks that can be used to compliment the company's various paving ranges.

These are only available in two special colours: Brindle Red -10 (top) and Brindle Blue -11 (bottom), as illustrated, in the following sizes:

HN870A: 210 x 100 x 38mm (8¼" x 3¹⁵/₁₆" x 1½")
HN871A: 210 x 65 x 38mm (8¼" x 2⁹/₁₆" x 1½")

General Note: Paving

A well-laid foundation is essential for effective and lasting results. A fall of at least 1 in 60 is recommended. For a clean architectural appearance, the joints can be mortar-pointed. For a softer, natural appearance, paving should be laid edge to edge, unpointed, with sand brushed into the joints. This method also facilitates drainage. Cement and mortar stains are difficult to remove from paving so extreme care must be taken to keep surfaces clean. Four clear days should be allowed to elapse after construction before foot traffic is allowed over all laid areas. For vehicular traffic, special laying instructions are available on application.

ARCHITECTURAL STONEWORK PAVING & STEPS

Haddonstone's standard paving and steps can be used to great effect in numerous garden and landscape applications.

Custom sizes can be created to meet customer requirements or the slabs can be cut on site by professional contractors.

Smooth Paving in custom sizes at the Army Air Corps Memorial, Hampshire.

HN1 Treads with HN3 Risers.

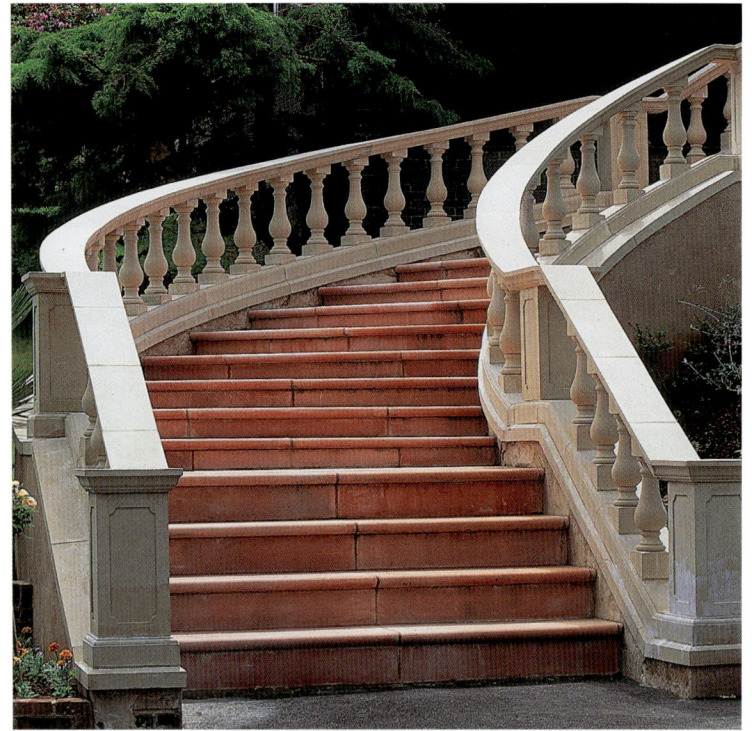

Terracotta coloured HN1 Treads with HN3 Risers.

Steps

IMPORTANT: Haddonstone steps must be continuously bedded.

Treads are available, as standard, in a plain bull nose or a moulded design as shown, in lengths of 1000mm (39⅜") and in standard widths of 300mm (11¹³⁄₁₆"), 375mm (14¾") and 450mm (17¹¹⁄₁₆"). These treads can be supplied with mouldings returned to left or right-hand ends. Square-edged risers are also available to suit. We have a range of curved treads and risers to meet individual requirements.

Treads and risers are produced in TecStone as standard.

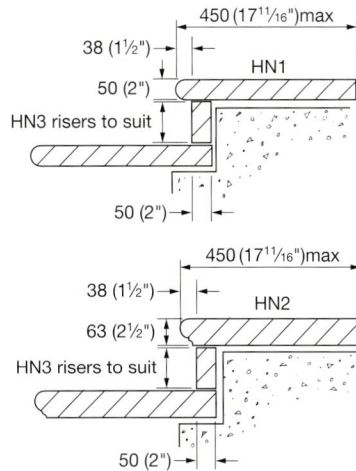

HN1 Treads with HN3 Risers.

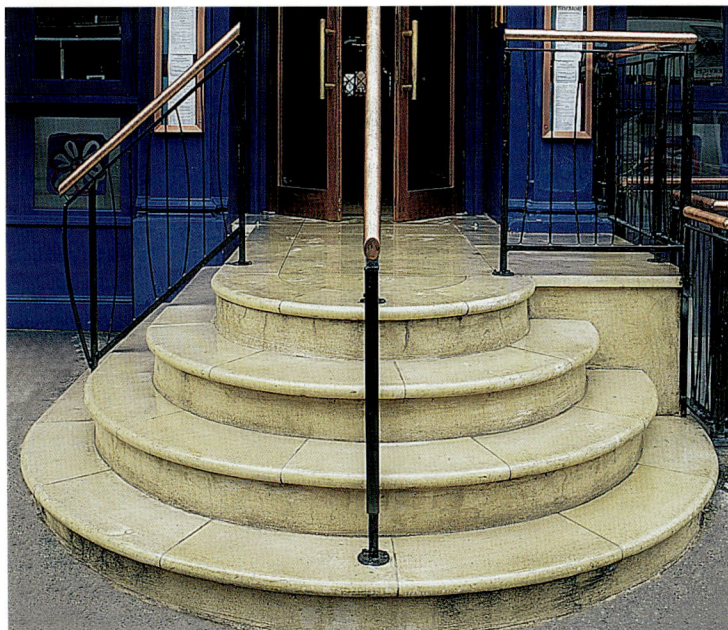

HN1 Treads with HN3 Risers.

Spiral Steps

Haddonstone has introduced a spiral staircase that is both simple and elegant.

With the riser and locating ring being an integral part of each step, a complete staircase can provide a functional design solution for both traditional and contemporary projects. Principally designed for interior use, the steps are available in widths up to 1200mm (47¼").

We strongly recommend that professional advice is taken to ensure that any proposal is designed to be structurally sound. For further information please contact your nearest Haddonstone office.

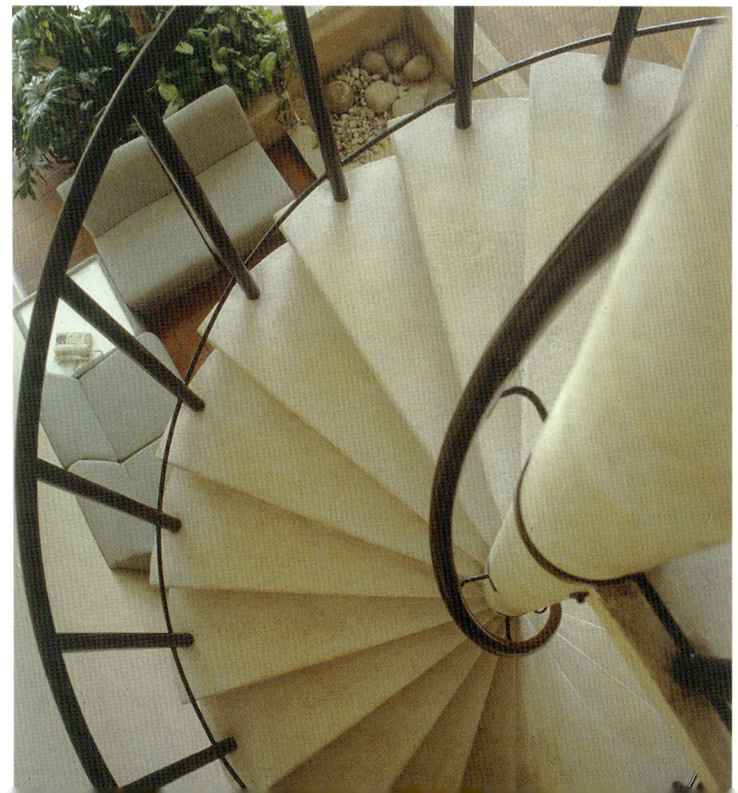

169

ARCHITECTURAL STONEWORK TECLITE

HADDONSTONE HAS LAUNCHED A REVOLUTIONARY NEW CAST STONE MATERIAL CALLED TECLITE.

Before:

Although TecLite closely resembles traditional cast stone and natural stone in appearance, the use of thin wall construction and GRC/GFRC technology means the component weight is reduced by approximately two thirds when compared with similar Haddonstone pieces.

TecLite is a cement based material containing drawn glass fibre (Glass Fibre Reinforced Concrete) which benefits from a high strength to weight ratio. TecLite is, therefore, ideal for retro-fit, timber-frame and new build projects where component weight is an issue.

TecLite products can be used in conjunction with standard Haddonstone architectural components as the colours are complementary. Consequently, users can incorporate both Haddonstone and TecLite components in the same project with absolute confidence. TecLite products can be used to achieve the same crisp detailing normally only associated with Haddonstone designs.

After: TecLite has been used extensively at this Leicestershire residence – completely transforming the exterior of the property.

Standard TecLite designs for interiors and exteriors include:

- DOOR SURROUNDS
- COLUMNS, HALF COLUMNS AND PILASTERS
- ENTABLATURES AND PEDIMENTS
- COPINGS AND PARAPET COPINGS

- STRING COURSES AND PLINTH COURSES
- QUOINS AND BLOCKS
- WINDOW SURROUNDS, CILLS, HEADS AND KEYSTONES
- CUSTOM-MADE DESIGNS TO INDIVIDUAL SPECIFICATIONS

ARCHITECTURAL STONEWORK
TECLITE DETAILS & DRESSINGS

CAPPINGS

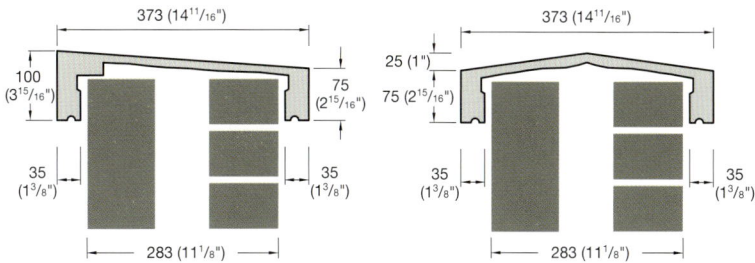

TLT390
24kg/m (16 lb/ft)

TLT395
As TLT390 except 393mm (15¹/₂")
width to suit 303mm (11¹⁵/₁₆") wall
25kg/m (17 lb/ft)

TLT790
23kg/m (15 lb/ft)

TLT795
As TLT790 except 393mm (15¹/₂")
width to suit 303mm (11¹⁵/₁₆") wall
24kg/m (16 lb/ft)

WINDOWS HEADS & CILLS

Haddonstone is able to offer a comprehensive range of window heads and cills in TecLite. Window surrounds are also available. For further information please contact your nearest Haddonstone office.

QUOIN

Surface-Fixed Quoin TLQ120

Weight: 9kg/course (20 lb/course).

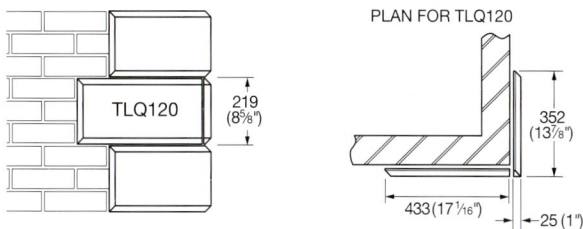

PLAN FOR TLQ120

ARCHITECTURAL DETAILS

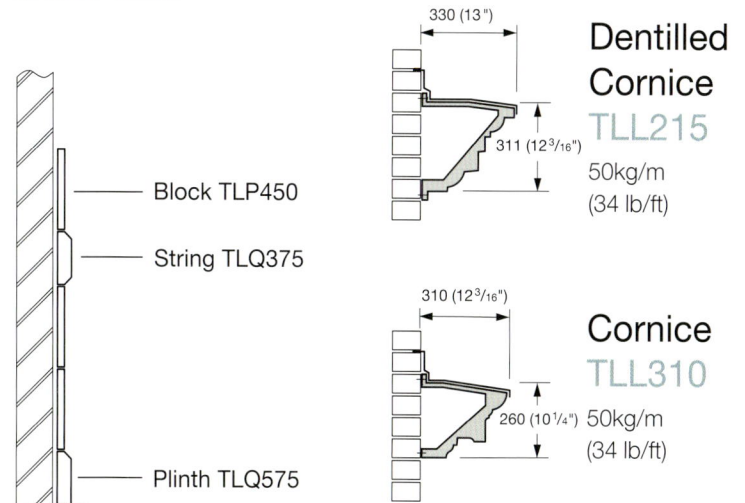

Block TLP450

String TLQ375

Plinth TLQ575

Block TLP450
444 x 219 x 20mm
(17¹/₂" x 8⁵/₈" x ³/₄")
Weight: 4kg (9 lb).

String TLQ375
894 x 144 x 40mm
(35¹/₄" x 5¹¹/₁₆" x 1⁹/₁₆")
Weight: 10kg/metre (7 lb/ft).

Plinth TLQ575
894 x 144 x 40mm
(35¹/₄" x 5¹¹/₁₆" x 1⁹/₁₆")
Weight: 10kg/metre (7 lb/ft).

ENTABLATURES

Dentilled Cornice
TLL215
50kg/m
(34 lb/ft)

Cornice
TLL310
50kg/m
(34 lb/ft)

Cornice
TLL510
39kg/m
(27 lb/ft)

Architrave
TLL450
(for use in conjunction with TLL215, TLL310 and TLL510).
15kg/m
(10 lb/ft)

Standard Jamb
TLQ309

Weight: 36kg (79 lb)
TLQ309B for left (shown)
TLQ309C for right

Feature Jamb
TLQ310

Weight: 36kg (79 lb)
TLQ310B for left (shown)
TLQ310C for right

Fluted Jamb
TLQ311

Weight: 36kg (79 lb)
TLQ311B for left
TLQ311C for right

Canopy Head
TLQ303

Weight: 80kg (176 lb)
Can be used with TLQ309,
TLQ310 and TLQ311

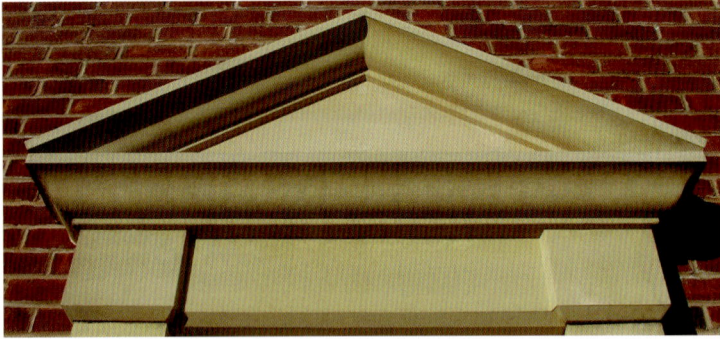

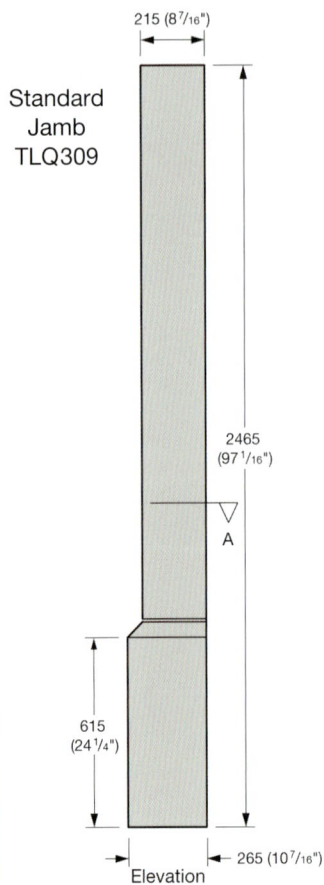

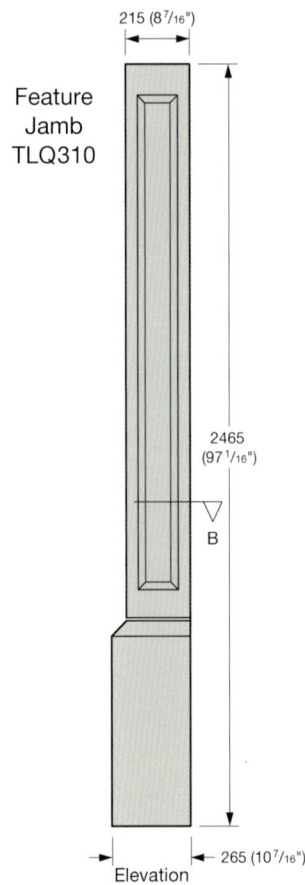

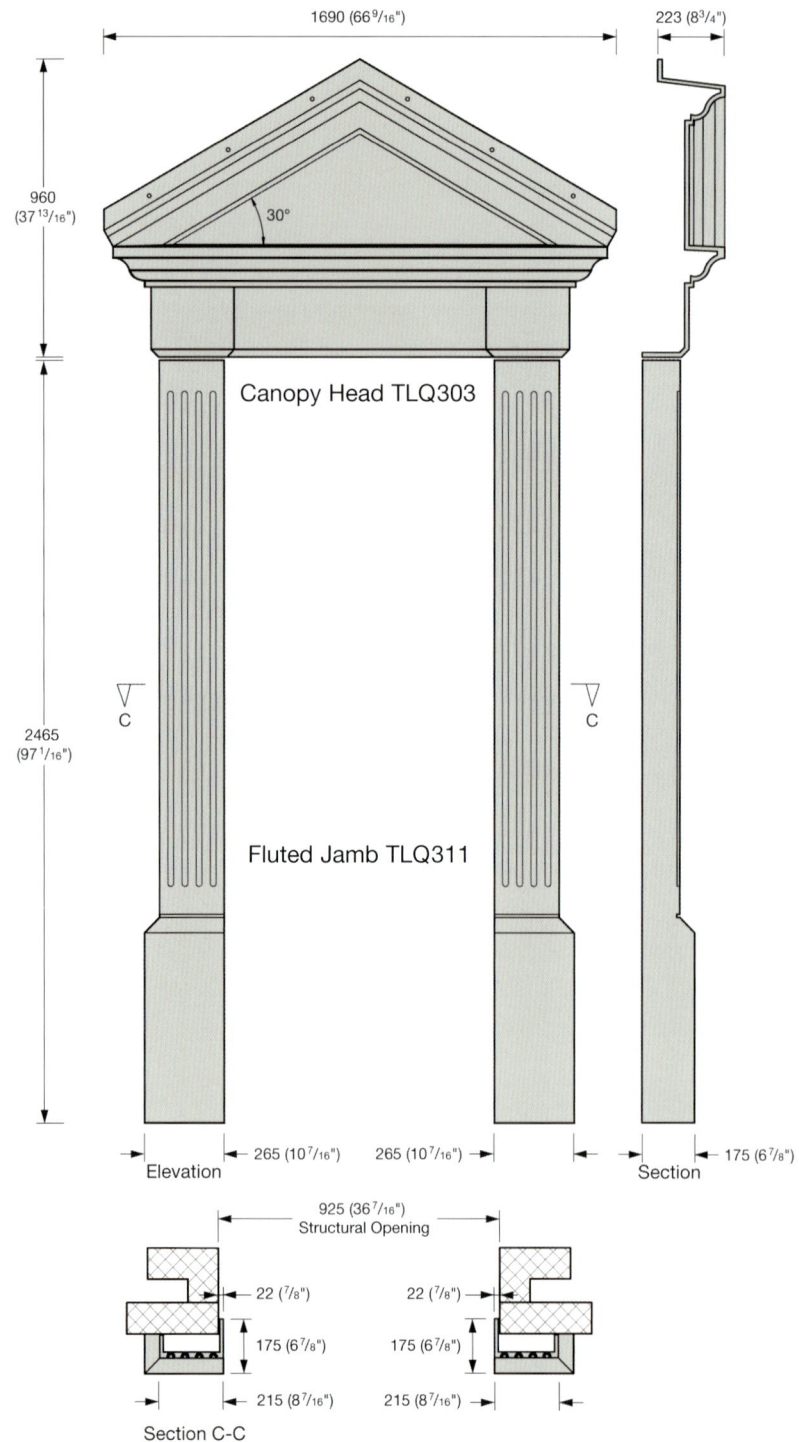

Standard Jamb TLQ309

215 (8⁷/₁₆")
2465 (97¹/₁₆")
615 (24¹/₄")
Elevation
265 (10⁷/₁₆")
75 (3¹⁵/₁₆")   125 (4¹⁵/₁₆")
Section A

Feature Jamb TLQ310

215 (8⁷/₁₆")
2465 (97¹/₁₆")
Elevation
265 (10⁷/₁₆")
75 (3¹⁵/₁₆")   125 (4¹⁵/₁₆")
Section B

Canopy Head TLQ303

1690 (66⁹/₁₆")
223 (8³/₄")
960 (37¹³/₁₆")
30°
2465 (97¹/₁₆")

Fluted Jamb TLQ311

Elevation
265 (10⁷/₁₆")   265 (10⁷/₁₆")
Section
175 (6⁷/₈")

925 (36⁷/₁₆")
Structural Opening
22 (⁷/₈")   22 (⁷/₈")
175 (6⁷/₈")   175 (6⁷/₈")
215 (8⁷/₁₆")   215 (8⁷/₁₆")
Section C-C

All jambs supplied as shown - 615mm (24¹/₄") plinth section can be cut to form shorter jambs as required.

TS Tech Sheets available.
Fixing kits available.

Fluted Jamb
TLQ311

Weight: 36kg (79 lb)
TLQ311B for left
TLQ311C for right

Canopy Head
TLQ302

Weight: 44kg (97 lb)
Can be used with TLQ309,
TLQ310 and TLQ311

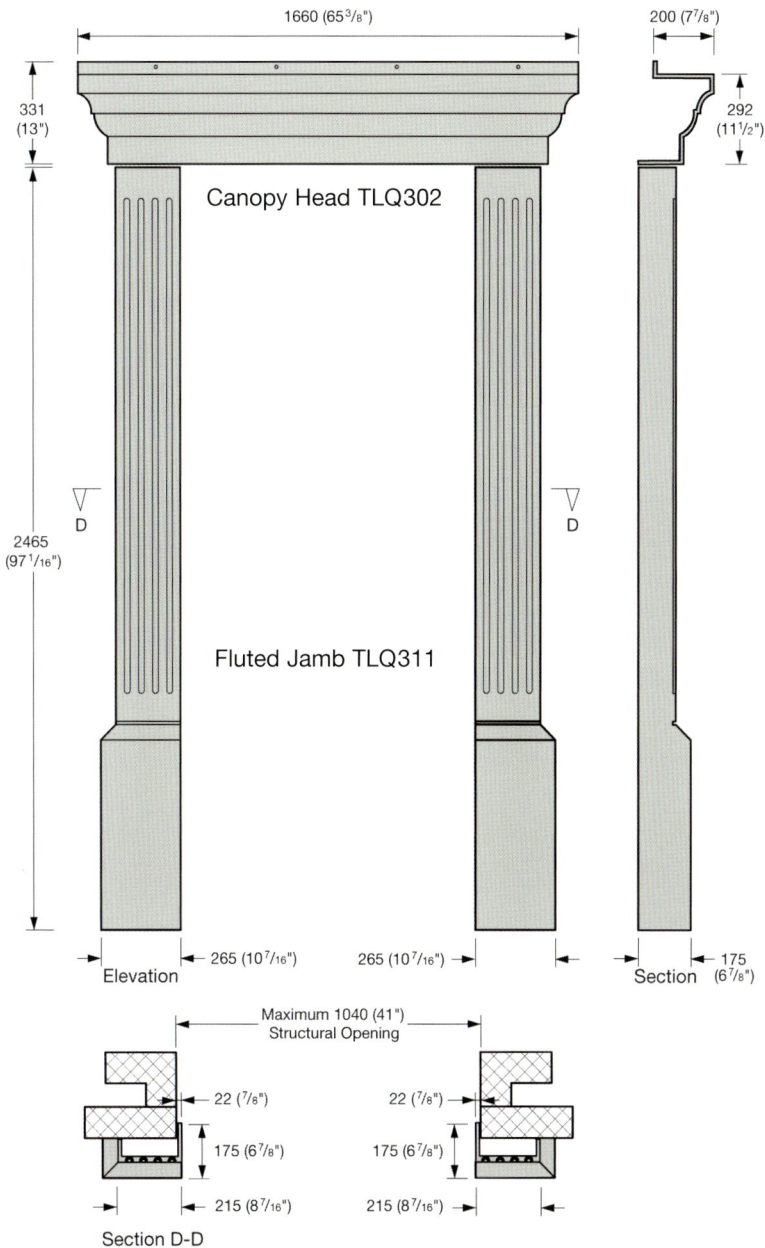

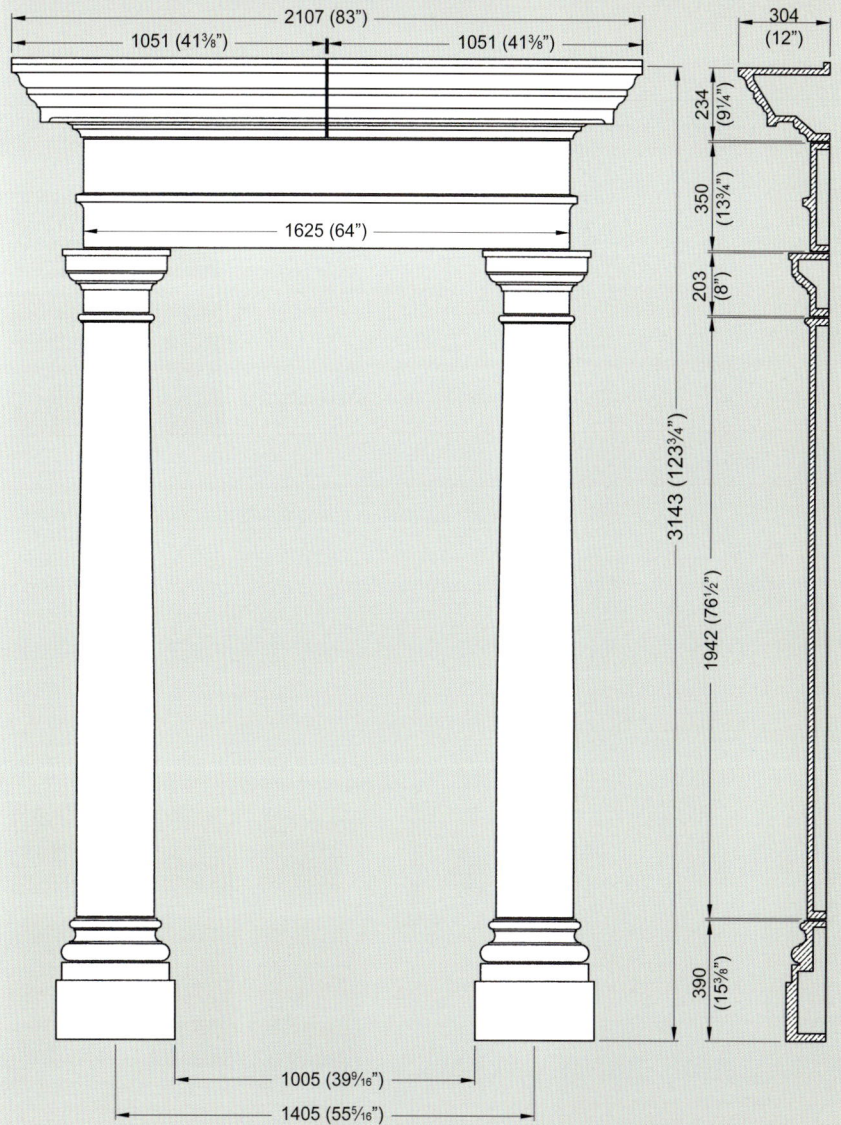

Canopy Head TLQ302

Fluted Jamb TLQ311

1660 (65³/₈")

200 (7⁷/₈")

331 (13")

292 (11¹/₂")

2465 (97¹/₁₆")

D

D

265 (10⁷/₁₆")   265 (10⁷/₁₆")

175 (6⁷/₈")

Elevation

Section

Maximum 1040 (41")
Structural Opening

22 (⁷/₈")   22 (⁷/₈")

175 (6⁷/₈")   175 (6⁷/₈")

215 (8⁷/₁₆")   215 (8⁷/₁₆")

Section D-D

IMPORTANT NOTICE: Canopy Heads TLQ301, TLQ302 and
TLQ303 are interchangeable. Each has been designed to be used in
conjunction with Jambs TLQ309, TLQ310 and TLQ311.

Door Surround
TLQ320

Total weight: 220kg (485 lb)

2107 (83")

1051 (41³/₈")   1051 (41³/₈")

304 (12")

234 (9¹/₄")

350 (13³/₄")

203 (8")

1625 (64")

3143 (123³/₄")

1942 (76¹/₂")

390 (15³/₈")

1005 (39⁹/₁₆")

1405 (55⁵/₁₆")

SPECIALIST
SERVICES

As can be seen from the scope of this catalogue, Haddonstone is justifiably regarded as the world's leading manufacturer of landscape ornaments and architectural cast stone.

Many clients are, however, unaware of the additional specialist services the company is able to offer including: Archives; Garden Cremation Memorials; Wrought Ironwork; Technistone tiles for interiors; Engraving Services; Restoration; Fireplaces, Mantels and Hearths; and a collection of primarily architectural designs created specifically for US customers.

Hopefully, the reader will find the following pages most enlightening.

Previously, when creating a new catalogue, Haddonstone has simply removed some of the more esoteric designs from the standard collection ~ banishing them to a dark corner of the company's archives never to be seen again.

Now, responding to numerous requests from clients, Haddonstone has opened up a veritable treasure chest of intriguing designs which are all available in restricted numbers.

The contents of this Archives section range from a wall mask inspired by the works of Giuseppe Arcimboldo to a fantastically decorated pool surround reminiscent of the works of Raphael at the Vatican in Rome.

Royal Pedestal
A560
Height: 1650mm (65")
Weight: 254kg (560 lb)

Victoria Vase
A695
Height: 445mm (17½")
Weight: 41kg (90 lb)

Victoria
Pedestal B695
Height: 520mm (20½")
Weight: 95kg (209 lb)

Leazes Park Urn HA455
Height: 890mm (35")   Weight: 310kg (683 lb)
Please note: requires mechanical lifting on site in all instances.

Herb Basket
A410
Width: 510mm (20")
Weight: 55kg (121 lb)

Flowered
Basket A310
Width: 510mm (20")
Weight: 31kg (68 lb)

Ascott Urn
A180
Height: 455mm (18")
Weight: 46kg (100 lb)

Wilton Urn
A760
Height: 455mm (18")
Weight: 35kg (77 lb)

Scaled
Jardiniere A570
Height: 510mm (20")
Weight: 125kg (276 lb)

Corinthian
Table D456
Top diam: 800mm (31½")
Weight: 127kg (280 lb)

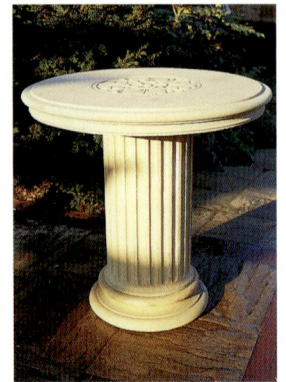

Doric Table
D455
Top diam: 800mm (31½")
Weight: 144kg (317 lb)

Highland Park Bench HD407

Length at top: 1555mm (61¼")
Height: 489mm (19¼")
Weight: 166kg (366 lb)

Highland Park Trough A417

Height: 457mm (18")
Weight: 175kg (386 lb)

Small Highland Fountain GC220

Height: 400mm (15¾")
Weight: 106kg (233 lb)

Large Highland Fountain GC210

Height: 430mm (17")
Weight: 196kg (432 lb)

Dolphin Table Top D470
Dolphin Supports D475

Length of top: 1500mm (59")
Weight: 357kg (786 lb)

Hoop
HA945

Height: 430mm (16¹⁵/₁₆")
Weight: 141kg (311 lb)

Channel
HA925

Height: 430mm (16¹⁵/₁₆")
Weight: 91kg (200 lb)

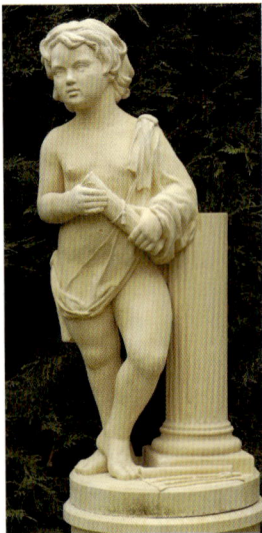

Architecture
HE770

Height: 915mm (36")
Weight: 95kg (209 lb)

Astronomy
HE775

Height: 915mm (36")
Weight: 95kg (209 lb)

Painting
HE780

Height: 915mm (36")
Weight: 95kg (209 lb)

Sculpture
HE785

Height: 915mm (36")
Weight: 95kg (209 lb)

Dovecote X600

Illustrated on M7 Column
& Gothic Bases, see p33.
Height overall:
  3645mm (143½")
Weight: 270kg (595 lb)

Recommended pedestal: HB390 Height: 380mm (14^{15}/$_{16}$") Weight: 70kg (154 lb)

Mount Edgcumbe Finial E530

Height: 1635mm (64½")
Weight: 435kg (959 lb)

Newlands Urn
A500

Height: 545mm (21½")
Weight: 50kg (110 lb)

Bishop's Finial
E192

Height: 660mm (26")
Weight: 35kg (77 lb)

Florentine Finial
E300

Height: 1210mm (47½")
Weight: 135kg (298 lb)

Peregrine Falcon E580

Height: 705mm (27¾")
Weight: 62kg (136 lb)

Elephant
HE575A
Base HE575B

Overall height:
900mm (35⁷⁄₁₆")

Overall weight:
386kg (850 lb)

Large XVIII Century Lion
E455

Height: 622mm (24½")
Weight: 217kg (478 lb)

Leazes Park Lion HE457 (left-hand)
Leazes Park Lion HE458 (right-hand not illustrated)

Height: 980mm (38⁵⁄₈")
Weight: 1000kg (2203 lb)

Sphinx Q995
(left-hand)

Length of base:
1060mm (41¾")
Height: 810mm (31⁷⁄₈")
Weight: 190kg (419 lb)

Sphinx Q996
(right-hand)

Length of base:
1020mm (40⅛")
Height: 780mm (30⁷⁄₈")
Weight: 190kg (419 lb)

Heron with Raised Head X150 Heron Stalking X160

Supplied with 520mm (20½") wide hexagonal bases for sinking into lawn or pond.

X150 Height above ground: 1070mm (42")   X160 Height above ground: 760mm (30")
X150 Weight: 45kg (99 lb)   X160 Weight: 45kg (99 lb)

Raphael Pool Surround C490
Illustrated with Eton College Fountain and Festoons of Fruit.

External width: 2650mm (104")
Height: 690mm (27")
Weight: 1460kg (3219 lb)
TS Tech Sheet No. P90 & P91

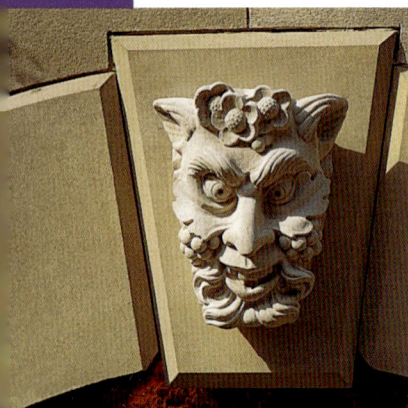

D'Hulst Mask
E345
D'Hulst Fountain C265
also available
Height: 345mm (13½")
Weight: 14kg (31 lb)

Cherub Wall
Mask E330

Diam.: 240mm (9½")
Weight: 10kg (22 lb)

Lotus Fountain with Boy-with-dolphin Centrepiece
HC354

Width of bowl:
  1200mm (47¼")
Height (excl. centrepiece):
  420mm (16½")
Weight: 332kg (731 lb)

Obelisk Pebble Bowl Fountain
GC153

Height: 935mm (36¾")
Weight: 82kg (181 lb)

Arcadian Egg Fountain
GC111

Height: 500mm (19¾")
Weight: 80kg (176 lb)

Seahorse Bowl Fountain
GC561

Height: 770mm (30¼")
Weight: 50kg (110 lb)

Nautilus Fountain
GC170A

Recom. pump: X201
Height: 280mm (11")
Weight: 24kg (53 lb)

Lion Mask Wall Fountain
GC510A

Recom. pump: X190
Diam.: 292mm (11½")
Weight: 6kg (13 lb)

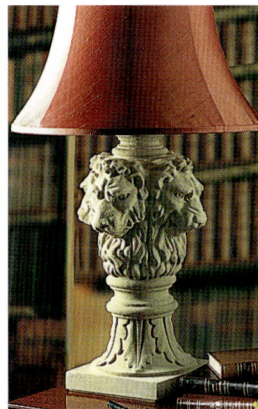

Acanthus Table Lamp F100

Stonework height:
400mm (15¾")
Weight: 9kg (20 lb)

Lion-head Table Lamp F250

Stonework height:
475mm (18¾")
Weight: 17kg (37 lb)

Elizabethan Smokers' Stand F300

Supplied with brass ash-tray and handled bucket as standard.
Height: 570mm (22½")
Weight: 30kg (66 lb)

Supplied with brass bayonet lamp holder, plug and approx. 2m (78") of cable (not USA). Shade not included.

Haddonstone Table Support F270

Height: 705mm (27¾")
Weight (each): 91kg (201 lb)
Glass Table Top not supplied.

Scrolled Table Support F290

Height: 405mm (16")
Weight (each): 58kg (128 lb)
Glass Table Top not supplied.

Large Corinthian Table D451 Illustrated with Venus statue, see page 66.

Table Top:
Diameter: 1370mm (54")
Weight: 186kg (410 lb)

Support:
Height: 675mm (26½")
Weight: 250kg (551 lb)

SPECIALIST SERVICES
GARDEN CREMATION MEMORIALS

Haddonstone has introduced a unique range of Garden Cremation Memorials. Exceptionally crafted, yet unobtrusive, each design provides both a beautiful ornament and a discreet receptacle for a loved one's cremated remains. Each design incorporates a plinth which can accommodate one or two proprietary Poly-Urns (one supplied with memorial).

To personalise each memorial a stone inscription panel is recess fixed into the pedestal. As standard, this is supplied inclusive of a engraved inscription detailing a first name, surname and years of birth and death. Various options are also available. For further details please refer to: **www.haddonstonememorials.com**

In addition to Garden Cremation Memorials, Haddonstone engraves some standard ornaments, see page 184.

Memorial Obelisk & Pedestal MEM500
(with standard engraved inscription)

Ped. base width: 338mm (13 1/4")
Height: 1650mm (65")
Weight: 120kg (264 lb)

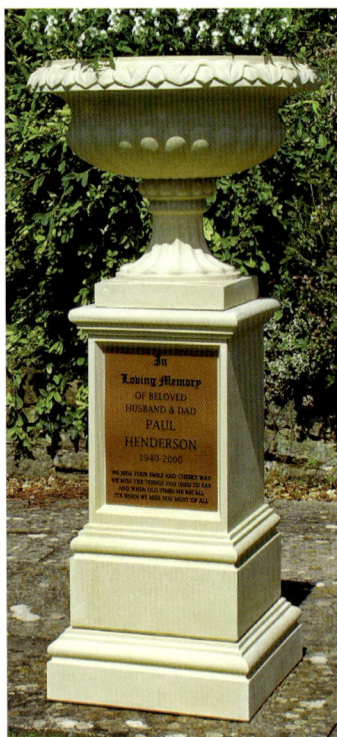

Memorial Vase & Pedestal MEM300
(with optional perspex plaque)

Width at top: 510mm (20")
Ped. base width: 338mm (13 1/4")
Height: 980mm (38 5/8")
Weight: 88kg (194 lb)

Memorial Classical Sundial & Pedestal MEM100
(with optional ceramic photo plaque and engraved inscription enamel infill)

Top diameter: 375mm (14 3/4")
Ped. base width: 338mm (13 1/4")
Stone height: 880mm (34 5/8")
Weight: 81kg (178 lb)

Memorial Celestial Sundial & Pedestal MEM200
(with standard engraved inscription)

Top diameter: 375mm (14 3/4")
Ped. base width: 338mm (13 1/4")
Stone height: 880mm (34 5/8")
Weight: 81kg (178 lb)

Memorial Block (Rope) MEM750 (right)

(With laminate plaque and gold-effect flower vase)

Dimensions: 247 x 280 x 140mm (9 3/4 x 11 x 5 1/2")
Weight: 15kg (33 lb)

Classical (detail)   Celestial (detail)

Memorial Bird Bath & Pedestal MEM400
(with standard engraved inscription)

Width at top: 485mm (19")
Ped. base width: 338mm (13 1/4")
Height: 927mm (36 1/2")
Weight: 96kg (211 lb)

SPECIALIST SERVICES
HADDONCRAFT FORGE

Haddoncraft Forge offers a range of high quality decorative wrought ironwork. Standard designs include: landscape structures, obelisks, towers, rose arches, weathervanes, baluster bars (see page 130), gates (see page 135), railings, fire baskets (see pages 188-189 and candelabra. Haddoncraft Forge also offers a bespoke service.

For further information visit: **www.haddoncraft.co.uk**

A full colour Brochure and Price List is available upon request.

Charleston Seat WD430

Inspired by the exuberance of the 1920s, Haddoncraft designed and created this unique seat in wrought iron.

Height: 1020mm (40 1/8")   Length: 2110mm (83")   Weight: 73kg (161 lb)

Obelisks

Available in three standard heights:

Large WE300 (not illustrated)
Height overall: 2250mm (88 9/16")
Height above ground: 1900mm (74 13/16")
Width: 560mm (22")
Weight: 26kg (57 lb)

Medium WE200 (illustrated in Scrolled Jardiniere, see page 20)
Height overall: 1300mm (51 3/16")
Height above ground: 1100mm (43 5/16")
Width: 300mm (11 13/16")
Weight: 9kg (20 lb)

Small WE100 (not illustrated)
Height overall: 750mm (29 1/2")
Height above ground: 600mm (23 5/8")
Width: 250mm (9 7/8")
Weight: 6kg (13 lb)

Towers

Available in three standard heights:

Large WE700 (not illustrated)
Height overall: 2900mm (114 3/16")
Height above ground: 2400mm (94 1/2")
Width: 420mm (16 9/16")
Weight: 32kg (70 lb)

Medium WE600 (illustrated in Elizabethan Jardiniere, see page 18)
Height overall: 2100mm (82 11/16")
Height above ground: 1600mm (63")
Width: 320mm (12 5/8")
Weight: 13kg (29 lb)

Small WE500 (not illustrated)
Height overall: 1350mm (53 1/8")
Height above ground: 1100mm (43 5/16")
Width: 300mm (11 13/16")
Weight: 9kg (20 lb)

Regency Three Seater WD710

Classic design incorporating a segmented hoop back and slatted seat.

Height: 985mm (38 13/16")
Length: 1600mm (63")
Weight: 39kg (86 lb)

Regency Two Seater WD700
(not illustrated)

Height: 985mm (38 13/16")
Length: 1070mm (42 1/8")
Weight: 29kg (64 lb)

Wentworth Three Seater WD810

Designed by Haddoncraft in the Gothic style, featuring ogee arches.

Height: 985mm (38 13/16")
Length: 1600mm (63").
Weight: 39kg (86 lb)

Wentworth Two Seater WD800
(not illustrated)

Height: 985mm (38 13/16")
Length: 1070mm (42 1/8")
Weight: 29kg (64 lb)

SPECIALIST SERVICES
TECHNISTONE FLOORING & TILING

Haddonstone is the UK and US distributor for Technistone interior flooring and tiling – principally for use in hotels, offices, airports and prestige private residences. For standard colours, see below.

The robust Technistone material is ideal for use in top quality residential, architectural and interior design projects. Applications range from complex mosaic patterns to large scale tiled floors. Each combines smooth surfaces, precise joints and consistent colour. **Standard tile sizes are** 300 x 300 x 10 mm and 600 x 600 x 10mm.

Examples of Technistone flooring and paving can be seen at both Haddonstone's offices in East Haddon near Northampton and at Pennine Stone Ltd, Askern Road, Carcroft, Doncaster DN6 8DE. For further information, visit:

www.technistone-tiles.co.uk

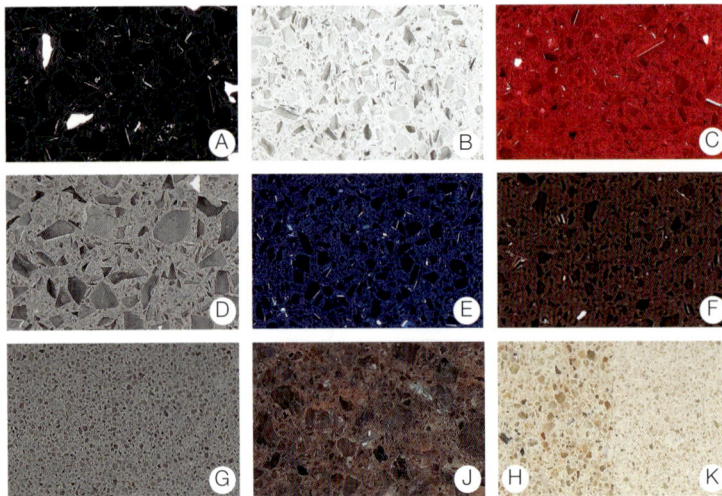

ENGRAVING

Haddonstone has often provided the finishing touch to a project with the supply of a plaque incorporating a house name, number or year. These plaques have been achieved by casting in the letters or numerals required, see page 164.

Haddonstone is now delighted to announce that it has the capability to provide an engraving service for designs with an appropriate flat surface such as the Hadrian Seat shown in either TecLite (product code prefix TL) and TecStone designs (product code prefix G or H). This engraving service is available by quotation only. House number and house name plaques are also available. See page 164 for house number plaques.

SPECIALIST SERVICES
RESTORATION

Haddonstone's meticulous care and attention to detail has earned the company a reputation for the provision of stonework for the restoration and replacement of stone damaged by exposure and neglect. Moreover, Haddonstone normally costs far less than carved stone.

As you will see elsewhere in this catalogue, many of the architectural and ornamental pieces in the Haddonstone Collection have been replicated from damaged originals at some of the world's most famous buildings and landscapes.

Working with designers, contractors and clients Haddonstone can create replica designs by utilising the company's skilled craftsmen and extensive mould making facilities in both the UK and USA.

Stonework was created specifically for this private Herefordshire property.

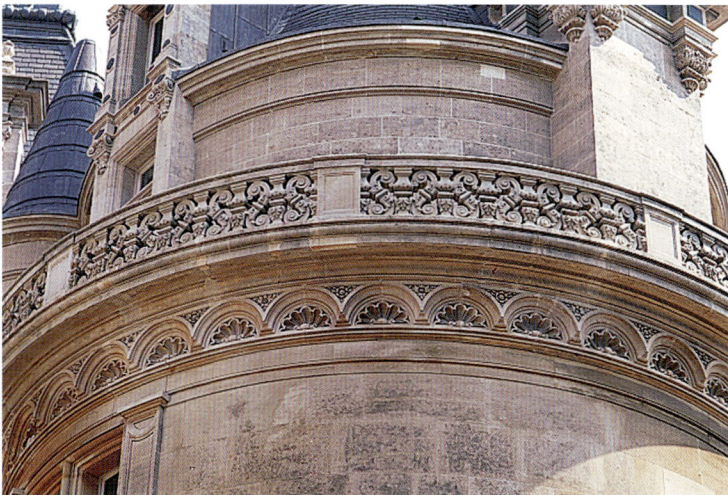

Haddonstone carried out replacement work on this ornate carved sandstone parapet at the National Trust property of Waddesdon Manor near Aylesbury.

Haddonstone replaced a badly eroded fountain with this exquisite replica at the prestigious Stoke Park Golf Club in Buckinghamshire.

Haddonstone's restoration expertise allowed the replication of this ornate stonework façade detailing in Highbury Quadrant, London.

Special bay windows to match existing at Haslemere School in Surrey.

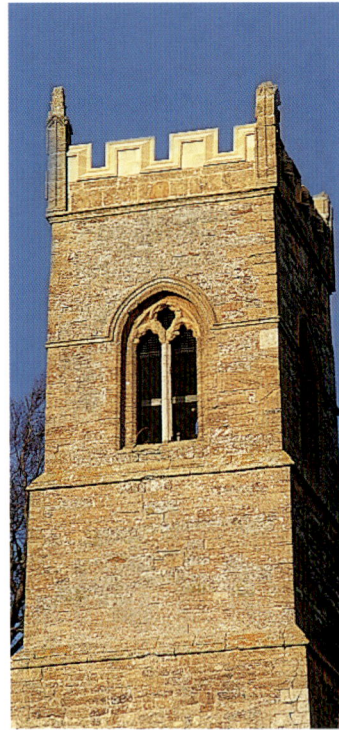

Replacement church crenellations.

Custom retail refurbishment project.

Replacement balusters at Albert Court, near the Royal Albert Hall, London.

The restoration of the XIX century Boat Houses at Didlington Manor in Norfolk includes custom-made Haddonstone balustrading.

Refurbished Northamptonshire house incorporating custom-manufactured stonework to match original detailing.

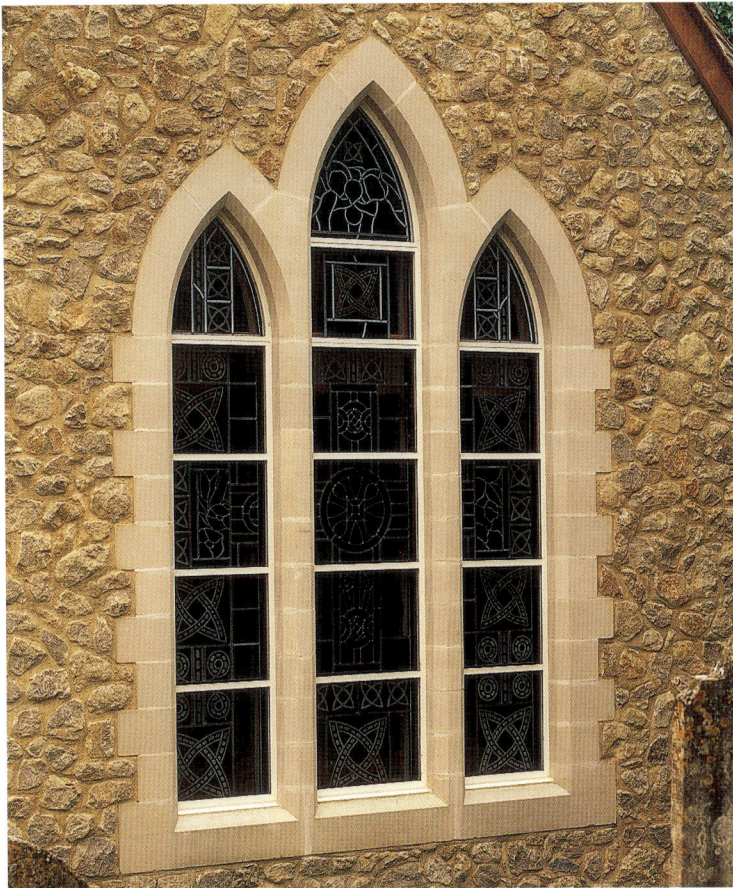

St Mary's Church in Kent incorporates custom-made window surrounds.

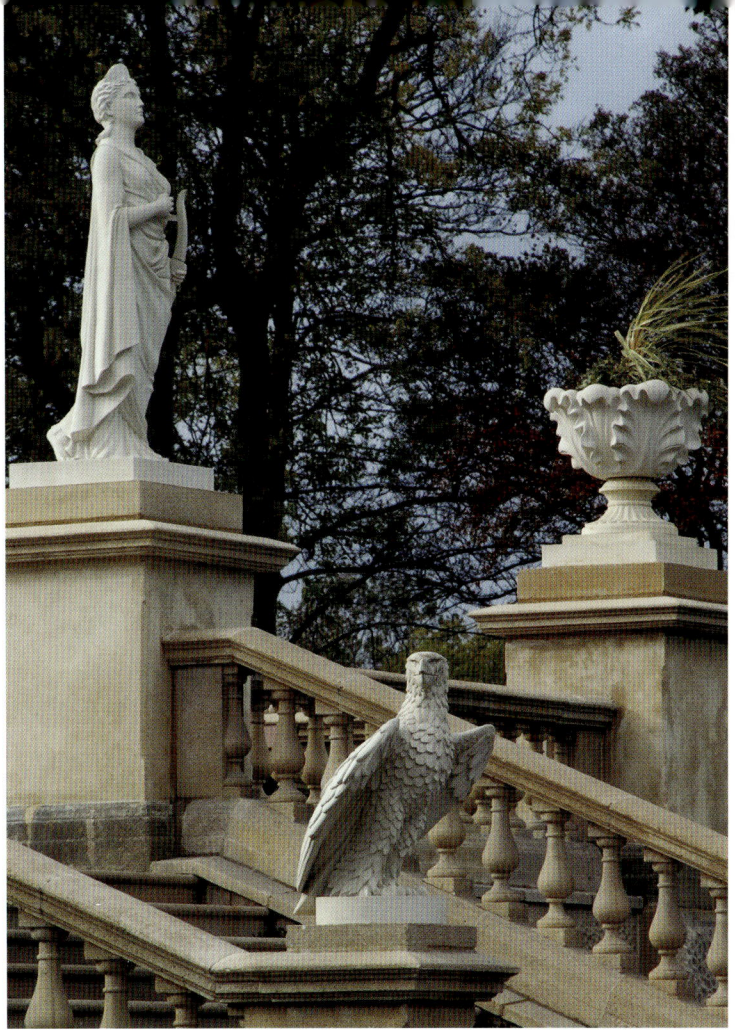

Restoration at Leazes Park, Newcastle included statues, eagles and urns.

Haddonstone recreated this unusual terrace balustrading for St Michael's School, Tawstock, North Devon. The project also features standard Clarence Urns.

SPECIALIST SERVICES
FIREPLACES AND MANTELS

Haddonstone's range of fireplaces, mantels, chimney piece surrounds and hearths has again been dramatically expanded to offer customers a choice of nineteen surround designs from the simple and stylish to the ornate and elegant. Most of these can be supplied with or without slip rebates, allowing thirty four variations.

Haddonstone slips allow for an opening of 572 x 420-470mm (22½" x 16½"-18½"). Full details and dimensions are given on the appropriate Tech Sheet.

Hearths and Back Hearths are available to suit all styles or can be supplied separately for use with a customer's own stove. Fireback Tiles are also available.

A separate Fireplaces, Mantels & Interiors brochure is available on request from Haddonstone Ltd. Alternatively, view on-line at:

www.haddonstone.com/view-catalogue

Louis XV Chimney Piece HF150W including Kerb and Hearth shown with non-standard Fire Basket

Deco Chimney Piece HF135W including Slips and Hearth, shown with Firebox X891.

Vanbrugh Chimney Piece HF634W including Hearth shown with optional Fire Basket WF250, Obelisks WF700 and Slips WF800 by Haddoncraft Forge

Tall Manor Chimney Piece, Plain HF411W including Hearth, with optional Back Hearth HF4A and Fireback Tiles HP450.

Adam Chimney Piece HF110W including Slips, Hearth, shown with optional Fire Basket WF200

Tudor Chimney Piece HF608W including Slips and Hearth, shown with optional Fire Basket WF200.

Hearth HF440

Manor Chimney Piece, Keystone HF425W including Slips and Hearth

SPECIALIST SERVICES
HADDONSTONE (USA) LTD

Haddonstone (USA) Ltd was founded in 1990, initially importing products into its New Jersey warehouse from the United Kingdom based parent company. Today, 95% of all Haddonstone products sold in the US are manufactured by Haddonstone in the US.

Haddonstone opened an impressive manufacturing facility in Colorado during 1996 to provide mold-making, Haddonstone production and extensive storage space. The site has been subsequently extended to enhance existing facilities whilst also introducing TecStone and TecLite production areas.

Haddonstone (USA) Ltd has now created an Architectural Supplement containing an extensive range of designs created specifically for the US market, complying with Building Codes as necessary. These designs are offered in addition to the company's standard collection.

Designs in the Architectural Supplement include:

- Non Standard Balusters
- Balustrading system
- Parapet Screening
- Gate Piers
- Quoins
- Pier Caps and Pier Strings
- Copings
- Plinth and String Courses
- Cladding and Blocks
- Columns and Pilasters
- Porticos
- Door and Window Surrounds

Craftsman at work in Haddonstone's Pueblo studios.

There is also a range of fireplaces and mantels that have been specifically developed for the North American market.

The Architectural Supplement is available on request from Haddonstone (USA) Ltd or can be viewed at:

www.haddonstone.com/view-catalogue

Haddonstone's plant in Pueblo, Colorado.

A selection of recent architectural projects incorporating both standard and custom designs from Haddonstone (USA) Ltd.

S

HADDONSTONE

Haddonstone Ltd.,
The Forge House,
East Haddon,
Northampton NN6 8DB

Telephone: 01604 770711
Fax: 01604 770027

PROJECT

CLIENT

DRAWING TITLE
3RD FLOOR ARCHED
WINDOW – DETAIL 'C'

SCALE
AS SHOWN

DATE

DRAWING No.
L-5504

DRAWN BY

ELEVATION

3410

USEFUL INFORMATION

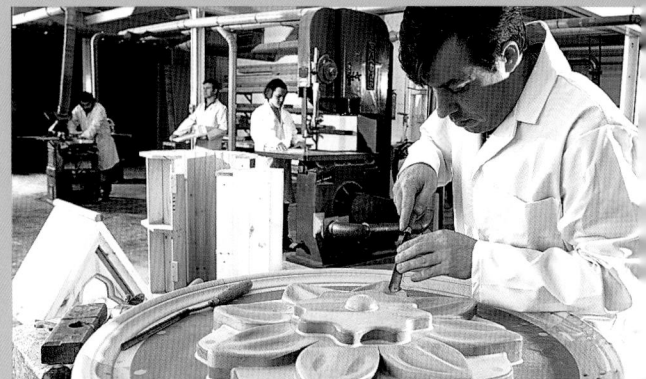

There have been more imitations of stone than any other natural building material. This persistent emulation has most consistently been for reasons of economy, availability and fashion.

Some of the historical substitutes for stone are now themselves the subject of conservation. Their history is distinguished and fine early examples can still be seen at Buckingham Palace, Hampton Court, Ham House and St George's Chapel, Windsor.

Today, cast stonework is being used increasingly by architects and both landscape and interior designers as a substitute in the many applications where quarried stone is difficult, time-consuming and forbiddingly expensive to employ, including restoration.

This section looks at the history and development of Haddonstone, the colour and material choices available and the services the company can offer to both professional and private clients.

Haddonstone, TecLite and TecStone are available in the following colours:

	Haddonstone	TecLite (TL prefix)	TecStone (G or H prefix)
Portland 01	●	●	●
Bath 02	●	●	●
Terracotta 04	●	●	●
Coade 05	○	●	●
Slate 06	○	●	●
Sienna 08	○	○	○
Wheat 09	○	○	○

○= USA only: non-standard at additional cost
Standard colours are Portland 01 and Bath 02. All other colours are made on request for specific customer orders.

Please note that throughout this catalogue the photographs show Haddonstone pieces of various ages and stages of maturity. The special qualities of Haddonstone ensure a rapid weathering of ornamental pieces, although the speed of weathering is dependent on location and climate.

The colours reproduced in this catalogue are as accurate as the printing process will permit. Stone colour samples are available upon request.

NEW FORMULA STONEAGE

If you want to achieve the instant aged look, so desired by many customers, then New Formula StoneAge is designed to give new stone the look of the weathered antique.

Available as an antique grey concentrate, New Formula StoneAge is a water-based formulation. It should be mixed with distilled or de-ionised water before being applied by spray or brush. Supplied in 237ml (8 fl oz) containers.

Bath 02

Portland 01

Terracotta 04

Coade 05

Slate 06

USA only: Sienna 08 (non-standard)

USA only: Wheat 09 (non-standard)

USEFUL INFORMATION
CARE & MAINTENANCE

With careful handling, Haddonstone needs no special maintenance as long as it is not exposed to extreme conditions. For example, it is recommended that in very hot weather a planter should be watered only in the early morning or cool evening. Also, in freezing conditions, fountain bowls should be emptied. To avoid harming the stone surface rock salt, proprietary de-icers or chlorine products should not be used.

Haddonstone is less susceptible to the detrimental effects of weathering, which can damage the laminated structure of quarried stone, and can be aesthetically more pleasing as it often matures and develops character much earlier. Like quarried stone, Haddonstone can exhibit slight shade variations from piece to piece, reflecting the colour of the natural materials used in the production process. Customers should also be aware that natural dyes in composts containing peat, coconut husk or coir can produce a brown staining which is very difficult to remove. Many fertilizers contain ferrous compounds that can cause rust stains. Cast-in fixings and reinforcement used during the standard production process are non-ferrous, usually stainless steel.

Haddonstone planters are suitable for acid-loving plants if used with an appropriate non-permeable liner. When planters are used in interior settings, a non-permeable liner should also be used as planters are made with drainage holes and the material has natural porosity. When interior architectural stonework is used in public areas it is advisable to seal the surface of the stone with a clear sealer.

Efflorescence, also known as lime bloom, may appear as a white deposit on the surface of any product containing cement or limestone. This is temporary and will disappear as a result of normal weathering, or may be removed with a proprietary acid washing agent. Under certain exceptional conditions a hairline fissure may occur in the surface of the product, a characteristic of any material using a cementitious binder. In normal circumstances, this will have no effect on the structural integrity of the piece.

GIFT VOUCHERS & CERTIFICATES

Haddonstone has a range of gift vouchers in the following denominations: £25, £50, £100, £250, £500 and £1000. Vouchers can also be created for specific values on request. Haddonstone (USA) Ltd offers gift certificates in $100, $250 and $1000 values.

Vouchers or certificates can be redeemed against any items in the current edition of The Haddonstone Collection, custom-made stonework or transport. To order, simply contact the UK or US offices or visit www.haddonstone.com

Haddonstone Gift Vouchers make the ideal gift for all occasions ~ from weddings and birthdays to Christmas and retirement. They can even be issued as part of a company incentive scheme.

Please note: Haddonstone Standard Terms & Conditions apply. In addition: Haddonstone Gift Vouchers have no cash redemption value; no change will be given if the value redeemed is less than the value of the Gift Voucher; Vouchers are only valid for retail purchases direct from Haddonstone Ltd or Haddonstone (USA) Ltd; and, Vouchers are available to UK or US clients only.

Haddonstone was awarded the prestigious International Green Apple Gold Award (Building Materials) for Environmental Best Practice and Sustainable Development by the Green Organisation for restoration work at Scarborough Spa.

ENVIRONMENTAL & SUSTAINABILITY POLICY

Haddonstone is committed to an Environmental & Sustainability Management System which ensures that work activity processes do not make a significant impact on the environment.

Best environmental practice is adopted wherever possible. Consequently, Haddonstone undertakes the management of finite, naturally occurring resources by balancing needs with future sustainability. Objectives include: energy conservation; resource conservation; reducing pollution; waste reduction and re-cycling; and the minimisation of hazardous substance use. As a result, all environmental and sustainability aspects are identified and, where necessary, controlled to minimise or eliminate their effect on the environment.

A copy of the company's full Environmental & Sustainability Policy is available on request.

FIVE YEAR WARRANTY

Haddonstone offers a five year warranty on all cast stone garden ornaments purchased direct from the company on production of the product's original invoice or order acknowledgement. This warranty applies in the unlikely event that a product fails, due to a design or production fault. This warranty does not apply if Haddonstone assembly recommendations have not been followed or if a problem arises as a consequence of the actions of the client or a third party. Contact your nearest Haddonstone office for the full terms of this warranty which does not affect your statutory rights.

THE MATERIAL

Haddonstone is a unique form of cast limestone with a surface texture similar to Portland stone or natural limestone. In a number of important ways Haddonstone is markedly superior, one of its greatest advantages being price, which, piece for piece, is normally significantly less than that of quarried stone.

Haddonstone is able to offer three high-specification cast stone options in both the UK and USA:

*   Haddonstone (dry-cast stone)
*   TecStone (wet-cast stone)
*   TecLite (fibre-reinforced cast stone, see pages 170-173)

Haddonstone recognises the exacting requirements of its customers, both private and professional, and an ongoing research and development programme ensures that the highest standards are maintained.

The illustrations, technical information and data contained in this catalogue, to Haddonstone's best knowledge, were correct at the time of going to print. The right to change specifications at any time, without notice, is reserved as part of a policy of continuous development and improvement.

In 1991, Haddonstone was a founder member of the United Kingdom Cast Stone Association (UKCSA). The Association defines strict levels of technical performance, which are set out in the UKCSA Technical Manual. Haddonstone's minimum compressive cube strength at 28 days is greater than 35 MPa, whilst TecStone's is greater than 45 MPa. Both materials therefore exceed the requirements of the UKCSA specification and comply with the requirements of BS1217: 2008, BS5642: 1983 and BS EN 13198: 2003. In addition, TecStone — a denser material with a smoother finish to meet demanding design and performance criteria — also exceeds the requirements of ASTM C1364 Standard Specification for Architectural Cast Stone in the United States of America.

As part of Haddonstone's Quality Assurance procedures, the materials are regularly tested both in the company's own laboratory and by recognised independent laboratories. Thus, customers may have every confidence that the quality and durability of both Haddonstone and TecStone materials will meet their needs.

High-tonnage silos (below) store raw materials needed to produce Haddonstone.

THE MANUFACTURING PROCESS

Each Haddonstone design is made to order. If the order is for a standard design, production can commence as soon as a colour has been agreed. If a custom design is required then a mould needs to be made. If the design is relatively simple, a window cill or coping stone for example, then the mould will be made of wood in the company's wood shop. One of the skilled carpenters will interpret drawings to produce a precise mould, which is the exact reverse of the shape ultimately required. Timber moulds have a comparatively limited life compared to their fibreglass equivalents. However, the speed with which timber moulds can be produced, combined with their relatively low cost, normally makes this type of mould more economical for the client.

The production of a fibreglass, rubber-lined mould in the company's studio is much more time-consuming and is only undertaken if the design is complex or if there are likely to be numerous castings over time. The work is one of the most highly skilled within Haddonstone, benefiting greatly from artistic and practical skills. Before such a mould can be made, it is first necessary to have a model. This can come from a variety of sources: it could be created by the neighbouring wood shop; it could have been carved from scratch by an in-house craftsman, normally in plaster, either replicating an antique piece for a restoration project or afresh for a new design; it could be a pristine antique stone; or it could be a damaged original requiring restoration.

Once the master model has been created, the mould-making can begin. This is done by rolling clay to a set thickness and covering the entire model. Over this a fibreglass case is formed. As this case will be completely inflexible, it has to be designed in such a way as to allow its later removal. For this reason, some fibreglass cases can comprise more than ten sections. Then the fibreglass case is removed, the model extricated and all traces of clay removed. The case is then reassembled around the model, there now being a void where the clay had previously been. Into that void is poured a specially developed rubber which has enough fluidity to fill every cavity whilst avoiding any air bubbles which would be seen in the finished design. After the rubber has set, the fibreglass case is, once again, removed and the model extricated for storage. When the fibreglass and rubber case is reassembled, the void now left in the centre is the precise shape and size of the finished design. Particular care is taken to ensure that any seam is in a position where it is least noticeable. Whether wooden or fibreglass, without a first-class mould it is impossible to create a first-class product.

For semi-dry cast Haddonstone, the principal materials are limestone, white cement, sand and a small quantity of water. This produces a Portland colour with other colours requiring the addition of pigment into the mix. Other key ingredients include plasticisers to improve workability and aid compaction as well as waterproofers for durability. To ensure complete control of the production process, every single batch of raw material delivered to the Haddonstone manufactory is quality checked, before it is used. The constituents of the mix are stored in high-tonnage silos adjacent to the production area, before being mixed in small quantities via computer controlled batching equipment and taken to a workstation. At this stage, the mix has the feel of damp sand or earth.

The stone is gradually packed into the mould using a number of ingeniously crafted tools. Whilst this is normally done by hand, some moulds can be packed using pneumatic hand rammers. Once packed,

The *How It's Made* TV crew filming stone being packed into a mould at Haddonstone's Northamptonshire manufactory.

the stone is left in the mould until the next working day. The process of delaminating or stripping is probably the most visually rewarding of the entire production process, particularly for a fibreglass mould. The fibreglass case is first stripped away, leaving the rubber around the stone. The rubber is then carefully peeled away to reveal the stone design in all its glory. No finishing is required as the quality of mould manufacture ensures that the design is perfect. It is at this stage that the first of many quality control checks is undertaken and the product is given a bar code label, which will remain with it until delivery to the customer. The stone is now strong enough to be transported outside the production area.

Like other companies in the industry, Haddonstone originally relied on the vagaries of the English climate to ensure that the stone cured correctly. However, the effects of temperature, precipitation and wind made this a very inexact science. For this reason, the company introduced a vapour curing system in 1999 that gives the stone the equivalent of fourteen days strength overnight. Not only does this give the company a guaranteed curing system, it also reduces delivery lead times and storage problems.

Although some customers opt to collect their orders, most rely on Haddonstone's own transport fleet, the majority of which include a demountable forklift to aid off-loading on site. Export orders are dispatched by container or in specially constructed wooden crates. A similar operation to Haddonstone's manufactory in Northamptonshire exists at the company's US manufactory in Colorado. In the UK and USA, Haddonstone also manufactures products by a wet-cast process, called TecStone. Here, the mix is poured into the mould. This process gives a finish, once acid etched, much more akin to Coade stone and is ideal for larger products, complex statuary and contemporary designs where clients prefer a surface finish which does not weather quickly. Most recently, Haddonstone has developed an artificial stone reinforced with glass fibres, called TecLite. Products made by this process have thinner walls and are consequently lighter.

CUSTOM-MADE STONEWORK

HADDONSTONE CAN MANUFACTURE ARCHITECTURAL STONE PIECES TO PRACTICALLY ANY SHAPE OR SIZE. THE ONLY CONSTRAINT IS YOUR IMAGINATION.

Haddonstone has a vast range of standard architectural components. Alternatively, by utilising the company's extensive mould shop and manufactory, Haddonstone can produce custom-made items, replicating simple or intricate designs, to individual specifications in any quantity.

If you are involved with commercial developments, private housing, refurbishment or restoration, Haddonstone has Technical Departments in the UK and USA, manned by experienced staff, who would be pleased to discuss your requirements.

The expertise of Haddonstone's craftsmen, together with on-going investment in research and development of state-of-the-art mould-making and casting technology, equips the company to solve most problems ~ including the constant need to contain costs.

While experts have, more than once, confused Haddonstone with carved stone, a glance at the company's prices would have made such confusion impossible!

DELIVERY

In the UK, Haddonstone has its own fleet of curtainside lorries all with tail-lift or fork lift facilities. This enables the company to deliver products throughout mainland Britain from a central location close to the motorway network.

At Haddonstone's manufactory near Northampton, pieces are carefully packed onto pallets before shrink-wrapping ready for mechanical offloading on site. Heavier pieces are delivered in sections for assembly on site. Delivery is kerbside only and does not include siting and installation, which are the sole responsibility of the client.

Haddonstone (USA) Ltd services its customers by offering crate and freight options ex-warehouse, by Haddonstone truck or common carrier dependent on location, as well as containers or trucks floor loaded with shrink-wrapped pallets direct to site.

POINTING MIX

Haddonstone's pointing mixes are used to achieve a good colour match in joints between Haddonstone, TecStone or TecLite components. They are totally unsuitable for use as a bedding mix.

Pointing mix is mixed by hand to achieve the best match to Haddonstone, TecStone or TecLite in terms of both colour and texture. This would normally be the recommended pointing mix, being available in Portland, Bath, Terracotta, Coade and Slate colours as standard. See Haddonstone's "Pointing Recommendations Sheet" for further information, available online at:

www.haddonstone.com/pointing

CPD & CONTINUING EDUCATION

Haddonstone is a member of The Construction Industry CPD Certification Service, offering UK architects and other construction professionals high quality material to complement the CPD policies of institutes and associations including RIBA, RIAS, RICS, RSUA and BIDA.

Haddonstone offers a unique CPD presentation for architects, designers and contractors as well as a tour of the manufactory. Topics covered range from the latest manufacturing methods to current industry standards, thereby assisting the professional client in the use of cast stone to achieve practical design and construction solutions.

In the US, Haddonstone offers online learning for professionals via AEC Daily Continuing Education.

BUILDING WITH HADDONSTONE

With its inherent strength, Haddonstone can be used in structural situations. However, the usual practice is to use Haddonstone purely as a decorative façade supported, where necessary, by reinforced concrete or structural steelwork. This task is not difficult but should be carried out only under the supervision of an architect or a structural engineer. If you intend to use the products structurally, let Haddonstone know when you place your order, giving as much detail as possible. You can then be advised on any ways in which Haddonstone can simplify this work, saving you time and money.

Working in conjunction with the architect and structural engineer, the company can manufacture TecStone components as structural units by incorporating reinforcement.

Where possible, Haddonstone is supplied in component form to ease handling on site. Consideration should be given to the weight of individual components when deciding on lifting and handling procedures, with due regard to the relevant regulations. Haddonstone's CD contains Technical Sheets and Assembly Advice which provide specific detailed information. We also recommend reference to Eurocode 6 and PD 6697: 2010.

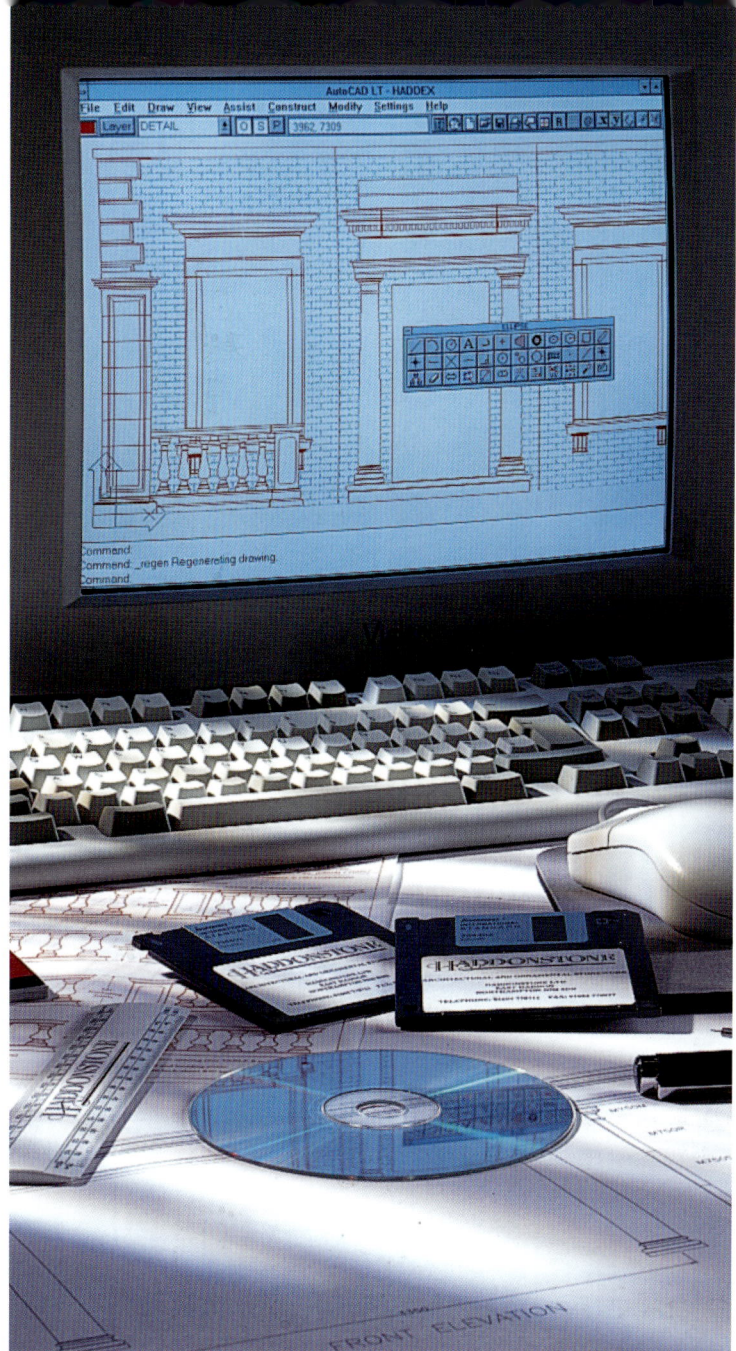

HADDONSTONE CD

Haddonstone has created an informative CD to bring all the company's product and technical information together, for the first time, in one easy-to-access form. The disk contains: Haddonstone product information; Technical Specification Sheets; Assembly Advice; CAD drawings; panorama views of the company's acclaimed Northamptonshire show gardens; and a corporate video. The CD is available by contacting your nearest Haddonstone office or distributor.

TECHNICAL SHEETS

To provide professional clients with every assistance in the use of Haddonstone, the company has produced a comprehensive range of Technical Sheets. These are available via Haddonstone's CD.

CAD WITH HADDONSTONE

Over 500 Haddonstone architectural components are now available to architects and designers for use with CAD systems including AutoCAD DWG, DXF or Apple Mac.

This enables architects to design in the classical style whilst using the latest technology to save hours of valuable research and drawing time.

Architects can download the data from Haddonstone's website:
www.haddonstone.com/CAD
Alternatively, the information is included on the Haddonstone CD.

Designs now covered in this FastrackCAD database include balustrading, columns, entablatures, gate piers, copings, landscape ornaments, balls and bases.

A BRIEF HISTORY

Artificial stone, or cast stone as it is most commonly called today, has a long and illustrious history that intertwines with the great boom in classically inspired country house building from the eighteenth century onwards. There have been more imitations of stone than of any other natural building material. This persistent emulation has most consistently been for reasons of economy, availability and fashion, particularly in applications where quarried stone is difficult, time consuming and forbiddingly expensive to employ. In the eighteenth and nineteenth centuries, designs created by leading manufacturers such as Coade, Blashfield, Austin & Seeley, Doulton and Pulham were used at prestigious country house locations such as Belton, Burghley, Croome, Ickworth, Kedleston and Stowe whilst artificial stone today is still being manufactured by Haddonstone to enhance country houses across the nation, from Mount Edgcumbe in Cornwall to Aske Hall in North Yorkshire.

A growing appreciation of the past and the resultant need to conserve historic landscapes and gardens, as well as a desire from the public to create their own accurate representations of gardens from the past, led to the re-emergence of artificial stone manufacture during the latter years of the twentieth century.

Haddonstone was established by Robert 'Bob' Barrow (1932-1996) in 1971 to produce high quality decorative cast stonework. The company had a range of just seven designs to offer during the first year of business, six of which continue to be best sellers today: the Plaited Basket, Elizabethan Jardiniere, French Urn, Regency Urn, Scaled Jardiniere and Straight 51" Seat. The company exhibited for the first time at the prestigious Chelsea Flower Show the following year. Haddonstone's collection has subsequently grown to over one thousand standard designs, with the company gaining an ever increasing reputation for its expertise in the manufacture of custom made architectural stonework. Today, Haddonstone is recognised as an international market leader with group companies in the United Kingdom and the United States of America.

The Haddonstone collection comprises the standard range of designs and is the most comprehensive of its kind produced anywhere. Every single item is the work of highly skilled craftsmen. Pieces from the range have been chosen for the construction and renovation of some of the world's most famous buildings, including palaces, stately homes, National Trust properties, international hotels, state buildings and gardens, as well as private houses and gardens of every description.

The demand for landscaping and architectural elements has led to Haddonstone's continuing expansion. From modest beginnings in 1971, by 1987 the company had moved its manufactory to a purpose built complex at Brixworth in Northamptonshire, UK. The two hectare (five acre) site incorporates Haddonstone's 5,000 sq m (54,000 sq ft) manufactory, studio and mould shop complex together with an

Photograph by David Newell-Smith

An early public relations photograph of Bob Barrow, Haddonstone's founder.

extensive stockyard and loading area. The premises were extended in 1988, 1991, 2000 and 2002 to provide some of the most advanced cast stonework mould making facilities in the UK together with a laboratory, vapour curing chamber and both TecStone and TecLite production facilities. The manufactory is located just six miles from the Haddonstone Group headquarters and show gardens at East Haddon.

Haddonstone (USA) Ltd was formed as a subsidiary of Haddonstone Ltd in 1990, operating from a 1,100 sq m (12,000 sq ft) warehouse with yard and offices in Bellmawr, New Jersey. During 1996 a 2.5 hectare (6¼ acre) site was acquired in Pueblo, Colorado on which a manufactory was constructed. This incorporated a purpose built mould shop, production facilities for both Haddonstone and TecStone, a large stock-yard and loading docks. In 2000 a purpose built vapour curing chamber was added to the production unit and the size of the stockyard was doubled. In 2003 the Colorado facility in the USA underwent a major expansion with the creation of additional offices, a new mould shop and an expanded TecStone production area.

For further information on the history of artificial stone from the eighteenth century to the present, copies of Simon Scott's acclaimed book 'Artificial Stone: a successful substitute for natural stone?' are available from Haddonstone offices in both the UK and US or can be ordered at **www.haddonstone.com**

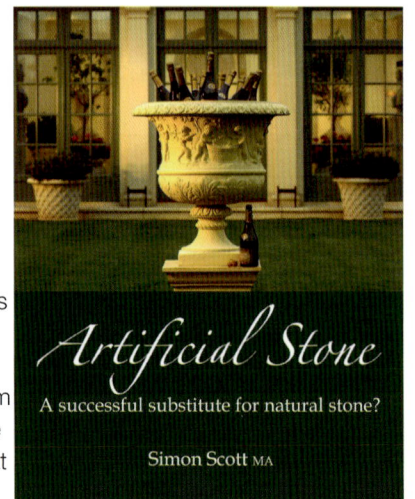

Artificial Stone
A successful substitute for natural stone?

Simon Scott MA

HADDONSTONE WORLDWIDE

Haddonstone has a group company in the United States of America ~ Haddonstone (USA) Ltd ~ with offices and warehouses in both New Jersey and Colorado, where the US manufactory opened in 1996. In addition Haddonstone has representation across North America, Europe, the Middle East, the Far East and Australasia.

Haddonstone has well-established Export and Pacific Rim Sales Departments supporting the company's world-wide activities. These Departments can provide dedicated technical assistance to customers in countries or territories where the company does not have representation. The company is thereby able to provide any customer with a quotation for the following services:

- Ex-works
- UK delivery for onward shipment
- Direct delivery to most countries in the world

Haddonstone can also arrange for foam packing, export crate packing or containerisation. Please contact the UK-based Export Department if you have a project to discuss or would like further information.

The Pearl in Qatar - a significant recent export contract for Haddonstone.

HOW TO FIND US IN THE UK

At Haddonstone we welcome visitors from around the world to our acclaimed .75ha (2 acre) show gardens and interior showroom at East Haddon, set in the picturesque countryside of rural Northamptonshire in England. For more details see "VISIT US" on page 04 or visit:

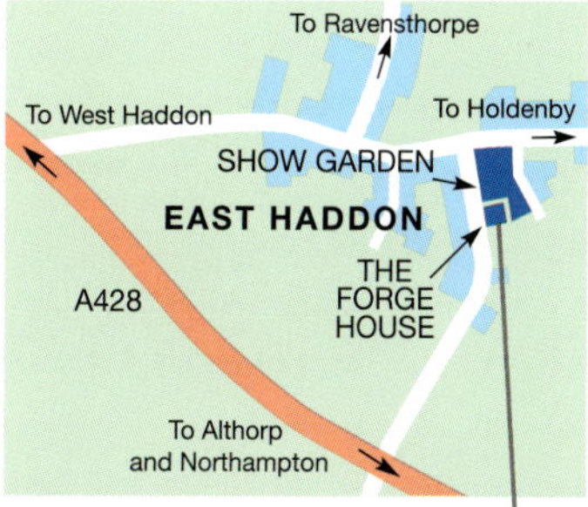

www.haddonstone.com/ visit-haddonstone

Examples of Haddonstone, TecLite, TecStone and Technistone can also be viewed at:
Pennine Stone Ltd,
Askern Road, Carcroft,
Doncaster DN6 8DE.

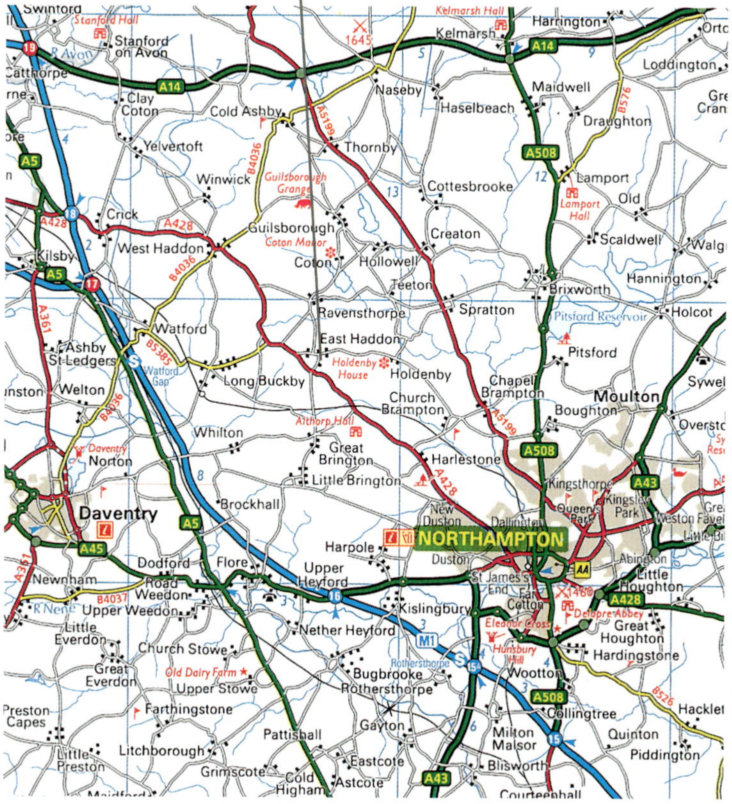

INDEX

Page numbers may refer to the first page in a section.